The Great Chicago Fire

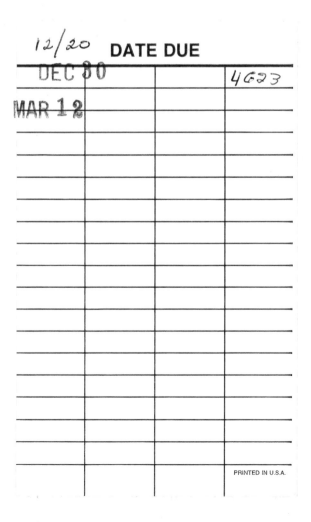

UNIVERSITY OF ILLINOIS PRESS · URBANA AND CHICAGO

The Great Chicago Fire

Ross Miller

For Julia and Sasha

First Illinois paperback, 2000
© 1990 by Ross Miller
Reprinted by arrangement with the author
All rights reserved
Manufactured in the United States of America
⊖ This book is printed on acid-free paper.

Research for this book was supported by a grant from the
Graham Foundation for Advanced Studies in the Fine Arts.

Portions of this book appeared in different form in the
Art Institute of Chicago's Museum Studies 13, no. 2 (1988),
and in *Chicago Architecture, 1872–1922: Birth of a Metropolis,* ed.
John Zukowsky (Munich: Prestel Verlag, 1987).

Previously published in hardcover as *American Apocalypse: The
Great Fire and the Myth of Chicago* (University of Chicago Press,
1990).

Library of Congress Cataloging-in-Publication Data

P 5 4 3 2 1

Contents

Acknowledgments   vii

Introduction   1

1 / The Chicago Fire
The Making of a Legend   12

2 / Reluctant Modernism
The Past as Present   38

3 / Derrick Time
Architecture, Memory, and the Poetics of Ruin   63

4 / The Fire as Image
Architecture and the Problem of Loss   106

5 / The Shanty and the Skyscraper   136

6 / Wright's Piano
Imagining the New Chicago   169

7 / Chicago Black and White
The Court, the University, the Midway, and the Street   195

Notes   251

Photo Acknowledgments   273

Index   281

Acknowledgments

I am indebted to the following institutions and individuals for their support of this project: the Graham Foundation for Advanced Study in the Fine Arts and Carter H. Manny, Jr., its director; the Wesleyan University Center for the Humanities and Richard Vann; the University of Connecticut Foundation, Hugh Clark, and Thomas Giolas; and the Yale University Visiting Faculty Program and Alan Trachtenberg.

Primary research was conducted at the Art Institute of Chicago, with the invaluable assistance of Robert Sharp, Mary Woolever, and John Zukowsky; the University of Chicago Libraries; the Chicago Historical Society; the Newberry Library; the Yale University Art and Architecture Library; the Chicago Architecture Foundation; the Huntington Library; the Getty Center for the History of Art and the Humanities; the National Center for the Study of Frank Lloyd Wright; and the New-York Historical Society. Special thanks to Robert Vrecenak, head of the interlibrary loan department at the Homer Babbidge Library, University of Connecticut, for his tireless pursuit of rare primary texts. This book was made richer through the generous work of David Phillips, who has collected the finest private source of Chicago photographs and literature.

In addition, many individuals provided support at critical times: John Abbott, Charles Boer, John Gatta, Paul Jay, Stephen Karcher, Jay Livernois, George Ranalli, Thomas Riggio, Stephen Saletan, Stanley Tigerman, Anthony Vidler, Ted Wolner, and Lynn Woodbury. The Staff of the University of Chicago Press made this project successful.

I wish especially to thank James Hillman and Philip Roth for helping me to reimagine this work.

Introduction

The Great Chicago Fire has long enjoyed mythic status. A rich folklore recounts Mrs. O'Leary's actions on the evening of October 8, 1871. Drunk or simply careless, she left her lantern in the barn when she finished milking her cow; the animal kicked over the light and began the blaze that quickly destroyed most of the city. Left out of the fable is any mention of a summer-long drought, a pathetically inadequate fire department, and a dangerous wood building stock.

In 1956, the city installed a modest monument at the site, DeKoven and South Jefferson streets, at the dedication of its new fire academy. It had taken over eighty years to commemorate formally an event indelibly associated with Chicago. The delay in acknowledging the event reveals something essential about the nature of the city and the sources of its imagery. If given the choice, Chicago's boosters would not have picked a destructive fire, or later in Chicago's history, a machine gun, to present their city to the world. Yet these are the images that have attached themselves to Chicago. It was through adversity and violence that Chicago transformed itself from a western outpost to a city of international rank. The city had a reputation as an open western town from the first days of its founding. Far from being excluded from municipal portraits, the shocking particulars concerning sex, drink, wheeling and dealing were reprocessed into legend. Chicago exploited its Dodge City rawness at the same time it competed successfully as an advanced center of commerce, banking, and industry—like Ben Franklin in Paris, simultaneously playing the contradictory roles of hick and sophisticate to great advantage. The fire accelerated an established process of mythologizing in which the negative aspects of frontier settlement were refitted to conform to a positive drama of steady development.

The composite tale of survival which was distilled from reams of printed matter about the fire corresponded conveniently to the larger myth of America. Both contain a curious yoking of two seemingly incompatible legends: one of origins, the romance of the frontier's virgin lands, and another of ends, including the prophesied destruction of the world. With its roots in the Puritans' millennial vision of settlement in America as a "City upon a hill," the threat of imminent destruction was twinned with the euphoria of settlement and new beginnings. In Chicago, a thriving, cosmopolitan downtown still coexisted with Mrs. O'Leary's rural homestead. When the fire occurred, Chicago contained all the stages of settlement, origins and ends in surreal proximity to one another.

The events in Chicago during the fire and the years of rebuilding were the focus of intense national interest. Reporters, photographers, and illustrators were sent to the ruins to report to a curious national and international readership. The fire ruins reminded readers of scorched Civil War battlefields, photographs of which had been made in great detail and circulated all over the world only a few years before. The availability of skilled documentary photographers made certain that there was some palpable record of what had occurred. Written accounts had to be considered against the unnerving images captured by the camera. Recollected reality seemed to be not quite so arbitrary as it had in the past, before reporters were able through a lens to document visually what they had seen.

Why does the Chicago fire qualify as a great event? What makes it important? There have been other devastating fires in America; Boston (1872) and Baltimore (1904) were both later savaged by flames, as earlier New York and Philadelphia had been. It was not the novelty of urban disaster that fascinated people. The Great Fire and Plague of London (1666) and the Lisbon Earthquake (1755) had long before established the vulnerability of cities to sudden calamity. As late as the early part of this century, fire and epidemic remained the twin natural threats to urban development. Yet Chicago remains emblematic of American vulnerability to natural disaster and its capacity for renewal.[1] The city managed to insinuate itself into a larger narrative, consciously exploiting its own tragedy as an archetype of the modern struggle against adversity. Within hours of the disaster, journalists, politicians, and a young, elite commercial class were cobbling together language that would reshape events positively. Genuine invention represented by local on-the-scene reporting and documentary photography was mixed with unapologetic cannibalizing of images like the phoenix, appropriated from post–Civil War Atlanta. Why was Chicago so successful in its self-conscious legendizing—a process that still continues?

Myths grow abundantly between fact and emotion. The period of raw emotional engagement with tragedy is relatively brief. Inevitably, the event is analyzed and reduced into a set of conventions. As interpreters haggle over the verifiable record, distilled in large part from the eyewitness reports of survivors, the set of agreed-upon facts grows smaller. Most rumors and tales evaporate as they are subjected over time to the rules of evidence, and historians are left with a plausible sense of what happened. But at a price. Half-truths and fantasies seek their own narrative and eventually find their own permanent form; legends only enlarge.

The events that lend themselves to mythologizing are large, tragic, and widely discussed. Fire has always generated myths evoking the primordial human appetite for control over nature. Prometheus was an Adam obsessively seeking something specifically denied by the gods. The freedom offered by fire is intimately associated with its double, destruction, which threatens imminent punishment when the flames inevitably get out of control. Elias Canetti commented on the human fascination with fire: "Fire is sudden; it can originate anywhere. No one is ever surprised when fire breaks out; here, there, or somewhere, it is always expected. Its very suddenness is impressive and people invariably search for a cause. The fact that often none can be found adds to the awe inherent in the idea of fire. It has a mysterious ubiquity; it can appear anywhere and at any time." The fear of fire revives memories of a time before science and technology attempted to explain and order mystery.

In myth, fire is linked to the imagination. Fire releases magic. Canetti again: "Fire spreads; it is contagious and insatiable. The violence with which it seizes whole forests and steppes and cities is one of the most impressive things about it. Until its onset tree stood by tree, and house by house, each distinct and separate from the next. But fire joins what was separate, and in the shortest possible time. Isolated and diverse objects all go up in the same flames. They become so much the same that they disappear completely. Houses, trees, creatures—the fire seizes them all."[2]

From its grain elevators and packing plants to its steel mills and stockyards, Chicago at the time of the fire was a Promethean city, celebrated for its ability to process raw material.[3] Other cities might have had one or two of its industries, but the concentration of them all in Chicago made it unique. By the 1860s, all railroads led to Chicago. The Chicago River, dwarfed by crowded commerce, appeared to be "a little muddy creek, crowded with huge masted wanderers from far-off waters nosing the black-posted banks."[4] Chicago's commerce would continue to dominate the river, its railroads, to dominate the land, and its towers, the sky. Chicagoans appropriated a vocabulary full of references to iron horses, cliffs, canyons, and mountains to describe an increasingly artificial environment, only recently sprung from the frontier. From the blast furnaces to the steam engines that powered the railroads, fire continued to be emblematic of Chicago's fate.

An event becomes legend as familiar themes are replayed through new details specific to the particular locale. The Chicago fire transposed Puritan myth to a gritty nineteenth-century urban setting, providing a real event for millennial rhetoric already in place. As a city in desolation, Chicago had a fortunate fall. At the time of America's most aggressive push westward, some of the country's best writers, like Nathaniel Hawthorne, had already imagined imminent disaster: "The Titan of innovation—angel or fiend, double in his nature, and capable of deeds befitting both characters."[5] Manifest Destiny had a dark imperial side. But in Hawthorne's American apocalypse, the End presented opportunities; out of a "heap of ashes and embers" people were free to invent, uninhibited by anxiety of the past.[6] In this fable, the End created a new point of origin, shifted significantly westward. Hawthorne's imaginary holocaust was Chicago's reality. Its inhabitants experienced what seemed to them to be a Biblical test—their only context for the extremes of fifteen-hundred-degree convection fires and cyclonic winds. New Jonahs and Jobs watched buildings melt and people evaporate in the heat. But instead of experiencing universal destruction, they and their city were saved. The "day after" became the first day of the new Chicago. The Biblical parallel ended in full view on the streets, where scenes of purposeful action provided vivid evidence that Chicago had cheated the apocalyptic prophesies of its own preachers. Within hours of the end Chicago was open again for business.

In the same year as Hawthorne's story, Edgar Allan Poe published "The Premature Burial" (1844). He too was drawn to the shadow side of American progress. His story is oddly predictive of Chicago's situation: "There are certain themes of which the interest is all absorbing, but which are too entirely horrible for the purposes of legitimate fiction. These the mere romanticist must eschew, if he do not wish to offend, or to disgust. They are with propriety handled, only when the severity and majesty of Truth sanctify and sustain them. We thrill for example, with the most intense of 'pleasurable pain', over the accounts of the Passage of the Beresina, of the Earthquake at Lisbon, of the Plague at London, of the Massacre of St. Batholmew, or of the stifling of the hundred and twenty-three prisoners in the Black Hole at Calcutta. But in these accounts, it is the fact—it is the reality—it is the history which excites. As inventions, we should regard them with simple abhorrence."[7]

The fact of a city in flames lay outside the reaches of the "legitimate fiction" of "mere romanticists" whose careers rested on not offending or disgusting their carefully prepared audience. A newly emerging middle-class readership preferred its dose of violence and disaster displaced to an earlier time and shifted to the usual hot-blooded Mediterranean locales at a good distance from home. Poe distinguishes between the Victorian hack and the modern artist, able to explore the real not just to fit what was seen and felt to convention. He continues: "I have mentioned some few of the more prominent and august calamities on record; but, in these, it is the extent, not less than the character of the calamity, which so vividly impresses the fancy . . . . The true wretchedness, indeed—the ultimate woe—is particular, not diffuse."[8]

Only the real event, reimagined and given its own language, is capable of eliciting "pleasurable pain." Poe was exploring the conditions of a future realism which he was not yet capable of writing himself. In the America of Hawthorne and Poe, the celebrated examples of tragedy were still too remote. On October 8, 1871, the civilizing force that had subdued the land went out of control. The narrative of Chicago's development and destruction offered a native tale of delicious pathos, in which the glory and tragedy of America's ambition was compressed into a single, memorable date.[9]

The swell of rhetoric and mythologizing that surrounds an emblematic event is a phenomenon first seen on a large scale after the Chicago fire. A western city in ruins provided the material for a sobering countermyth to the American vision of endless progress. The facts, featuring mass destruction and a loss of life on the scale of a Civil War battle, were daunting. There was no appetite yet for the sort of numbing retelling of atrocity that we experience today on the local evening news. People had a difficult time finding a language to tell the story.

The evangelists were there first with their standard end-of-the-world themes, although they didn't quite fit the facts of Chicago's remarkable survival. Elaborating on the record left by eyewitnesses and journalists, politicians followed with their own secular New Testament version of a city destroyed and reborn. A consideration of what had actually happened was quickly subordinated to a developing narrative that attempted to resolve into a unity the city's conflicted identity.

Chicago was at the time of the disaster a growing but still provincial city. The fire accelerated its rush into the modern. Legendizing of the fire was compensation in part for all that was thought lost. Tales of the fire were consolidated with earlier stories of the city into a secular myth that offered a certainty once provided by faith. A modern Chicagoan, Saul Bellow, suggests we have not yet outgrown our need for large events and the language that seems always to envelop them: "How we all love extreme cases and apocalypses, fires, drownings, stranglings and the rest of it. The bigger our mild, basically ethical, safe middle classes grow the more radical excitement is in demand. Mild or moderate truthfulness or accuracy seems to have no pull at all." [10]

Authenticity is always connected to specific cases. Events in real time shape the imagination, but never, as Bellow suggests, seem to be sufficient. We crave legends. Ironically, the very thing that stimulates interest—the suffering of individuals in a real situation—becomes generalized or distorted, its particularity lost. Almost immediately, an authentic piece of history is adapted to large abstractions already present in the culture. The celebrated event is adapted to provide airless abstractions with an air of reality, until an accretion of meanings makes the original facts almost unrecognizable.

In our own time, the mythologizing has become almost instantaneous. Two versions immediately surfaced of a widely-reported and photographed event in Tiananmen Square, Beijing, on June 4, 1989. The government praised a martyred army which had fought armed "ruffians" without killing a single student. On the other side, an observer of the massacre described in detail the murder of unarmed men and women. He told western reporters that before the events of May and June all his heroes had been in books; now he had seen some for himself. Information transmitted by fax, telephone, television, and newspapers made us all feel like eyewitnesses to a distant event.

Legendizing of experience is most common as a political phenomenon, particularly, but not confined to, the Orwellian rationalizing of totalitarian regimes. When America's Challenger space shuttle exploded seconds after launch on January 28, 1986, the President canceled the evening's scheduled State of the Union message and delivered some reassuring words about how the seven brave American heroes had died instantly, gathered into the arms of a waiting God—high-tech Icaruses plucked safely out of the air. Later investigation revealed mechanical error and further provided the unnerving speculation that the crew, rather than dying instantly, had been killed upon impact with the cold ocean.

The Challenger disaster has achieved iconographic meaning. Mention of Challenger now sets up immediate associations emblematic of strong antitechnology sentiments that had existed in American society before the disaster. It gave form to suppressed criticism of postwar American development that had rarely surfaced before. When three astronauts in the late sixties were burned to death in a fire on the launch tower, the event received close attention, but it was reported simply as a "regrettable accident." It lacked the necessary mythic qualities.

Events never generate myths; myths conjure the significance of events. Rockets blowing up on the launch pads in the early days of NASA did not cure Americans of the obsession to conquer space. But after years of fierce economic competition from Asia, post-Vietnam disenchantment with the military, and suspicion of large corporations, the Challenger fiasco seemed to epitomize the fallen status of America. NASA had seemed to be the Cadillac of space exploration; the failure of an "O ring" brought images to mind of an old Plymouth leaking fluids on the driveway. In the act of mourning the astronauts, the Challenger disaster allowed the public to mourn themselves and the decline of American technology. In less than a generation America had lost its first war and its industrial and political dominance. The Challenger became emblematic of once-amorphous dissatisfactions.

Cataclysms provide a focus absent from most lives. They have the aspect of theater, as we are forced to live outside ourselves. In retrospect, a single dramatic event, simply survived and seen uninquiringly, provides a certain unity to experience. One does not even have to have been there. Assassinations are individual cataclysms whose effects spread out quickly and involve millions. Through the destruction of a single gifted life, people see themselves at a distance, dramatized. They can see themselves seeing. John Lennon's death in 1980 represented to many the end of a hip pacificism and an imagined musical innocence. The deaths of Martin Luther King, Jr., and Robert Kennedy, within months of each other in the spring of 1968, crystallized the meaning of the sixties— the fatal mix of idealism and rage. John F. Kennedy's 1963 murder in Dallas revealed to a country that had been too enchanted with itself to notice, its own violent underside.

The Chicago fire was at the intersection of two contradictory ways of thinking about the modern. The immediate effects of the disaster had left those directly involved in a more elemental relation to the things around them. Buildings did not shelter them, authority did not protect them, and rhetoric did not immediately soothe them. Modern Chicago can be defined by the tension between the desire to recover a primitive sense of factuality and the necessity of finding a workable myth to sustain recovery.

How can this sense of inbetweenness be expressed? Walt Whitman was the first to find a form that expressed the double sense of disaster, in which one is conscious of the death of the old myth and the birth of the new. Whitman's Civil War poems examine the relationship between the classical view of the heroic and his own commitment to write about things as they were. They are in awkward balance:

On, on I go, (open doors of time! open hospital doors!)
The crush'd head I dress, (poor crazed hand tear not the
    bandage away,)
The neck of the cavalry-man with the bullet through and
    through I examine,
Had the breathing rattles, quite glazed already the eye,
    yet life struggles hard,
(Come sweet death! be persuaded O beautiful death!
In mercy come quickly.)
From the stump of the arm, the amputated hand,
I undo the clotted lint, remove the slough, wash off the
    matter and blood,
Back on his pillow the soldier bends with curv'd neck
    and side-falling head,
His eyes are closed, his face is pale, he dares not look on
    the bloody stump,
And has not yet look'd on it.[11]

Whitman is interested in seeing the thing itself, unmediated by language or sentiment; in effect, he is seeing it twice.[12] He wishes to record what the soldier, and perhaps by extension his Victorian audience, cannot yet bear to look at. But his report of crushed heads, clotted lint, stumps, and death rattles is not unrelieved. Typographically, Whitman sets up an opposition between an older form of romantic discourse, set off in parentheses ("Come sweet death! be persuaded O beautiful death!"), and his attempt to get at the facts through the use of unmediated description. He is emulating the photographer, and not the bard.

But the tension remains between the modern impulse to find form for what we see and the continued force of the unseen, the stuff of myth. Perhaps realism, the belief that we can ever see beyond myth and reimagine what we have seen through language, is our contemporary illusion. The realist sees the world in fragment, the mythographer finds unity. Experience of a catastrophic event puts these two in conflict. Poe used the metaphor of premature burial to include the contradictory impulses of seeking experience and fearing the results. We rubberneck at horrors.

The Chicago fire, like the Civil War for Whitman, challenged conventional ways of seeing. The results were too graphic—photographed and reported in detail—to ignore. Old formulas didn't work, and Chicago became a place hospitable to innovation on all levels. For as long as a generation after the fire, the city was a blank slate, liberated "for the first time since the days of Cadmus, free from the plague of letters—an enviable field for the authors of the next generation."[13] Chicago experimented with literary realism, a stripped-down and high-technology architecture, pragmatism, and the scientific study of society. All had a strong empirical base which valued observation over received opinion. While the rebuilding included much mindless replication, the disaster had created an environment of productive disorder. The visible ties with the past had been severed. Innovation became necessity.

But Chicagoans proved to be reluctant modernists. A generation after the fire, Chicago, after much competition, was awarded the honor of hosting the World's Columbian Exposition (1892–93). It was a building project on a scale not seen since the city had lain in ruins. The choice of a neoclassical style to clad what were essentially modern, steel-framed buildings was seen by Louis Sullivan and other modernists as a permanent retreat to a retrograde style. But of course the retreat proved not to be permanent. The history of architec-

1. Claes Oldenburg, Proposal for a Skyscraper for Michigan Avenue, Chicago, in the form of Lorado Taft's Sculpture "Death" (1968).

ture since then has shown a consistent movement back and forth between periods of invention and nostalgic returns. Architecture has always been used to create an impression of stability and order, particularly when they are patently absent in fact. Daniel Burnham's stewardship of Chicago's White City followed two decades of often violent innovation and change, including the fire, the rebuilding, the nationwide economic panic of 1873, and the growing labor agitation which culminated in the Haymarket Riot (1886).[14] Chicago's myth of unity was consistently challenged by events.

The city continues to claim the imagination as a double—sometimes tragic and other times almost farcical. Chicago still reveals itself through violent contradiction. Nelson Algren explains it: "With us ugliness and beauty, the grotesque and the tragic, and even good and evil, go their separate ways: Americans do not like to think that such extremes can mingle."[15] Simone de Beauvoir, when she visited Chicago after

World War II, was told by an American friend that the city was "all facade." After only twenty-four hours she had seen enough of the city, both the lakeside and the Polish district on the west, to see through the illusion. "In a big elegant restaurant on the Loop, where Martinis and grilled lobsters are served, I had difficulty in believing that it was still the same town. . . . If I had not been so insistent last night, I would not have known any more of Chicago than this *decor* made up of lights and stone, this facade at once so opulent, so polished and deceptive. At least I had glanced behind the painted scenes and had a glimpse of a real city, with its tragic daily life, fascinating like all cities where men must live and struggle in their millions." [16]

2. Red Grooms and Mimi Gross, *City of Chicago* (1967).

The Chicago Fire
The Making of a Legend

The Great Fire of October 8, 1871, provided Chicago with a convergence of fact and myth. In truth, the city suffered a terrible calamity. Frederick Law Olmsted, sent by *The Nation* to observe the damage, reported: "It will be seen that a much larger part of the town proper was burned than a stranger would be led to suppose by the published maps."[1] But even Olmsted, the acclaimed landscape architect, not given to gushing pronouncements, was taken with the fire's mythic proportions: "Very sensible men have declared that they were fully impressed at such a time with the conviction that it was the burning of the world."[2] Within days, the fire replaced the Fort Dearborn Massacre of 1812 and the frontier trials of the city's founders in the 1830s as Chicago's seminal moment. And whereas few alive in the 1870s had any firsthand memory of the massacre and only a few select families could count themselves founders, the fire included everyone. It was a universal experience, in which simple survival was made to seem heroic. An eyewitness recalled the scene as a "chapter of horrors that can only be written as it was, with a pen of fire."[3]

Chicago was quickly transformed, even before any of the rebuilding began; it became the only American city whose myth of founding and development was absolutely contemporaneous with its modern condition. Boston's origins went back to the Puritans, New York's, to the Dutch, and Philadelphia's, to a large English land grant. As a result, the roots of Eastern cities were emotionally remote from most of their nineteenth-century citizenry.[4] This was not true of Chicago. A Chicagoan needed to look no further back than October 8, 1871, for his city's origins.[5] The fire allowed him to think of himself as both pioneer and modern. It so compressed time—making the heroic past seem present and the present appear immediately part of the mythic past—that a Chicagoan might, if he chose, be released from his own history. History was thus so personalized that the city's resurrection seemed directly to apply to him. Through one dramatic act, the present was no longer necessarily subordinate to the past.

What separates Chicago's history of emerging modernity from that of other nineteenth-century cities is the clarity of its imagery.[6] While others suffered the modern through a host of neurasthenic symptoms—their bodies if not their minds agreeing with Marx's sense of the era's airlessness—Chicagoans felt its freeing possibilities.[7] Their initial view of the modern was positive. From the omnipresent engravings of the phoenix rising from the ashes to the apocalyptic talk of preachers and reporters, Chicagoans had a way to picture the way they felt. And because these images were not the mere fancy of artists and intellectuals, but ideas supported by the materiality of change seen everyday in the tons of rubble and shells of new buildings, each Chicagoan had a way to authenticate his sense of the transformation. But the question remained as to how long the city would be able to maintain its heady sense of common fate and enterprise before the specter of Chicago's double identity—as both queen of the inland lakes and gritty frontier city on the make—haunted it again. Because it is precisely this doubleness, even in the face of the postfire city's ever more dissonant realities, that provides modern Chicago with its character—a doubleness observed and systematically denied, that is as old as the city.

At the time of the fire, Chicago had just recently consolidated its position as the West's preeminent city. The opening of the Illinois and Michigan Canal (1848), and the founding of the Galena (1850), Illinois Central (1851), Michigan Southern, and Michigan Central (1852) railroads, which transformed the city from a retailing market into a prominent wholesaling center, were not far in the past. In fact, Chicagoans were nearly as close in time to their city's beginnings as a town in 1833 as they were to its recent renown. But Chicago always seemed to encourage visionaries who were less concerned with immediate realities than future opportunities. It was little more than a glorified army outpost when Charles Butler, one of the city's earliest financiers, arrived in 1833, but there was still something compelling enough about the place for him to invest one hundred thousand dollars and declare, "The experienced observer saw the germ of a city, destined from its peculiar position near the head of the Lake and its remarkable harbor formed by the river, to become the largest inland commercial Emporium in the United States."[8]

Butler was looking back fifty years when he recorded these

impressions. His brother-in-law William Ogden, Chicago's
first mayor, was another of the city's early prophets who
turned a profit on land investments. The infant city's heady
promise coexisted with the base realities of a muddy western
settlement. The visionary emporium of Butler and Ogden
was a spot where "wolves during the night roamed all over
where the city now stands."[9] Chicago always contained such
contradictions. One had to look beyond the present condition
or back into an idealized past to locate a consistent reality.
Had Butler's vision of Chicago materialized, it might well
have resembled Thomas Cole's painting *The Architect's Dream*
(1842) or the Court of Honor at the World's Columbian Exposition of 1893. The vision of the city's founding appeared to
be unified through the fortunes of its dynastic families, like
the trader Kinzies, real-estate baron Palmers, and packer
Swifts. The desired singleness of purpose always seemed to
compete with the gritty actuality at hand.

This duality between vision and reality became, at a very
early date, the way Chicagoans saw themselves. As long as a
unified vision of a progressive modern city was denied, they

4. Prefire Chicago: Illinois Central Yards.

5. Prefire Chicago: Shipping on the Chicago River.

would look to the future or the past to avoid the present, dress richly to forget recent poverty, and build grand facades for show on firetraps and structurally flawed buildings. An ingrained and finally institutionalized schizophrenia was, in part, compensation for the strains of the city's meteoric growth and expansion. Although a visitor in 1857 could declare, "Truly there is but one Chicago," he could not avoid mentioning progress's mixed results. "Miserable hovels are mixed up with the most beautiful and costly stores and edifices, such as I never saw in any other place."[10] The "one Chicago" frustrated devotion; the costs of development, both material and human, were too apparent. "The only drawback, perhaps, to the comfort of the money-making inhabitants, and of the stranger within the gates, is to be found in the clouds of dust and in the unpaved streets and thoroughfares, which give anguish to horse and man."[11]

Chicago's incongruities became a part of any portrait of the city. Praise, set off by examples from the city's other side, began to structure the ways people thought and wrote about Chicago. It was not as if Chicago was the only American city with dark recesses. Cable's New Orleans and Norris's San Francisco were just as bleak. Only in Chicago's case there was a certain pride in the city's divided nature because of its faith in an eventual coherence that would vindicate its struggles. Here was a city founded and developed from a dialectic of forces; as in America itself, unity would emerge from diversity. The mud, foul weather, and depravity, which in lesser

6. Prefire Chicago: Buildings along the Chicago River.

places would resist civilization, gave Chicago's development its special character. A city that seemed perpetually divided was employing its inherited contradictions to prevail. A local commentator reported: "The wickedness and the piety of Chicago are, in their way, marvelous. It is a city of church-building, church-going people, and yet contains more people who are not church-going in proportion to the population, than any other place. The Sabbath day in Chicago is, so far as the eye can discover externally, as quiet and orderly as in any New England city; yet, all laws for Sunday observance have been repealed, and in no other American city are there so many people who devote the day to festivity. Everything undertaken here is done promptly and on a grand scale."[12]

J. W. Sheahan, a Chicagoan who later published an account of the fire, writing in the September 1875 issue of *Scribner's Monthly*, employed the contemporary idea of a divided Chicago. Where others used the contrast between hovels and mansions, Sheahan divided the city between churchgoer and religious truant. But there is a critical difference. Sheahan noticed none of the cultural anxiety expressed in earlier accounts. Something had happened that changed the ways Chicagoans presented and perceived themselves. Not that the facts were different; only the attitudes toward development had changed. Chicago had found a way to see itself. Instead of trying to resolve its divisions like the cities of the East Coast and Europe, it would make its conflicts the basis of its identity. The differences of tone and attitude that Sheahan reported would never have amounted to much more than the stuff of Sunday supplements, if not for the Great Chicago Fire of 1871.

The fire provided substance for the inchoate sense of Chicago's uniqueness. For instance, Sheahan discovered in the events of the fire substantiation for the city's four-decades-long claim to "greatness."[13] Others viewed the calamity as a dramatic justification for the posturings of its pioneer generation. The fire became the key to understanding the city, so that an event that did nothing to resolve the city's deep divisions along class and ethnic lines did something more radical by providing a model for initiative and innovation. It implied to Chicagoans that their history would not evolve in millenia, like the history of European cities, nor in centuries, like that of established American cities, but in bursts which liberated individuals to do their best. Divisions that might paralyze other places provided the very condition for Chicago's existence. Change on the largest scale was to be permanent in modern Chicago.

Starting on the Southwest Side's DeKoven Street on the evening of October 8, the fire raged late into the next day and night, ending in the northeast on Fullerton Avenue, frustrated finally by Lake Michigan and a persistent rain shower.[14] Two thousand acres were lost. Eighteen thousand buildings were destroyed and ninety thousand people were left homeless.[15] City coroner Stephens and Cook County physician Dr. Ben C. Miller estimated deaths at nearly three hundred, noting the difficulty of identifying bodies charred beyond recognition.[16] Clearly, the fire was a major disaster, but the city could consider itself lucky because so few lives were lost, in large part due to the wind's consistent northeast heading. Although the winds never achieved a velocity of over thirty miles per hour, the blaze was aided by a convection effect, or "fire devils," which greatly added to its destructive energy.[17]

The eyewitness accounts understandably stressed the dramatic and life-threatening aspects of the disaster. Chicago's "sluggish river seemed to boil."[18] The event was immediately made to take on mysterious powers. "The wind blowing a stiff gale has possession of the flames, and the beautiful buildings, Chicago's glory, lay before them . . . and within an incredibly short space of time nearly a mile of brick blocks was consumed as if by magic."[19] Not only the act of nature it surely was, the culminating act of a ninety-eight-day drought during which less than two inches of rain had fallen since July

7. Magazine illustration: "Scene on the Chicago River. Grain Elevators on Fire" (1871).

fourth,[20] nor the result of the carelessness of man, who had overbuilt the city with flammable materials and protected it with a spectacularly inadequate fire department;[21] the fire took on the attributes of a full-blown act of God or the devil, complete with Biblical overtones. An account published in the *Post* of October 17 suggests the tone of the response: "From the roof of a tall stable and warehouse to which the writer clambered, the sight was one of unparalleled sublimity and terror. He was above the whole fire. The crowds directly under him could not be distinguished because of the curling volumes of crimsoned smoke, through which an occasional scarlet rift could be seen. He could feel the heat and smoke and hear the maddened Babel of sounds, and it required but little imagination to believe one's self looking over the adamantine bulwarks of hell into the bottomless pit."[22] The Great Fire was a one-and-a-half-day apocalypse, an enormous event that instantly confirmed the city's importance both to its citizens and to all outsiders who watched or heard about its trials, a disaster comparable in their view to the destruction of Rome, Babylon, or Troy.[23] But this was a particularly American apocalypse. Instead of leveling the city and destroying forever man's vainglories, this act of magic, devil, or God was decidedly latitudinarian. The Kingdom of God to which Chicagoans awoke the next morning was not among the angels in heaven, but still in Chicago. Twenty years after

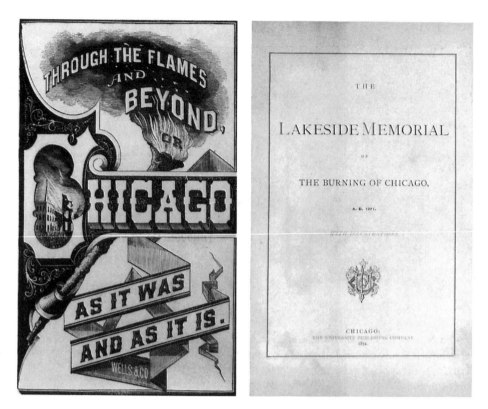

8. Title page of *Through the Flames and Beyond*.

9. Title page of *The Lakeside Memorial of the Burning of Chicago* (1872).

the fire, the Chicago evangelist David Swing wrote, "When we awoke we were in a new world . . . the tens of thousands of sleepers sunk away in weariness and grief, but when they awoke they saw around them a Nation full of kindness, and a great circle of states and empires all colored deeply by an undreamed of civilization."[24] Swing echoes here an idea of worldly trial and redemption that has its American roots in William Bradford's *Of Plymouth Plantation* (1630), itself a retrospective account of a great human test.

What the Puritans found in the trials of a sea voyage, Chicagoans like Swing and Kirkland discovered in the fire. The Puritans' tabula rasa was simply projected onto Chicago's cooling ashes; the fire was to be a repeat of the initial American apocalypse in which all dissonance had vanished, only this time not so that the righteous could claim the next world but so that all could have a new chance to prosper materially. Chicago perhaps could finally after the fire shed the ragged image of a western town, the contradictions and persistent double identity as a place of rare highs and frequent lows, and begin its own urban idyll.[25] This was a popular form of late nineteenth-century urban pastoral. Darker Theocritan pastoral images appeared later as writers confronted the more fragmented reality of the city. Like those who survived the ocean's perils that claimed so many lives aboard Bradford's ship, Chicago's survivors were extraordinary individuals who "resisted beastly drunkeness"[26] and overcame the rage of their fellow citizens "maddened by the sight of pillage or arson who fell upon the miscreant and beat him to death."[27] Tales of the fire began to read like a modern morality play in which good, it seemed, was destined to overcome evil. The difference was that this was living theater which threatened to get out of hand.

A sense of impending chaos led the federal government to call out the army. Although General Sheridan denied that there was any widespread civil unrest, his presence helped insure order.[28] His confident show of force was a sure sign to outsiders that Chicago was going to survive intact. In response, there began almost immediately a tremendous outpouring of aid from other states, foreign countries, and national businesses. Within hours of the fire, Chicago began rebuilding, content with its new notoriety, and finally confirming to others the greatness it had projected for itself nearly four decades earlier. So it was quite natural to find in the first comprehensive report of the fire, Elias Colbert and Everett Chamberlin's *Chicago and the Great Conflagration,* language linking the city to America's beginnings. The authors declared that reconstruction would issue from the "firm foundation rock of her business, the Plymouth Rock of her society."[29] This was a time to start over, like the country's first settlers had. The authors exploited the ancient precedents: "Let any man figure to himself what he would endure if he were stripped not only of everything that may make him conventionally 'respectable' or eminent, but of the wherewithal to supply the first conditions of physical existence—food and shelter—and all his neighbors stripped of all that could alleviate his sufferings, and he will form a notion, faint and far off indeed, but far truer than description, however ample, could give him, of what has befallen, and for many days to come will befall, myriads of men as capable as himself to suffer and enjoy."[30] The city's swift recovery lent support to such self-important analogies. Chicago had been tested—its people stripped to essentials—and had been found more than equal to the challenge. Some wrote unlikely improvisations on Biblical myths concerning the end: "That towering wall of whirling, seething, roaring flame, which swept on and on—devouring the most stately and massive stone buildings

10. W. D. Kerfoot's Real Estate Office (1871), the first building constructed after the fire.

as though they had been the cardboard playthings of a child."[31] Others like Swing wrote of the beginning of a "new world." In all local accounts, the fire established Chicago as the most American of American cities. Instantly, it became the newest Old city of the New World, incarnating in microcosm the country's century-long westward expansion.

Facts of the initial reconstruction only gave further substance to the city's boast. Within days of the disaster, the General Relief Committee was established to provide refuge and create distribution centers to handle the influx of donations and charitable aid. In answer to the Chamber of Commerce's October 10 call to rebuild immediately, there were already on November 18th over five thousand cottages completed or under construction.[32] And by October 1872 there was over thirty-four-million dollars worth of new building on the South Side, almost four-million on the North, and nearly two-million on the West.[33] Trade quickly increased, and real estate values inflated to a level at or above prefire assessments. Chicago's forty years of constant development had paradoxically made the land more valuable without structures than with. Expensive buildings constructed before the fire were now more valuable as rubble. Potter Palmer, the city's most successful and flamboyant real estate speculator, recouped and extended his fortune after losing all his buildings to the fire.[34] The city even grew, using debris from the fire as landfill to extend its boundaries.

While Chicago's physical plant was severely affected, its importance as a commercial and industrial hub remained essentially undisturbed.[35] It still had unrivaled geographic superiority for railroad, canal, river, and lake travel. Grain, lumber, and stock, according to the Chicago Board of Trade, was 75 to 80 percent intact. Almost 90 percent of manufacturing, machinery, and products was unaffected.

Within a year after the fire, Chicagoans were planning a memorial to their city's aborted destruction. Although the memorial was never completed, only two years after the fire the Inter-State Industrial Exposition (September 25–November 12, 1873) was held to celebrate Chicago's material progress since the fire. The Exposition's exhibits were offered as factual evidence for the city's maturing mythology of resurrection. Even visitors caught it. A British traveler (quoted in the *Chicago Tribune,* January 18, 1874) called Chicago the "concentrated essence of Americanism," America reborn.[36]

Fairs, plans for memorials, and reconstruction's impressive statistics were only the palpable manifestations of a phenomenon attributable to the fire. The conflagration was made to validate Chicago's claim to uniqueness. Here was a city that not only could survive adversity but welcomed such a powerful event to clean away the negative aspects of development. On the Sunday following the fire, Henry Ward Beecher, preaching at Chicago's Plymouth Church, declared that the city "could not afford to do without the Chicago Fire."[37] Beecher, like Swing, used the fire, strongly dramatic in its effects, as a model of change. This American apocalypse was a scene of great disruption, but one that would create both material and moral opportunities.[38] Chicago's use of this idea was especially stunning because the transition from bad to good news was almost instantaneous. Chicago's experience with disaster secularized the Biblical idea of history's end and incorporated it into a growing civic mythology. Chicagoans had survived their city's fortunate fall into the future.

This secularized theology freed the city from doubt and gave its citizens a way to view positively two decades of cyclical reversals, including financial panics and labor unrest. Such a faith became the conceptual underpinning of all who would come to think and write about Chicago. Perpetuated around the time of the fire was a myth that proposed to exclude the city from history's ravages: Chicago was conflict's beneficiary, not its victim. Initially just in sermons but later universally, the city began to be seen as fortune's child, the happy survivor of the "day after," and the future's pride. Chicago was the American city that was not only free of a long and deadening history, like its western counterparts, but was also released from its own past mistakes. Illustrators portrayed it as the phoenix rising. If they could seize the opportunity, Chicagoans thought themselves in a position to regain the energy represented by Butler's pioneering generation without the attendant problems. The fire then could be viewed as modernization's necessary hygiene, a cyclical fact of modern life. What men could not correct, nature would. Could anything stop a city that had successfully resisted a test of Biblical severity that was enough to "reverse the Westward current of human migration and unsettle the business of the world?"[39] Swing had the answer: "Twenty years would transform a painful experience into rather a pleasing dream."[40]

The fire's immediate legacy was that Chicago would not be allowed to get old and decadent. Even Colbert and Chamberlin adopted the developing apocalyptic tone. Future visitors to the city "will find her changed from the Chicago of yesterday in such manner as the wild and wanton girl, of luxurious beauty, and generous, free ways, is changed."[41] The earliest speculators and developers had provided the original impetus for improvement, which left alone was fast becoming detrimental to the city's moral development. A change was required. "The people of Chicago were, before the fire, fast lapsing into luxury—not as yet to any degree as the people of New York—but still more than was for their good. The fire roused them from this tendency, and made them the same strong men and women, of the same simple, industrious, self-denying habits, which built up Chicago, and pushed her so powerfully along her unparalleled career. All show and frivolity were abandoned, and democracy became the fashion."[42] In one great act, the American promised land had arrived on the streets of Chicago. Tired men and women were transformed. Young again like the city, they could now get back to work and abandon their "dawdling lives." Viewed in this way, the fire became a timely moral corrective. And given Chicago's more earthy interests, it also aided in the "correction of besetting faults, which it is fair to assume would not have been corrected if the city had not been burned."[43]

The "Great Awakening" after the initial Puritan settlements took three long generations to develop; in Chicago, the awakening after the fire occurred almost immediately. Thirty-six hours of flames and hot winds were more than equal to Jonathan Edwards's words: "If God should only withdraw his hand from the flood-gate, it would immediately fly open, and the fiery floods of the fierceness and wrath of God, would rush forth with inconceivable fury."[44] Chicagoans had seen the "fiery floods," and their experiences made Edwards's rhetoric palpable. The city made metaphor literal by the very materiality of its history. Through the fire's urgency, Chicago was compelled to experience in microcosm the eighteenth-century American passage from a sense of spiritual degeneration to attempted purification. Only what were once words and images to Edwards's congregation were now facts. Chicago could see itself not only in terms of its own particular history but as a paradigm for the larger development of America as a nation. In no small measure, the city was the national testing ground for abstractions through which the country was coming to know itself. The local commentators all took advantage of their rush to prominence. The moralists and theologians among them argued the fine points, but all initially appeared to agree that any city that survived such a calamity would in the end, like Edwards's parishioner contemplating his nasty fate, be better off. The facts supported such optimism. On a strictly economic and political basis, Chicago in the months and years after the fire could be shown to have made a startling correction for four decades of nearly random, unplanned development. To this end, Colbert and Chamberlin wrote that real-estate speculators who had suffered severe losses might in the future be less reckless; their buildings would be made of better materials. The fire because it "checked the two [*sic*] rapid spread of the city in all directions" would lead to a rebuilding of the city's central business district.[45] In addition, by getting rid of failing or marginal businesses, the fire could be seen literally as a "purifying" act.[46] In fact, the politicians, including Mayor Joseph Medill, who immediately after the disaster ran on a "Fire-Proof" ticket—arguing for a strict building code which included the elimination of flammable architectural ornamentation—won by a five-to-one margin.

Colbert and Chamberlin's report, published within months of the fire (December 1, 1871), was the document of record. *Chicago and the Great Conflagration* combined authoritative facts and figures describing the disaster graphically with more evocative chapters like "Good Out of Evil" and "The New Chicago." As a result, the authors articulated an instant history, a seemingly objective account that gave people a way to view a common experience. Instant history is now a common phenomenon; a population comes to learn how it feels by reading about itself. Primary experience is thus distanced and is made somewhat suspect until given the authority of interpretation. For instance, by reading about the damage done to "individual fortunes," the population was encouraged to bemoan its own bad luck and at the same time consider the city's greater destiny. By doing so individuals were spared painful personal introspection and encouraged to sublimate their own fate to Chicago's. The city's recovery then could be thought of in the same dramatic terms as its aborted destruction until the question became simply one of "how long it will require for the country to produce the bricks and the stone to lay up her walls."[47] To Chicago's worldly believers, restitution was expected in this world, not the next. After assembling their contributors' eyewitness accounts, the editors of *Harper's Weekly* (November 4, 1871) added their own imprimatur to the city's increasingly sophisticated mythos: "It will all come back again in time, if not to every loser, certainly to those who believe in the future of Chicago. It will be made a better city than it ever could have become but for this fire. A better building system, a more shapely development, a spirit of enterprise and determination, literally tried as by fire, will bring all these results."[48]

Let the rest of the country wait for Judgment Day, *Harper's* editors implied, for Chicago had already had its, and had wound up on the other shore potentially in better shape than ever.[49] All the elements were in place. Tried by fire, Chicago merely lacked a gifted enough interpreter to consolidate the myth of its apocalypse with the facts of its extraordinary trials. Chicago found him, though, conveniently enough in the person of William Bross, Illinois's ex–lieutenant governor and an eyewitness to the fire. In the guise of a formal history, Bross provided seemingly objective language to describe the city's first modern decade. More civic propaganda than were the later artistic attempts of the eighties and nineties, his *History of Chicago* (1876) cleverly fit four decades of free-form growth to the fire's thirty-six hours of violent change.

Although there had been prefire efforts to understand the city in terms of its larger history, most notably Judge Henry Brown's *History of Chicago* (1844) and Juliette Kinzie's novel *Wau-Bun* (1856), they were largely anecdotal or broadly autobiographical. Bross personified the city and centered the story directly on Chicago. He had intuited a new fact of urban life. Whereas the West had formerly depended on man to name and frame it, very much in the spirit of James Fenimore Cooper's pioneers, Chicago in the 1870s reversed this defining practice. The city now bestowed fame, and did not need to borrow it from the celebrity of its visitors. Bross tried to argue that Chicago, like Paris and London, could now claim to make individuals significant by their mere presence on its streets. But unlike the fancy European cities that cultivated class and position, Chicago gave equal status to all those who survived the fire. Bross's upbeat report of the event and the city's immediate rush to rebuild encouraged the growing romance of how Chicago was to be after the fire.[50]

Bross in his *History* simply affirmed and gave language to a newly experienced sensation of urban identification. Individuals, in this formulation, were immediately aggrandized by their association with the city in which they lived. Bross hoped that "Chicagoan"—given the heroic agency of the fire—would one day soon rival "Parisian" and "New Yorker" for the mystery and romance of its associations. A contemporary preacher put it this way: "You could tell a Chicagoan in any city in the world, for he would not talk a minute scarcely until he would let you know he was from Chicago."[51] A man's identity became in the nineteenth century subordinated to the city in which he lived. More important than family or religion, the city was central in the 1870s. Credit Bross that he saw this critical shift of allegiances as one of the dominant aspects of modern life. His *History* is an attempt to establish Chicago's claim to such radical dependency, not with a comprehensive account of the city but with highlights of its accomplishments augmented by facts and illustrations to support his claims. He writes for a new Chicagoan who needs a language to understand his home. By understanding the city's mythos, the anonymous individual—emigrating from the countryside in ever-larger numbers—might find mirrored his own rationale for existence and striving.

Bross's work, soon supplanted by A. T. Andreas's comprehensive three-volume *History of Chicago* (1884–86), was a crucial document if only because it provided a conceptual bridge between what Chicago was and what it wanted to become. Using the fire as a dramatic demarcation dividing the city's past from its future, Bross established, for the first time, a grammar for the 1870s. His *History* focuses on the fire as the culmination of a forty-year-long reorganization of man and materials. The negative side of such mass development can surely be extrapolated from Bross's statistics, but the overall impression for the author was decidedly positive. Positive, not because Bross neglected familiar Chicago contradictions but because he was skillful enough to manipulate an individual sense of trauma toward an identification with the commonwealth. He recorded the displacement of farm land caused by the sale of hundreds of thousands of new city lots (25 × 125 feet each)[52]; he duly noted a thousandfold population increase in just over four decades; and he correctly projected that such an influx of people would severely strain existing services and resources. But when he made these observations or considered the growing gap between rich and poor, success and failure, he provided his reader with a higher rationale, implying that it would be a mistake to think of Chicago as being determined by even its recent history. The fire had seen to that by leveling all in its way. It is a theme Swing picked up in recalling the day of the fire: "This was not a poor man's fire. It smote the rich and the middle class. After destroying six hundred great business houses, great churches, hotels, and theatres, it crossed the river and attacked the most fashionable homes in the North Division."[53] So too did the novelist and historian Joseph Kirkland echo the theme of unity out of chaos in his own retrospective account when he observed, "After all the ages of men's alienation, isolation, enmity, the race is at last one, in heart; and it needed the Chicago fire to make patent the blessed fact."[54]

Both Swing and Kirkland were merely repeating—admittedly in their own personal terms—Bross's formula for the events. Swing, without mentioning the October 7 West Side fire of a day earlier, was quick to point out the universality of suffering. This was not a "poor man's fire," unlike the one preceding the Great Fire which did an estimated one-million-dollars worth of damage.[55] The Great Fire was different because, in Kirkland's words, it ended the "ages of men's alienation" and made the race "at last one." Substitute Chicagoans for "race," excusing Kirkland's elevated diction, and you can understand how successful Bross was in promulgating his own ideas about Chicago and the fire. For it was Bross's aim in his *History* to universalize suffering and triumph. He wished to see Chicago (like the Puritan's Plymouth) after the calamity as a blank slate, a place to make new arrangements, educated but unbound by history. The ex–lieutenant governor's tone is characteristically direct and practical: "There has not been, for the last twenty years, so good a time for men of capital to start business in Chicago as now. Thousands anxious to locate in this focus of Western Commerce have been deterred from doing so for the reason that the business in each department had become concentrated in comparatively a few hands. With few exceptions, all can now start even, in the race for fame and fortune. The fire has leveled nearly all distinctions."[56]

All the facts were there to support the city's ascendancy in all areas of urban development, from railroads, manufacturing, heavy industry, and trade, to numbers of hotels and domestic buildings. Bross wrote that all could point with "confidence and pride" to their combined accomplishments. But the story was not all in the facts. Facts might be enough for the Bostons, New Yorks, and Philadelphias. Bross called them "finished" cities. Like their older European models, the East Coast urban centers were no longer developing. In Bross's view, they were culturally set in place. But not Chicago. Chicago was unfinished and being made over every day.[57]

Bross's implications were clear. Here was a place dynamic enough to welcome disaster rather than to suffer the stultifying stratification of other cities. The fire "leveled nearly all distinctions" and instantly provided new opportunities for growth. William Bross was important because his was the first "official" account of the Chicago legend, one repeated, embroidered, and improved upon, but not essentially altered. It reads: Out of periodic adversity, from the original calamity, the Indian massacre at Fort Dearborn, through financial panics and economic reversals, to the Great Fire, Chicago not only survived but prospered. Bross simply extended the legend to include Chicago's most recent history and described it in modern language.

Chicago, in his view, became the archetypal American city, going through the usual urban growth process, only dramatically faster and more efficiently. While it had taken the oldest American cities centuries, and Chicago initially decades, to transform from frontier to metropolis, in the 1870s it took only years. Bross reminded his readers: "It should be noticed that what I predicted would be accomplished in five years was mostly done in three, and much of it in two. The unsightly acres still to be seen on State street, Wabash avenue, and some portions of Michigan avenue, were burned over by the disastrous fire of July 14th, 1874. Nearly all the open spaces made by the great fire of 1871 are now covered with buildings."[58] Within three years the city was repaired and responding to the opportunity created by yet another fire. The legend implied that Chicago was special and disaster-proof. The apocalyptic moment provided it with a serial necessity for starting over. It was its special identity, a stimulant to dynamic change unavailable to all those "finished" cities back East and in Europe. For Chicago, devastation, manmade or natural, became merely opportunity's mother, allowing all to "start even, in the race for fame and fortune."

Change, the modern's defining characteristic, was what Bross called the city's "permanent impulse."[59] Chicago's condition in the 1870s was a paradox—change was permanent and the search for permanence frustrated. This modern feeling of being temporary was keenly experienced by individuals, who alternately experienced the sensation as stimulating and depressing. It was to become, in many ways, the driving emotional force behind the city's art and a prod to two decades of intense creative expression, culminating in the great architecture of the late 1880s and the 1890s.

Edward Payson Roe was the city's first novelist to combine Chicago's growing sense of a unique identity with the anxieties occasioned by life after the fire. More a melodrama than a fully developed work of fiction, Roe's *Barriers Burned Away* (1872) is the emotional counterpart to Bross's history.[60] Where Bross showed Chicagoans how to see the fire, Roe suggested the ways they might feel. Their accounts are remarkably similar.

Structured as a conventional sentimental tale complete with righteous and tragic deaths, noble poverty and empty wealth, Roe's novel uses the fire in a clever way. Other nineteenth-century American novels were conveniently resolved through war, pestilence, suicide, and other deus ex machina devices; *Barriers Burned Away* employs the fire as a perfect indigenous solution to the characters' differences of sensibility, class, and ambition. The novel ends with Chicago ruined. Its population, rich and poor, is left nearly naked to wander the beach. Christine Ludolph, a spoiled American with an inherited title, has lost her father and possessions to the flames, but she feels oddly free. In the heat of the fire she declares, "I wish to take leave to-night of my old life—the strange, sad past with its mystery of evil; and then I shall set my face resolutely toward a better life—a better country."[61] Her "utterly pagan" room in ruins, Christine feels liberated. She can now embrace Dennis Fleet, the poor but honest young man who has been working in her father's art business and who has distinguished himself over time as a responsible and talented artist. In hours, the fire accomplishes reconciliations that for years have seemed impossible. Christine declares, "Love has transformed that desert place into the paradise of God."[62] But the author has us understand that, although the result is unchanged, Christine has cause and effect reversed. Love does not "transform" Chicago; rather the city in its blasted state makes it once again possible for people to make elemental connections. Precisely because people are left wandering on the beach, stripped of inessential possessions and pretenses, are they suddenly in a free environment. The fire is seen as a necessary precondition for love.

E. P. Roe in *Barriers Burned Away* simply fictionalized prevailing attitudes about the fire and Chicago's modern condition. Along with other eyewitnesses to the calamity, he saw the fire as a fortunate fall in temporal terms. Christine Ludolph is Roe's example of a character who rises to a "higher life" through severe moral and physical tests. Chicago in ruins is her paradise.

Yet such a fortuitous accident was not merely a product of Roe's imagination. As we have seen, positive views of disaster were prevalent after the fire. Roe simply employed them as his characters' reactions. A Presbyterian minister, he gave authenticity to the twisted emotional logic of the time. Although the fire was by all indices a material catastrophe, it was viewed widely as ultimately good. His book became a bestseller in 1872 because Roe succeeded in capturing the city's longing after meaning. He confirmed his audience's sense of having survived something extraordinary. The book works at achieving a strong sense of reality, an objective accomplished through a self-conscious echoing of contemporary reports. Roe struggles to express the fire's sounds. He recalls that, "The rush and roar of the wind and flames were like the thunder of Niagra, and to this awful monotone accompaniment was added a Babel of sounds."[63] Compare Roe's fictional treatment to the *Harper's* account published a few months earlier: "Every one knows how inadequate is human language to express the grandeur of Niagra—we can only *feel* it. And yet Niagra sinks into insignificance."[64] Out of the fire's Babel, Roe found an adequate language, one with which Chicagoans were already conversant.

The novel's struggle for authenticity made it part of a general movement to establish the fire as a universally accepted emblem of Chicago's modern state. Whereas the sublime was formerly only to be found deep in nature, it now could be discovered in the urban core. To Bross's later metaphor of the city's "permanent impulse," Roe offered a collateral image. For Roe, the fire was the culmination of an extended time of change, "a chaotic period—the old world breaking up," and the beginning of new social and cultural arrangements.[65] His own decade of the 1870s would be a concentrated time of "breaking up," in which the fire only hastened transformations that were slowly occurring anyway and simply heightened existing conflicts, inherent in modern life, to the point of explosion.

Roe's work is important not only because it is the first fiction of the period but because *Barriers Burned Away* is itself, like the city, balanced precariously between old and new. In many ways the work embodies standard Victorian conflicts: battles of influence (pious mother versus worldly, beaten father); conflicts of ambitions (success versus the good); and the virtues of the country pitted against the dangers of city life. However, influenced by the real example of Chicago after the fire, Roe gives an importance to place that is at least embryonically modern.

Roe stresses the generational differences between Dennis Fleet and his parents. The elder Fleets had moved west from Connecticut and had found enough initial prosperity to support Dennis's first three years at college, "under the great elms in Connecticut."[66] But life on the prairie gets bad. The father, driven to drink and depression by his failure to achieve, settles into paralyzed inaction. The mother survives through inspired resignation, imagining "to herself grander things which God would realize to her *beyond* this earth."[67] When Dennis arrives home, forced to leave college, he is surprisingly optimistic. In the first of a series of displacements, Roe simply exchanges Chicago for Dennis's mother's city "beyond this earth." While she waits for—and is soon dispatched to—the "celestial railroad," Dennis takes the "express train . . . toward the great city."[68] "The world was all before him, and Chicago, the young and giant city of the West, seemed an Eldorado, where future, and perhaps fame, might soon be won."[69]

The second major displacement occurs when Dennis enters the city. Although his father followed the earlier lure of self-sufficiency in the West, Dennis knows better. Roe's novel is a counterpastoral in which money (Dennis only has two dollars in his pocket) is the "ample seed corn . . . for a golden harvest."[70] Money displaces the idyllic land. Unlike anti-urban novels of the period, Roe's views Chicago, particularly after the fire's general hygiene, as the West's inevitable center. Although Dennis, having abandoned his legal studies and all hopes of becoming a refined professional, has trouble learning the rules of "practical Chicago" and considers a "return to pastoral life,"[71] he stays because "even in the midst of a great city the sweet odor of spring find their way."[72] Roe has transposed the acts of pioneering and discovery from the western prairie to the heart of the city.

Dennis's struggle, for this and other reasons, is distinct from his parents'. While they have succeeded or failed through their attempts to flee the city, Dennis's success is measured by the degree to which his values—true art and virtue—can be made to prevail in town. His forced retreat from a practical career and his choice to become an artist illuminate Roe's sense of modern Chicago. In this sketchy portrait of an artist, the author attempts to portray the growing conflict between enduring spiritual values which proved lethal to the older generation—the legion of Mrs. Fleets in nineteenth-century sentimental fiction—and the developing secular religion of business and commerce.[73] Dennis, like many other Chicagoans of the century's last decades, is caught between the high culture—religious ideas of the good and artistic ideas of the beautiful—that inspires him and the energizing low culture of the burgeoning city. The novel's most interesting aspect is, in fact, Roe's insistent attempt to reconcile, through his portrait of Dennis's and Christine's difficult love, the undeniable power of Chicago street life with a series of higher ideals not formerly associated with the new American cities. The fire's extraordinary reality accelerated the process of reconciliation. The excitement of the apocalyptic moment created the appearance of a larger social compact which proved over time to be as impermanent as the fire's damage.

Life before the fire was perceived as bifurcated. There was an older generation of "aborigines"[74] who had brought with them to Chicago a mix of piety and ambition. Seen from a distance, pioneers like Butler and Ogden became models of respectability, combining Eastern education with the demands of Western settlement. They became the Chicago establishment. Set up in fine houses and rich enough for philanthropy, Chicago's first generation had time for pieties and church-going. Fortunes already in hand, they looked for ways to spend their money and perpetuate their newly minted good reputations. Their sons and daughters, with the pressure of making money removed, lacked any direction. Beginning in the 1870s, Chicago literature is marked with portraits of dissolute young men—often prodigal sons who before it's too late come to their senses—and airy young women. Playboys and dilettantes, especially before the fire, appeared to be Chicago's legacy.

However, there was another important group of young people. If Christine Ludolph, before her conversion on the beach, represents the former, Dennis Fleet is emblematic of the latter. Eastern-educated and full of ambition, like the city's first generation, Dennis only lacks opportunity. To Roe, Dennis and Christine are the two halves of Chicago's future. Christine's friends include the children of robber barons. She is always off to parties at brewer Brown's home; like Christine, "his daughter seemed to be living in a palace of ice." Miss Ludolph and her friends represent opportunity without ambition, while Dennis and young men like the poor son of his painting teacher have ambition without opportunity. Roe saw Chicago's divided generation as endemic to the city's accelerated development. There was something defective about such a vital place where those most able to lead were systematically excluded from power. Roe offers an explanation, through a gentle criticism of Dennis, "The defect in his religion, and that of his mother too, was that both separated the spiritual life of the soul too widely from the present life with its material, yet essential, cares and needs." [75]

Roe's criticism eventually led him and his contemporaries to embrace a pragmatic code that comfortably balanced the imperatives of the spirit with the more anarchic energies of a gritty city. And because of this it is no accident that Chicago literature of the late nineteenth century is filled with characters who are either accomplished or aspiring artists. For the artist, particularly a practical one like an architect, seems most suited to express the city's complex identity. Roe's *Barriers Burned Away*, with all its stylistic deficiencies, presents the archetype for the modern Chicagoan, and in many ways the model for the ideal American. Roe recognized that his central character could not simply be heroic. [76] Rather, he looked forward and tried to imagine the qualities necessary for the city's future: a composite character blending feminine piety with the power of male ambition. Through the eventual alliance of Dennis and Christine, Roe suggests the qualities necessary for any whole individual in the coming decades. However, these qualities, which were gender-specific in Chicago's first generation—witness the lives of god-fearing Mrs. Fleet and the beaten father—were no longer so in the 1870s. This marriage of essential qualities does not come about only through love (which distinguishes Roe's novel from other, pure melodramas) but through a natural disaster.

Before the fire Christine Ludolph "believed in nothing save art and her father's wisdom." [77] Her father, a dealer in objets d'art, deals with art as a commodity. Roe has us understand that as long as Christine is under his sway she will never create anything of value. In fact, she comes to realize this herself and winds up copying Dennis's more original paintings. But Dennis, too, is incomplete, although he possesses "a rare sensitivity to beauty. While others exclaim it, he savors it."[78] It is not until Dennis dedicates himself completely to art by studying with the master Bruder that his elevated sensibility becomes more than a self-destructive taint. The older painter Bruder eventually dies in poverty, even with his superior talent, because he lacked the more "practical" skills Dennis learns and because he was unable to "work more from the commercial standpoint than the artist's."[79] At the time of the fire, both Dennis and Christine have reached dead ends. Dennis has become practical. Painting to please others, he is rewarded with a two-thousand-dollar prize; Christine has confronted the emptiness of her former existence and views herself as a failure: "I have attained my growth, I can never be a true artist."[80] Dennis's prize-winning painting illustrates the impasse. Roe describes the improbable narrative: "The whole scene was the portrayal, in the beautiful language of art, of a worldly, ambitious marriage, where the man seeks more beauty, and the woman wealth and position, love having no existence."[81]

Interestingly, the "language" of the painting, the characters' frustrated state, was also Colbert and Chamberlin's sense of the entire city before the fire: "The fire roused them from this tendency, and made them the same strong men and women . . . which built up Chicago."[82] The fire recreated Chicago's initial condition of a frontier town; it destroyed old arrangements and, like the frontier of four decades past, provided a low-resistance environment for change. Roe's scenes on the beach are those of a new wilderness, created instantly by the fire's ferocity. "Here again was seen the mingling of all classes which the streets and every place of refuge witnessed. Judges, physicians, statesmen, clergymen, bankers were jostled by roughs and thieves. The laborer sat on the sand with his family, side by side with the millionaire and his household. . . . In the unparalleled disaster, all social distinctions were lost, levelled like the beach on which the fugitives cower."[83] Dennis's and Christine's coming together is part of this same process. All physical and social barriers are burned away. Dennis's painting and his two thousand dollars are lost. Christine is orphaned; her father has died in a vain attempt to rescue his burning property at the "Arts Building." Both young people must start again in this place where "all social distinctions were lost." Dennis begins happily, sweeping ashes with the newly humbled Christine at his side.

Without the lengthy trials of Bradford's sea passage, the worthy citizens of Chicago were instantly transported back to their frontier origins and forward towards a promised future of even greater prosperity. A new, improved Chicago was imagined, where the simple material drive of men like Mr. Ludolph would be married to the practical artistry of characters like Dennis Fleet. By creating the possibility of a new class, the disaster imitated the land's barren condition when it was first settled and provided Dennis's and Christine's generation with its own heroic identity. Neither rapacious, like the robber baron, nor effete, the new Chicagoan would emerge in this legend, tested by fire and ready to "meet this great disaster with courage and fortitude, and hopefully set about retrieving it."[84] The young Fleets and Ludolphs had the opportunity to merge their own destinies to Chicago's. The city's fate became theirs and offered them an "inherent nobility such as no King or Kaiser could bestow."[85]

E. P. Roe's *Barriers Burned Away* is a forward-looking novel that added to the ongoing Chicago mythos. While the eyewitness and historical documents discussed above provided a factual basis for the modern city, Roe offered his suspicions about how the modern individual might feel. He understood that the fire not only altered and enhanced the city architecturally but changed the way people experienced time. An accelerated temporal sense, earlier associated only vaguely with the move from country to city, became after the fire completely identified with life in Chicago. Dennis Fleet reflects the change. When he first came to town "it seemed to him that he had lived years in those two days."[86] However, it was not until the fire that he realized these impressions were essential elements of modern Chicago, where "on that awful night events marched as rapidly as the flames, and the experience of years was crowded into hours, and that of hours into minutes."[87] The fire simply made explicit what he had been experiencing all along.

Time was different in the city. The fire, to Roe, was the emblem of a modern fact. He wished to view it simply as a palpable reminder of Chicago's almost perverse delight in change. While Europeans resisted change to the point of revolution and Easterners measured movement in centuries, Chicagoans thrived on their everyday possibility. For Roe, the fire was the physical fact of Marx's description of the modern—"all that is solid melts into air." But Roe's Chicago, after having gone through the fire, was a step ahead of such theory. A theoretical problem for Marx was every Chicagoan's new reality.

The fire generation, which identified completely its own destiny with the city's, was initially composed of eager modernists; it would take little time before a pronounced reluctance began to emerge. Yet, wildly stimulated by the fire's excitement, even conservative Christine Ludolph, a victim herself of the flames, dressed in tattered clothes and blackened with soot, is finally prepared to change: "All I possess, all I value, is in this city. It was my father's ambition, and at one time my own, to restore the ancient grandeur of the family with the wealth acquired in this land. The plan lost its charms for me long ago—I would not have gone if I could have helped it—and now it is impossible. It has perished in flame and smoke. Mr. Fleet, you see before you a simple American girl." [88] Resolutions she was unable to keep are made inevitable, and Christine is instantly transformed, as if by an alchemist's flame, into that "simple American girl" she had "perversely" resisted becoming. Thus, the Chicago fire efficiently seemed to erase the past. The actuality of suffering was immediately subordinated to the myth of an ever-resurgent city.

Reluctant Modernism
The Past as Present

The fire produced an odd sense of euphoria. All at once the population was released from the past—not metaphorically or theoretically, but in actuality, for some time at least. Joseph Kirkland recalled: "The banks, hotels, dry goods, hardware, and grocery houses, theatres, art-galleries, book-stores, music-stores, shipping and bridges, the Post Office with its mails, and the Government Sub-treasury with its millions, were now 'in one red burial blent.' And here, in the Court House, were all the records of all the courts since the county was constituted; and what is more, all records of the transfer of lands and lots, from the government to each successive holder down to that very day. Every leaf was burned."[1] Chicagoans saw money—millions of dollars—turned to dust, and their important legal transactions lost to all but memory. Here lies the key to the Chicago condition: in the same instant the fire created a possibility for radical freedom it also produced enormous anxieties in the face of such release. The initial euphoria was experienced by some as trauma. Frank J. Loesch tried to recreate his initial recognition of danger: "I watched for some moments, with a fascination which only the growing danger to myself drew me away from, the effect of the fire upon the city hall. The strong southwest wind was driving the heat in sheets of flame from the hundreds of burning buildings to the west of it, upon the southwest corner of the building, with such terrific effect that the limestone was melting and was running down the face of the building with first a slow then an accelerating movement as if it were a thin white paste."[2]

Both Kirkland and Loesch wrote from memory, looking back over decades. To each the event was still vivid. Kirkland's phrase, "every leaf was burned," recreates the sense of promise the moment must have held for him. Loesch's writing has the same authority, with a stronger power of observation. He mixes the compulsion to witness the spectacle with palpable images of its horror, like the great stone buildings "melting" into a "thin white paste." The two accounts taken together capture something of the fire's manic-depressive effect. The event encouraged such extremes while providing a ready-made context for them. One did not have to imagine the scene; it was provided full-blown. Looking at the eyewitness, first-person reports, we see a collection of voices joined together by similar concerns. What links them all is a consideration of freedom and its limits. Often brilliant in fragments, these responses to the fire are Chicago's first real literature. They are rare glimpses of the reality of Chicago life, unmatched in their raw honesty. Only Dreiser and Norris were later more successful in capturing the city's unrepressed vitality. But unlike later artists, those who first wrote about the fire were unable to understand what they saw—vivid scenes of license and uncommon generosity—outside of the most conventional frame of reference. It is as if they were scared, unable at the moment of greatest opportunity to assert themselves beyond the already established ways of thinking about the city. A curious form of self-censorship or internalized limits is operating here. Heroes themselves, they still were more content deferring to those who went before.

Although only four decades had passed since the city's founding, and a significant number of Chicago's first citizens were still alive, the past was remote enough in 1871 to be comfortable. It had already been processed and mythologized, in contrast to the observed fury of the present. Men like Butler and Ogden were now safe, rather misty presences from a time gone. Chicago's pioneer past had already been rendered into legend by the city's first successful novelist, Juliette Kinzie. While the fire undoubtedly stimulated people to think of radical freedom—the physical record of the past having been obliterated—it also disturbed a safe and self-aggrandizing portrait of a time gone.

Almost immediately the fire was less an enduring physical threat—insurance, relief societies, and federal assistance saw to that—than a psychic one. No one had seemed prepared to challenge Chicago's hard-worked myth of self, until another was found to replace it. A frame had to be worked around these observations to make them consistent, not in every detail but in tone, with the way the city had come to be seen. Before the fire Chicago had already been worked over imaginatively, and the boom-town chaos given a certain unity by Mrs. Kinzie. Although her novels were widely circulated, it was by her own example that she seemed to crystallize the city's unusually swift passage from frontier town to metropolis. While she wrote stories about the Fort Dearborn massacre and numerous Indian skirmishes, it was her life with John Kinzie that made the most formidable impression. She and her husband were the bridge between the swamp days and Chicago's new respectability. The fire, if not controlled through language somehow, could threaten all that.

Juliette Magill Kinzie represented a critical stage in Chicago's development. Her work and the public example of her civilized life reassured Chicagoans that they had passed safely from a period of enforced savagery into something approaching the American mainstream portrayed by Ralph Waldo Emerson and other Concord intellectuals. Born September 11, 1806, in Middletown, Connecticut, into a literary, political, and intellectual family, she retained a strong sense of America's past and of the country's first efforts at conceptualizing its history into a literature of its own. In fact, her own life could have been out of a novel by Cooper. She was forced to travel west, after her family suffered some unexplained financial setbacks, where in the early 1820s she met the rough frontier trader John H. Kinzie (born 1803). Kinzie was a second generation westerner who worked for the American Fur Company. Through their marriage, the Kinzies incorporated the two Chicagos.

John's family contained all the elements of the city's early history. He was from an old frontier clan that had fled the East after choosing the wrong side during the Revolutionary War. John had inherited the family's steadfastness and managed to weather periodic financial disasters. When in 1833 he resigned his appointment as Indian agent at Fort Winnebago, Wisconsin (the locale of Mrs. Kinzie's 1870 novel, *Mark Logan*), and returned to Chicago, he found the city in the first stages of development. Public auctions of government land taken from the Indians commenced in October of that year.[3] One parcel alone, the School Section, near the Kinzie family holdings, was divided into one hundred forty blocks and brought the government $38,865.[4] These lots were further subdivided, thus multiplying their value. John H. Kinzie, prudently selling off the land garnered by his father, profited from the boom. Kinzie had already made his fortune before the financial panic of 1837.

John represented the old Chicago, raw and undaunted. His wife was intellectually and culturally advanced. Juliette Kinzie read widely and was fond of music. Particularly after John Kinzie's death in 1865, she became associated with the new Chicago, a city of dinner parties and charity balls. Broadly speaking, Mrs. Kinzie's novels rest heavily upon a Whig interpretation of history, which argued that the past was ever receding before an improved future.[5] More specifically, it suggested that Chicago's ratty beginnings might successfully fade into its progressive present, so the new Chicago could choose at will what it wished to remember. Mrs. Kinzie is especially coy on this point: "It never entered the anticipations of the most sanguine that the march of improvement and prosperity would, in less than a quarter of a century, have so obliterated the traces of 'the first beginning' that a vast and intelligent multitude would be crying out for information in regard to the early settlement of this portion of our country, which so few are left to."[6] Here Mrs. Kinzie is using a familiar nineteenth-century disclaimer; like Hawthorne in "The Custom House," Mrs. Kinzie, overwhelmed by a self-manufactured interest in her subject, reluctantly agrees to inform her reader. She appoints herself as one of the survivors of the "first beginning" prepared to furnish "information." Yet, as one would expect, the information is selective and significantly edited. The past in *Wau-Bun* and *Mark Logan* is a steady conflict between the forces of order (white settlers and converted redmen) and those of anarchy (Indians and depraved whites). Order wins out.

While Mrs. Kinzie wrote about and in her writings largely defined the old Chicago giving way to the new, she and her husband John lived out the legend. The Kinzies embodied the prefire gentry and provided the model for the city's first families. Because her "first beginnings" were "so obliterated," Mrs. Kinzie manufactured the past in her books and lived it out in society. She and John, followed by the real estate czar Potter Palmer and his socialite wife, provided Chicago with far more than a sense of its new wealth. They gave the city a completely sanitized and rebuilt past, free of sweaty pioneer men and less-than-virtuous women, dubious land transactions, and all the accompanying ambiguities of any frontier community, particularly one so quickly on the rise. The Kinzies gave Chicago a way to deal with its double history. Families like the Wahls, the Deweys, and the Pullmans all built mansions on the fashionable Near South Side before the fire; they were living by the Kinzie example. The new Chicagoans, represented most successfully by the elite on Prairie Avenue, were simply urbanized versions of Mrs. Kinzie's Mark Logan, who was so "spick and span" in his "neatness as to attest that he had taken no part in the labors which told so unmistakably on the toilets of the rest."[7] Mark Logan, the elegant bourgeois of the frontier, is the past Mrs. Kinzie reconstructed and the one the prefire elite wished to remember.

For some years preceding the fire, Chicagoans had for the first time a past that seemed unified and neat. Almost forty years had passed since the city was founded, and one could imagine from the safe confines of Prairie Avenue that the city had come into being without the bloody struggles and ferocious financial dealings. The crude, simple energies of men like John Kinzie seemed tamed, at least at night, when dressed in evening clothes they went out to poetry readings and concerts—like gorillas in suits, waiting impatiently for the next day's swing in the trees. No, prefire Chicago denied its own characteristic and central dualities; it was dressing up. Having manufactured a livable past that spoke only to the astounding progress made in so short a time, Chicago wanted nothing of the realities revealed by the fire.

Mrs. Kinzie and her class's idealization of the past and her availability as cultural doyenne gave the city an order and unity it did not possess in fact. Her marriage to John epitomized the Chicago will to sublimate its own raw ambition. Marriages of Chicagoans from different social classes extended well into the next century. With their new prosperity the best families could even go beyond New England to Europe's impoverished aristocracy to seek mates. Such marriages of ambition were the social counterpart to the city's manufactured and edited past. Through Kinzie-like marriages or alliances of low and high culture, Chicagoans appropriated elements of glamour and style that were absent from their own real history. These unions of cultural opposites were like yoked teams pulling together into what they thought were fields of boundless progress. It would take finally the Haymarket Riot (1886) and the Pullman Strike (1894) to put an effective end to Chicago's fantasy of class harmony.

But at least in the first thirty-six hours the fire challenged the processed view of Chicago as a completely unified city. Here was an event that was large enough to exist outside the dominant mythologies that organized the city's experiences. The fire was quickly remythologized, as if to keep pace with the city's rebuilding. While it detonated the imagination in ways that were finally impossible to suppress, the fire was still effectively controlled by language. It is useful therefore to look at some of the initial responses to the fire to see what was authentic about them and what was not. For in these realistic fragments lie America's modern literary roots and a clue to a grammar that tried to represent a city as it was, and not as what it pretended to be.

While much of the immediate literature about the fire is strong in observed detail, it is finally compromised by forced synthesis. Language had earlier been used by Mrs. Kinzie and others to domesticate the brutish reality of settlement. Frantic land dealing and the brutal removal of a native population was subsumed by the romance of the city's first families, still being lived out at the time of the fire by the Swifts, Fields, and Palmers. The conflagration's unpredictability—its ferocious reality—was perceived, at least subliminally, as a threat to the city's stability; the writing about it balances extremes. That almost euphoric enthusiasm which greeted the holocaust was transformed into bestselling fiction by Roe, codified into a formidable myth of resurrection by Bross, Colbert and Chamberlin, Sheahan and Upton, and theologized by Kirkland and Swing. Each of these commentators seemed to understand intuitively that the fire threatened Chicago's manufactured view of itself, as did even the fire's very first writers, who recorded what they witnessed in diaries, letters, and notebooks. Momentary euphoria was psychic compensation for the trauma on the streets.

The fire immediately reminded people of the city's essential improbability and fragility. Wooden pavement was severely scorched or entirely burned away. The rain that helped put out the flames created pools of mud, reminding survivors of the city's swampy foundation. What the fire removed, if not for the sustained industry of man, nature might reclaim. For all the talk and the literature about Chicago being propelled into the future through its unequaled opportunity to rebuild, there was the far more insistent reality around town that the city might have that day been bombed into the past. As survivors surveyed the scene and watched unrestrained mobs of people poking through the ruins, their faith in the gospel of progress was tested. The physical destruction seemed to be mirrored by an incipient social anarchy being kept under control by General Sheridan.

The sight of unrestrained activity in the streets is a part of most early accounts. But surprisingly, while there is a ferociousness to the detail, the accounts usually end with an almost classical balance. Anarchy in the streets, like a city in ruins, was unacceptable to Chicagoans. It reminded them too brutally of the unrestrained freedoms of their past, before the frontier reality had been made into the first families' urbane chatter and the stuff of popular literature. The truth was that Chicagoans had paid for their new respectability with an almost universal sense of shame about their raw beginnings. When they saw the mud reappearing along with a frontier anarchy on the streets, they were compelled to relive that shame.

The haste of rebuilding was preceded by a rudimentary literary attempt to control reality with words. Control of Chicago's double vision of itself—as simultaneously Whig progressive and shamefully primitive—was applied in response to the fire as it had been to the trauma of settlement. A secure middle ground was sought where the city's extremes of ambition and unrestrained freedom might no longer appear so threatening. The use of language as a mediating force was quickly associated with civic pride. While it generated good propaganda, the process of modifying details gleaned from personal witness severely undermined the production of good literature and later good architecture. A struggle to regain a squandered authenticity became fundamental to the city's artists, as they struggled with the compound legacies of frontier and fire.

Yet in the fire's immediate aftermath, commentators appeared untroubled by the event's potential to silence individual responses and were rather caught up in a patriotic fervor that moved them to falsify their own observations. As a result, personal experiences were lost to the communal memory and thereby made more remote. Instant distance from the trauma was achieved through the loss of particularity. A tribal calm was purchased at the expense of felt reality. Over a short period of time all experiences of the fire began to read the same, as predictable as the well-known accounts of the Fort Dearborn and settlement days. Individuals immersed their own unique experiences into a bath of common recollections until their sharpest edges wore down and finally eroded. With such shared impressions of the event, the fire was almost immediately put in service of the city's drive to rebuild.

People with little or no literary ambition wrote long letters detailing their struggles. They did not set out to write with the thought that the collective record of their outpourings would serve a city determined to propagate a message of rebirth, but they had so internalized the process that for every indecent extreme recorded they had to note a compensatory positive one to balance it off. Thus was played a psychic zero-sum game in which each retrogressive, negative experience was balanced by an experience that was good and forward-looking. Considering this, it is clearer why E. P. Roe's novel about the fire was so successful: his work was the game's most sophisticated and complete evocation. Still, there are to be found rawer, more poignant accounts of the disaster. Authors free from the necessity to make some final sense of the event or the need to place it securely within a formula managed to write quite powerfully. What remain are many brilliant pieces of a great comprehensive work waiting to be written. Arthur M. Kinzie wrote: "We saw in one place a very sick man. His wife was attending him, and had obtained an old piano packing-case, which she had placed on its side with the bottom toward the wind, and made a bed for her husband inside. A piece of candle fastened to a wire hung from the top, by the light of which she was reading to him. . . . It was a strange sight as we passed through the burned district that night. All the squares formerly built up solidly were now so many black excavations, while the streets had the appearance of raised turnpikes intersecting each other on a level prairie."[8]

Arthur Kinzie, a grandson of the city's first permanent white settler, joined judges, journalists, and other less prominent citizens like Mary L. Fales, whose October 10, 1871, letter to her mother was preserved by the Chicago Historical Society. Mrs. Fales, like Arthur Kinzie, was stimulated by the fire to observe with great clarity: "One young lady, who was to have had a fine wedding tomorrow, came dragging along some of her wedding presents."[9] The fire initially excited people to see the uniqueness of all that was around them: men in suits burying fine musical instruments, bums smoking expensive cigars, and women serving tea in the shell of a burned-out building. Everywhere the imagination was fed until it was sated by reality. But almost at once, those who survived the blaze and came to write about it sought relief in the known. They had had enough of their own agitated minds. "I have lost nothing myself by the fire but what I can recover, but on Monday afternoon I went to bed with a sick headache and a fever, which were the result of mental excitement rather than physical exposure."[10]

The result was a retreat to long-established conventions. A catastrophic experience with personal and intimate immediate effects, the Chicago fire was carefully integrated with the basic variations through which the city had come to see itself. William Bross's city of the phoenix soon joined Mrs. Kinzie's frontier romance of "first beginnings," obliterating the possibility of a true literature or architecture arising immediately after the fire. Individuals were sick with "mental excitement" and were, at least for the time being, unwilling or unable to resist the impulse to enter the future only after manufacturing a comfortable past. They lacked the will to sustain an original relationship to the event. Instead, they participated in an act of myth-making as old as the city.

Mrs. Alfred Hebard was typical of those who felt compelled to record their impressions of the fire. A private diary is the only work she is known to have written. One could not imagine a less self-conscious or less affected writer. Yet instinctively she internalized what she named the "Chicago Spirit." "The very awfulness of the peril passed through, the loss of material possessions and of everything but mutual good will, seems to have bound her people together, and left to all succeeding generations a priceless legacy—the Chicago Spirit."[11] Basically, the "Chicago Spirit" was an updated version of the frontier myth, only now the frontier yeoman was a temporarily displaced urbanite. Call him, for purposes of the myth, an urban wanderer. Dennis Fleet was the period's first fully realized type. Like his frontier counterpart, the urban wanderer is less concerned with physical danger—"to believe one's self looking over the adamantine bulwarks of hell into the bottomless pit"—than he is with the human threat.[12] His "Indians" on October 8, 1871, were his fellow citizens. Mrs. Hebard saw the division between safety and danger as clearly as the difference between indoors and out. Paradoxically, at the fire's peak, she perceives her house as physically vulnerable but still psychically safe: "Within the house the perfect quiet had astonished us—every man taking care of his own, silently and rapidly, few words being spoken; only some ladies unaccompanied by gentlemen consulting together in whispers what they should do if compelled to leave the house. Outside we found confusion."[13] She fears the street's intense heat and flames. But more importantly she is apprehensive about the "confusion" that awaits her outside the "perfect quiet" of her home, the unadorned and raw reality of the street.

The "Indians" of the fire were, by and large, the city's swelling numbers of Irish, German, and Scandinavian immigrants, the denizens of places like the South Side's Conley's Patch. Horace White, the *Chicago Tribune* editor, in a letter to the *Cincinnati Commercial* (October 1871) makes such identification explicit: "Vice and crime had got the first scorching. The district where the fire got its first firm foothold was the Alsatia of Chicago. Fleeing before it was a crowd of bleareyed, drunken, and diseased wretches, male and female, half naked, ghastly, with painted cheeks, cursing and uttering ribald jests as they drifted along."[14] Mr. Alexander Frear, a visiting New York state assemblyman, described a similar scene for the *New York World* (October 15, 1871): "The Horror and the brutality of the scene made it sickening. A fellow standing on a piano declared that the fire was the friend of the poor man."[15] To the city's respectable citizenry, Chicago seemed to erupt during the fire. Long-buried and suppressed forces bubbled up from the overheated ground. As fearful as the flames was the potential human threat.

The fire was an anarchic challenge to the carefully orchestrated picture of dynastic order presented by Mrs. Kinzie and others.[16] Eyewitnesses like Jonas Hutchinson were scared less by the physical danger of the fire, once it took a steady northeast heading, than they were by the specter of the old Chicago—thought buried in the ruins of Fort Dearborn—that seemed to rise precipitately from the rubble. He wrote: "As far as the fire reached the city is thronged with desperadoes who are plundering and trying to set new fires. . . . Several were shot and others hung to lamp posts last night. . . . The city is in darkness, no gas, 50,000 army tents are being pitched to house the poor. The like of this sight since Sodom & Gomorrha has never met human vision. No pen can tell what a ruin this is."[17] The fire heightened extremes; it challenged the ideal of four decades of supposed progress since the city's primitive beginnings. Even the privileged felt exposed and driven to excesses. In a letter written October 21, 1871, almost two weeks after the event, Mrs. Aurelia King has regained some control over her material. "Then too, there is a little touch of the ludicrous now and then which cheers us. Imagine your friend Aurelia, for instance, with a thousand dollar India shawl and a lavender silk with a velvet flounce, and not a chemise for her back—not a pocket handkerchief to wipe the soot from her face. A friend of mine saved nothing but a white tulle dress. Another lady has a pink silk dress but no stockings. I went to town yesterday, and was the envy and admiration of my Chicago friends because I had clean cuffs and a collar. I had to own at last that they were stolen."[18] Mrs. King offers a detached literary irony in the place of the earlier eyewitness accounts' barely submerged hysteria. She is comfortable once again and no longer "horrified" or "fevered." Rather, Mrs. King is cheered by some "ludicrous" consequences of the spectacle of a fortnight past. A thief herself—necessity's child—she does not for a moment identify with her fellow sufferers who were described so luridly by White and Frear. She is selective in her identification with fellow Chicagoans and does not suggest any solidarity with the poor of Conley's Patch. They and others from Chicago's forsaken ethnic neighborhoods were vocational thieves, while her thievery was compelled by extraordinary circumstances and was purely avocational. She has no special sympathy for the poor.

Thought buried or at least gerrymandered into their own

districts or wards by forty years of civic progress, the rabble were burned out into the streets and made once again visible. Typically the accounts take more notice of the dissolute than of the working poor in their descriptions of frantic exhibitionism. The poor become stereotyped and marked. On reflection, Aurelia King's self-description comes to have a certain poignancy for Chicago itself. Dressed with "a thousand dollar India shawl and a lavender silk with a velvet flounce, and not a chemise for her back," Mrs. King, like the city itself, struggled not for the truth but for appearances, even if she had to steal.

The Great Fire for an extended moment compelled gentrified Chicago to see its other half. The city, like Mrs. King, reacted by reasserting a tattered but unbowed gentility; Chicago wished to deny that social and cultural divisions really existed. True Chicagoans stole when they had to, but they stole clean clothes and not booze. At any rate, this was the preferred version of the event's less heroic side. However, the problem remained—what to do with the other Chicago, the part of town and population still untamed.

How was the city to reconcile its Whiggish sense of its own progress with the obvious signs of regression in its midst? Chicago had a ready answer: merely to evade the unparalleled opportunities for self-examination provided by the fire. Free to write anything, her writers endorsed the various fantasies of unity that were apotheosized a generation later at the World's Columbian Exposition (1893). Inhibited in part by existing canons of taste that stressed decorum over reportorial accuracy, and limited as well by conventional talents, those who wrote about the fire exhibited a considerable lack of will. They avoided any conscious acknowledgment of the city's double nature: an aspiring high-cultured gentry competing with what it was perhaps only a generation earlier, a low-cultured, highly energized but volatile proletariat.

Chicagoans searched for a duller middle ground. They eventually downplayed the striking characterizations that were already recorded because images of "blear-eyed, drunken and diseased wretches" (the long-forgotten failures of progress) were dramatically at odds with the aristocratic vision of William Bross, fleeing "on horseback down Michigan Avenue with his portrait under one arm and his lecture, 'Across the Continent,' under the other."[19] If either extreme had been chosen as an appropriate manifestation of Chicago at the time, an authentic literature with some of the proletarian bite of a Theodore Dreiser or the New England caution of a Henry Blake Fuller might have developed earlier. Instead a subliterature developed that was more sensitive to prevailing fashions and taste than to coldly observed facts. Epitomized by Bross's *History,* it became a major influence on Chicago's cultural and social development through, at least, the 1870s.

The post-fire literature, which borrowed as much from the language of boosterism as from art, might be called Boosterature. It sought not the truth but only neat reconciliations of opposites, sacrificing the strongly observed detail for the emblematic impression. It is not as if journalists, novelists, and other writers chose to falsify what they saw. Rather, at the time of the fire they were as yet unwilling to abandon their faith in progress to a now-familiar litany of urban failures, including the horrifying possibility that the denizens of the city's Conley's Patches were an ever-expanding population. As long as they had a choice, writers contrived to see the fire as simply a dramatic interruption on the road to success.

We have already seen how quickly talk of the city's physical restoration began, and later we will consider how swiftly the actual rebuilding commenced. In a complementary sense, it was thought at the time that Chicago's own hard-worked unified sense of self could as easily be restored once the human detritus was taken care of. In the same way they hoped money and sweat would rebuild the city physically, Chicagoans looked to language to restore their dynastic pretense of well-being. Chicago's architects were asked by developers to manufacture a safer, but essentially replicated, version of the prefire environment. It was left to those who wrote about Chicago to create a comfortable version of a hard, emerging reality of poverty and alienated labor. The reality all had seen in the glow of the flames now must be denied. In the glow of civic pride and the hypnotic effect of boosterism, writers began to reinterpret what they had seen.

Too much had been invested in detailing Chicago's rise from a swampy backwater to a major metropolis to let intervene something as explainable as a natural disaster. Excesses described in the event's first rush were gradually suppressed until it appeared that they hadn't happened at all. When J. W. S. Cleveland came to write about the fire (November 10, 1871) he seemed naturally to assume the booster's role. He reported, "Everybody seemed cool and collected and exerting himself to save his own and others' property, or seeking a good position for observation, and it is a sufficient refutation of the absurd stories which have since been circulated of outrages, lynchings, etc., to state the simple fact that my wife and her sister after I left them, which was about 3 A.M., were a long time walking about the streets in the vicinity of the fire as mere spectators, and finally returned home before daylight without ever a feeling of insecurity, or receiving an uncivil word from anyone."[20] Cleveland tried to minimize the disturbance. He selected impressions that supported a feeling of common cause. The extremes of human behavior reported by Jonas Hutchinson, Alexander Frear, and Mrs. Alfred Hebard, among other eyewitnesses, were treated by Cleveland as oddities unworthy of serious consideration. He simply refuted them anecdotally. How could there have been lynchings when his wife and her sister walked the streets undisturbed?

No single account of the fire attempted to explain the contradictory evidence. Reports of unusual civility were mixed with those of extraordinary brutality. The fire, in all its unsparing violence, had burned away the city's skin, leaving it exposed and vulnerable. Chicago had been a mass of contradictions for the four decades of sustained development. Desiring to be civil, like Boston, New York, and Philadelphia, Chicago had felt it must suppress even the suggestion of a mixed pedigree. Eastern cities had at least two hundred years to disguise their origins; Chicago, a mere forty. The fire revealed too much.

An effort toward immediate rebuilding, as chronicled by William Bross in *History of Chicago* (1876) and made into legend by E. P. Roe in *Barriers Burned Away* (1872), was part of a frantic attempt to graft a new skin before too much gore was exposed. Chicago's civil self, represented by the dynastic marriages of the Kinzies and Palmers, as well as by the hautebourgeoise manners of Mrs. Aurelia King, was threatened by its uncivil alter ego, suggested in its most unregenerate form by the inhabitants of Conley's Patch and other ethnic slums. Until the Haymarket Riot (1886) and the Pullman Strike (1894), among the most notable labor disturbances, forced Chicagoans to face more squarely their cultural and political divisions, evasion was the rule.[21]

Although it would take artists over a decade to find a subject equal to the city's complexity, the fire was still a turning point. Reluctance to exploit contradictions of class and the brewing political conflict can be explained by the pervasiveness and persuasive power of boosterism. A kind of anti-art itself, Boosterature had all the advantages of nineteenth-century melodrama—its insistent tragedies and happy resolutions—and with the fire's added impetus it was nicely up to date. Boosterism provided an instant model for writers who merely plugged in the city's recent events to give a simple feeling of urgency.

Chicago after the fire was like a city at war. Architects were drafted by the local developers and supported by the Eastern banks; writers enlisted. For at least the first years after the fire all were good soldiers carrying the banner of Mrs. Alfred Hebard's "Chicago Spirit." When the city's darker side needed acknowledgment, its portrayal was subsumed within the larger picture of Chicago's persistent struggle and triumph over adversity. Two works published immediately after the fire provide the most accurate sense of the prevailing mood. The Reverend E. J. Goodspeed's *History of the Great Fires in Chicago and the West* (1871), a journalistic and evangelical evocation of the city's recent past, and Mrs. Martha J. Lamb's *Spicy* (1873), a novel, manage a mixture of facts and fiction to control the fire's meaning. They offer partial blueprints to the event's insistent romance.

Goodspeed employed reflections on Chicago's "unenviable reputation abroad for wickedness" as evidence for the city's unequaled vitality.[22] Far from denying the "other Chicago"—whose existence became the foundation of the works of James T. Farrell, Upton Sinclair, and Nelson Algren— Goodspeed incorporated it into a larger tale of regeneration. "The annals of crime have been full and red. Only the week preceding the fire a mysterious murder occurred which sent a thrill throughout the community. Drinking was carried to excess, even Sunday dram-selling being tolerated by the executive to an alarming and shameful extent. Covetousness also prevailed under the forms of prodigality and avarice. The Sabbath was terribly profaned by our foreign population and the demoralization ran along all orders of society. Sinful or doubtful amusements received the devotion of multitudes." He continues: "Alas for our city! Pompeii could scarcely excel the madness of its passion, though law gives no sanction to iniquity, as it did in that vile nest of heathen immorality."[23]

Goodspeed's millenial language was deliberate. Where others saw disorder in Chicago's wickedness and chose to ignore it or will it away, Goodspeed saw signs of future redemption.[24] He viewed its struggle for civility and respectability as part of a larger historic drama into which all the pieces fit. A "mysterious murder" of a week earlier was given new significance; it and other events recorded by Goodspeed simply anticipated the fire. The city's entire history—admittedly "sinful" at times—contributed to this firey apotheosis. But unlike Pompeii, buried under ash for thousands of years, Chicago survived. The fire offered the city a second chance. Just as the

Kinzies and the other prominent families, including all the famous industrialists and commercial entrepreneurs, offered a model of civility to an aspiring bourgeoisie, Goodspeed's apocalyptic model provided to all the formerly excluded classes a heroic identity. Their earlier sins had been "blessedly" overlooked by a compassionate God; their very survival was evidence of the fact. Chicago was a Sodom and Gomorrah deemed worthy of survival, a Pompeii that God spared. Goodspeed is quick to argue the moral: "While we thus glance at the darker aspect of life here, in order to be just and true to facts, we turn gladly and boldly to another side of the picture, and hold up a people whose liberality, generosity, piety and morals will compare in their fruit—their actual outworkings—with those of any other people under the sun. It must be remembered that in the new West everything has had to be done, as it were, at once—every necessity to be provided for within a generation." [25]

His is a Genesis for the common man, to compete with the dynastic models of the great families. Both were created within one generation. For the Chicagoan of the 1870s, the past was present. There was no need to refer to experience further back than October 8, 1871. For Mrs. Kinzie and her class the fire created the opportunity to rebuild on a vaster scale and to further their considerable influence, without any unflattering comparisons to the pioneer generation's gigantic accomplishments. For Chicago's working class and expanding immigrant population the fire was a second chance. They had survived the "world's end," and the day after promised new hope. The rebuilding, soon severely limited by the national financial panic of 1873, at least in its original frenzy offered work to anyone willing to abandon the bad habits thought endemic to the lower classes. It is no accident that the accepted version of the fire's origin included a drunken Mrs. O'Leary forgetting her lantern in the barn. The fire, in Goodspeed's view, was simply a preordained means of mass conversion. Instead of time ending, in a millenial sense, this secular apocalypse—secular because the city of man miraculously remained—announced the start of modern time.

Goodspeed was sure of his calculations. What the initial settlement of the city had promised in civilizing the swamps, the fire would fulfill. He preached that "the indolent, debauched barbarians were among the most serious obstructions to the progress of the infant town, as their bloody and vengeful ancestors had hindered the early settlement. Men were unwilling to hazard their scalps in unequal contests with these wild savages unless there was some prize to be gained worthy the dangerous venture; and when they had become tamed they were still animals, corrupt and corrupting. The condition of the muddy banks of the Chicago river and outlaying prairie was not particularly inviting to persons of intelligence, who had been accustomed to the comparative civilization and improvements of the East. But one by one these obstacles disappeared."[26] The fire and its aftermath to Goodspeed were the culminating hours of the city's prehistory. Seen eschatologically, Chicago's past was subsumed by its present as surely as its physical plant was destroyed by the flames. Goodspeed concluded: "We then struggled with Nature to gain a little by Art; now Art and Nature have become one in the physical advantages which no conflagration can destroy, and Chicago with its great business division in mournful ruin, is greater, in the resources of regaining what she has lost, than any city ever built by human hands."[27]

Goodspeed's theologizing was quickly adopted and explained by the Reverend E. P. Roe in *Barriers Burned Away* (1872). As seen, Roe was able to dramatize in lay spiritual terms the kinds of conversions Goodspeed, almost a year closer to the event, could only suggest. Dennis Fleet's progression from an ambitious and ultimately successful artist to a humble raker of ashes at novel's end was the individual counterpart to Goodspeed's vision for the entire society. For along with the city's eventual material salvation was to come a spiritual reawakening, as typified by young Fleet and Miss Ludolph, his bride-to-be. Although the popular success of Roe's novel attests to the acceptability of Goodspeed's latitudinarian vision, there was another, perhaps more enduring view of the fire that avoided a specifically religious interpretation.

While Goodspeed and Roe sought to convert the "barbarians," others offered a more democratic solution. Mrs. Martha J. Lamb's *Spicy* (1873) was the second novel published after the fire and the first to offer a more modern answer to the problem of the liberated hordes. Mrs. Lamb combined the elements of Boosterature with all the timeless devices of nineteenth-century dime-novel melodrama to form an interesting whole. Although her work is far from having any recognizable literary merit, it is unencumbered by the sort of theologizing that exerts a deus ex machina hold on Roe's plot. Mrs. Lamb's narrative develops naturally from its own often inane logic. The background of the novel is clearly recognizable. Spicy's older sister Meddie naturally takes the booster's pose in comparing Chicago of the Civil War to the days before the fire: "In all modern history there is nothing quite so marvelous and captivating as the growth of Chicago." Impressed by the city's new reputation, she continues, "It appears almost incredible that the site of such a city as Chicago is today, should forty years ago, have been only a great, reedy, miasmatic marsh on the shore of an inland sea!" [28]

Such are the reflections of Mrs. Lamb's narrator on the eve of the fire. Gone are the intricacies of the novel's earlier plot, which includes an improbable ghost story of lost loves and conveniently timed deaths. [29] In their place Mrs. Lamb provides an almost journalistic concentration on details. The fire to her is equal in importance to the Civil War. She had to strain to argue Chicago's centrality to the Civil War, but she had in the fire an event whose explosive force insured its significance. Mrs. Lamb first insinuates the history of the city into the fate of the nation by claiming Abraham Lincoln as Chicago's own. "The convention in the Lake-Street Wigwam had nominated Abraham Lincoln, of Illinois, as its standard-bearer. Chicago honored and loved him." She continues the argument: "It was Chicago who first summoned him from comparative obscurity in a political sense, and watched with pride his wrestle with an able and cunning debater, until his sagacity and honesty and purity had been established beyond question. Chicago had sent him out a brave, earnest, hopeful, Christian man to save the country." [30] And when his work was done, "Chicago tenderly received his sacred ashes, with bowed heads and streaming eyes." [31] The logic of Mrs. Lamb's argument goes something like this: Chicago's development was "incredible"; out of the great democratic process came Lincoln (specifically through his debates with Douglas); the city that gave the nation Lincoln was now in flames; something of national importance was happening. What she found so important about the fire was a crucial elaboration upon the discoveries of Goodspeed, Roe, and Swing. By being less evangelical—using Lincoln's assassination as a one-day apocalypse, rather than Pompeii or scenes of the world's end—Mrs. Lamb mediated the mythic aspects of the fire with the purely practical. She provided comfortable mediation between the psychological extremes of October 8 and its more practical material concerns.

Mrs. Lamb developed a usable myth of the fire to inform the immediate period of rebuilding. She confronted directly Chicago's fears of disorder and of being revealed as a divided city. The anxiety addressed earlier by Juliette Kinzie and others in choreographed histories of the frontier is now captured by Mrs. Lamb in images of the roving mob. [32] "Nothing material could stand the surge of this tremendous sea. The panic-stricken and distracted mob were almost as terrible to behold as the roaring conflagration. They ran toward Lake and South Water Streets, and upon the bridges, and then turned at bay like affrighted animals."[33] But the mob, like Mrs. Kinzie's Indians and Goodspeed's barbarians, is subdued, significantly after they pass Lake Street, the site of Abraham Lincoln's Republican nomination. In fact, it is precisely when they reach Lake Street that Mrs. Lamb notes, "All distinctions of class or nationality were lost; every life was dear to its possessor."[34] Here Chicagoans are not converted as they were in *Barriers Burned Away*, but are "melted" by air "like a furnace seven times heated."[35] *Spicy* added to the practical histories and the novel of the fire a literature of the rebuilding. Certainly the millenial chords can be heard in Mrs. Lamb's account, but they only rumble below the surface. For her, the fire is far more interesting in its supposed practical results: it unleashed and then quieted the mob.

By suppressing a seemingly natural tendency to view the fire apocalyptically Mrs. Lamb added through her picture of the beneficial mixing of classes a more usable myth of radical democratization. The subdued mob, the "hackmen who were the monarchs of the occasion" were the ghosts of the Civil War, also a time of dramatic divisions.[36] Chicago's vitality, Mrs. Lamb implied, was based precisely on these generational eruptions, from frontier to Civil War to the Great Fire. By incorporating the two Chicagos—civil and uncivil—Mrs. Lamb made the fire into yet another occasion for renewal.

Mrs. Lamb also believed that the rebuilding could be facilitated if Chicagoans were convinced of the possibilities of future class harmony. Compare her description of Lincoln Park with E. P. Roe's beach after the fire. "The tumult and the roar had given place to a terrible silence. Seventy thousand people were huddled together. The delicate woman, the high-bred dame, the haughty banker, the revered clergyman, the tender infant, the hardy laborer, and the worst denizens of the worst localities."[37] All are forced to take care of themselves. Chicagoans, who had been found able to meet the periodic tests of the frontier and war, are now faced with an equal challenge. As a woman in Lincoln Park observes, "'ristocrats now; they would know how it felt to be poor."[38] The romance of classlessness is the perfect answer to the fears occasioned by the fire. Mrs. Lamb seemed to argue that while the event unleashed some negative energies it would finally serve, as had the frontier and the war, to liberate the city's best instincts. A decidedly Whig view of history in *Spicy* conformed very nicely to the way Chicagoans wished to see themselves. Chicagoans were different from other Americans, and particularly from Easterners, to whom they were financially indebted. They found unity—"Chicago Spirit"—in events of sufficient magnitude to fracture any other city or state.

Martha Lamb's vision of classlessness was built on Roe's presumption that after the fire "all social distinctions were lost." It was a happy although temporary resolution to the main human issue of the disaster. The fire in its incredible ferocity stripped away, in one sharp stroke, all the civic niceties of two previous generations. Rather than face the inevitability of a growing working class, and of a less successful cohort of chronically unemployed forced into the street, and therefore into public view, by the fire, Chicagoans chose Mrs. Lamb's fiction of class reconciliation. In this way, they could sublimate their initial personal fears and anxieties about their uncivilized brethren and immediately begin the task of reconstruction. But it would be a mistake to underestimate the trauma revealed in the fire's primary literature. The citizens of Chicago did clearly see themselves, if only for an instant. And like Gulliver, who failed to get the point that the howling Yahoo was his own unredeemed self, the Chicagoan tried to get on happily with his business.

The first novelists of the fire were selective in their choice of details. Both E. P. Roe and Martha Lamb relied heavily on the fire's journalistic record. Their decision to elaborate upon scenes of class harmony was influenced by the prevailing mood of civic boosterism epitomized by William Bross's *History*. And there was a documented public record to build on. Roe's and Lamb's writing was not that different in tone from Horace White's eyewitness account. He recalled: "I saw a great many kindly acts done as we moved along. The poor helped the rich, and the rich helped the poor (if anybody could be called rich at such a time) to get on with their loads. I heard of cartmen demanding one hundred and fifty dollars (in hand, of course) for carrying a single load. Very likely it was so, but those cases did not come under my own notice. It did come under my notice that some cartmen worked for whatever the sufferers felt able to pay, and one I knew worked with alacrity for nothing. It takes all sorts of people to make a great fire." [39] Horace White, the editor of the *Chicago Tribune* at the time of the fire, recounted here the celebrated case of working men with carts overcharging people in distress. This incident, with its suggestion of class conflict, was raised repeatedly in the eyewitness accounts. White himself acknowledged that there might have been abuses of this sort but they did not come under his "notice." He chose to stress the positive, already aware that the rebuilding would demand civic and not class solidarity. Noting oddly that "it takes all sorts of people to make a great fire," White determined to treat the event as spectacle.

While Chicagoans like Horace White indulged the apocalyptic rhetoric occasioned by the fire and to an extent were even flattered by it, they were also disquieted by the promise of unmediated change it seemed to imply. They were reluctant modernists who would gladly face the present as long as it was safely anchored in the past. What the writers accomplished, as did the architects later in the initial rebuilding, was to forestall a headlong rush toward the modern. The Virgilian pastoral in a decidedly urban context, of happy workers in partnership with their bosses, was one of the most dramatic images of this reluctant modernism. A classless world within a society of surplus was the Reverend David Swing's strongest memory of the fire, twenty years later. Swing happily reported that he had "transformed a painful experience into a rather pleasing dream."[40] He went on: "The scene at four o'clock in the morning was most wonderful in this, that fine residences were open to anybody. The inmates had left them. Pictures, books, pianos, clothing, table-ware, ornaments were alone, waiting for fire or some one to take them. It was not just to call by the name of thief the man or the woman who ran up a front step and looked around the parlor rapidly for something to transfer to basket or pocket. There were not thieves enough in the North Division to meet the demand of the night. If any there were, it was the most honest night any of them had ever lived."[41]

Here was a dream city, a Chicago where there would be so much wealth that Goodspeed's "barbarians" would be reformed by the mere sight of overwhelming plenty. Mrs. Lamb saw that same moment as an "instance of pure good-nature" that brought people together in the wake of disaster.[42] Fears of lynchings, looting, murder, and public drunkenness were lost in dramatized scenes of the heroic.[43] The fire's uniqueness was contained and thus controlled by language, until it seemed to be just another instance of the city's extraordinary past. The conflagration, like a giant crucible, to Swing, Lamb and other Chicago propagandists merely speeded up the process of conversion. Those who had failed to be converted from frontier louts to urban gentlemen or ladies might just as well have been outright victims of the flames, or have submerged themselves into the city's endless neighborhoods. Thus, the fire came to be viewed conveniently as an opportunity to consolidate the gains of the past, not to break from it.

Although the moral of regeneration is less spiritual and more practical the further you get away from the fire and the closer to the process of rebuilding, there is still in this earliest modern writing about Chicago a pronounced secular theology. It is a theology totally in service to man; Chicago had already survived the world's end, as all these accounts vividly describe. The literature of the fire, clothed often in spiritual language for lack of a more modern grammar, is about the resurrection of a city and by extension, its people. And befitting a Christian view of the world where all evil is forever in the service of ultimate good, Chicago's other, darker side is subsumed within the general feeling of rebirth. The real historical dissonance between the city's frontier wildness and its passion to gentrify is dropped for the moment in favor of a myth more useful to the business of reconstruction. "She has all the elements of a great city left, except the mere buildings," Mrs. Lamb optimistically declared. She continued: "Chicago has not lost her shrewd, enterprising, energetic, indomitable men of business. The brilliant, powerful city of a week ago has still its financial, commercial, social, and domestic roots stretched to the remote quarters of the earth; its marked quotations and opinions in all American cities; its prices of grains, hides, and lumber in Europe; its trade connections reaching through San Francisco to China and Japan, and its personal family ties everywhere. Her sorrow is a common sorrow. Her uprising from her ashes will be a common joy." [44] Chicago the phoenix is here a ubiquitous god, a rising Christ. [45] All who visited the city would see a "new life" infused into her "working heroes." [46]

The fire was the modern city's great generative event. On the most basic level it was a palpable demarcation between Chicago's past—frontier boom town—and its future; a harrowing, life-defining experience shared by all of its citizens. Like the physical rebuilding, modern time began on October 8, 1871. One's identity or sense of progress need not be referred further back than that date. No longer did a dynastic monopoly, epitomized by the Kinzies, control the memory of the past. The past was present, as recent as the fire. Present were the "working heroes," as surely as in Mrs. Kinzie's *Wau-Bun*, or Major John Richardson's *Hardscrabble: or, Fall of Chicago* (1856). The fire replaced the frontier as the testing ground for the Chicago character. A heroic past was no longer the exclusive property of an elite, but was as available as one's memory of yesterday. The profusion of eyewitness accounts, diaries, pamphlets, and poems by common people attests to the event's hold on the popular imagination.

However, this democratizing of the past was the start of a rift central to an understanding of the city's modern development. On one hand, the fire had liberated a sense of enormous possibilities, and on the other, created new limits. The old had been scorched and awaited rebuilding. An entire new class of people, with family histories in the city of less than a generation, had emerged. For the first time, the common laborer—characterized most often by the drayman or porter—was made visible to the city's dynasts. And while it is true, as we have seen, that the essential literary reaction was to turn away from the most extreme examples of lower-class behavior, those who made the city work were no longer invisible. Postfire scenes of cooperation between the city's haves and have-nots were themselves only overcompensation for physical terrors raised by the flames and projected upon the most unfortunate segment of the population. Such efforts to romanticize the event's harshest realities were part of a mostly unconscious process of containment. The privileged classes were not ready in 1871 to abandon a sturdy portrait of themselves, based on a formidable succession of dynastic leaders from the Kinzies to the newly ascendant Potter Palmers, for a shaky unknown that might include, in a more permanent political form, the very same cohort of their fellow citizens that had, as the flames blazed, given them such a fright.

The city had narrowly escaped annihilation. Goodspeed's picture of the city as a fortunate Pompeii was no mere metaphor; it was the survivor's reality. There was no place for even the suggestion of anarchy implied by the reported behavior of the city's more rambunctious citizens. The "Chicago Spirit" became a symbol of unity necessary for the long and demanding period of rebuilding. Chicago's rebuilding, which lasted well into the decade of the eighties, created a particularly American interaction between art and commerce. While it was possible, at least initially, to build simply a better and safer version of prefire Chicago, ignoring the more unpleasant aspects of those days in October, the city would eventually lose its claim on innocence. Unemployment, rising immigration, labor organization—the least gentrified aspects of a capitalist economy, all there before the fire—would over the next twenty years create a counterreality that would seriously put into question Chicago's professed solidarity.

Both in Chicago architecture—almost by definition a mediator between art and business—and literature there was a slow but deliberate investigation of the fire's legacy that eventually portrayed the city in its full complexity. Initially, however, there was an unwillingness to bear the full burden of consciousness. The city's writers and architects for an extended period following the fire fell under the spell of Kinzie and Bross, who still offered visions of harmony. By making the past present and simply shifting the historical focus from the settlement days to October 1871, Chicagoans were not compelled to focus on how different and inalterable their current reality was.

The choice of usable myths of regeneration successfully, for a time at least, promoted the old Chicago notion of a common reality, generated by the dominant gentrified class and imposed upon the rest. However, what had worked before, when memory of the heroic past was the exclusive domain of the privileged few, would become in time impossible. The Indians and barbarians of legend would not this time be vanquished but, in fact, would come to write their own histories. The fire had democratized experience and contributed to making each "heroic worker" potentially his own historian. There could never again be a dynastic monopoly on the truth. The variety of reactions to the event testifies to this, as it does also to the persistent and ingrained American habit of resolving unpleasant or threatening contradictions in favor of a manageable unity.

The rift that first appeared as people attempted to understand what they had been through divided those who still sought in the accustomed manner to level all experience for a common end and those—first called "realists" and later "modernists"—who attempted to authenticate the particularities of their own reality. The city endorsed and encouraged the former and discouraged the latter. Architects were hired to rebuild a city in the Europeanized image of the one that burned down. Writers were rewarded with a large audience when they formulated, as Roe and Lamb did, a comfortable legend for the present. But ultimately the fire had revealed too much. The rebuilding would continue to expose contradictions between the idealized Whig ideal of development and life's reality in the neighborhoods. Chicagoans found that they could more easily bury the fire's physical record than its psychological effect. Debris from the conflagration was used as landfill, entombed forever, for the expanding modern city, while the fire's memory, in all the vivid particulars of gallantry and depravity, became buried too.

With time writers began to reconsider what had happened the day of the fire. John McGovern's *Daniel Trentworthy: A Tale of the Great Fire of Chicago* (1889) compares the 1871 "destruction of Chicago" not to a supernatural event or to a natural disaster, but to the manmade French Revolution.[47] McGovern's novel, written in the wake of the Haymarket bombing and violence at the McCormick Works, offers no simple resolution. He sees in the class divisions and conflicts revealed by the fire a continuing problem for the city. The fire's intensity is a metaphor for the later eruptions of violence in Chicago. For McGovern and others looking back on the event, the fire was seen as a turning point.

But for the waning months of 1871 and for the rest of the decade Chicagoans would yield a hard-won and individuated sense of reality to the common myth of unity they felt necessary for the long period of rebuilding. Like a country recovering from war, where fierce nationalism takes hold, Chicago encouraged all to pull together. Such common will was unquestionably good for development. However, taken too far it could dull the mind. Witness an example from one of the fire's many commemorative poems:

> Fair seemed the old; but fairer still
> The new the dreary void shall fill,
> With dearer homes than those o'erthrown,
> For love shall lay each corner-stone.

The words carry the tone of a city too busy to pause for self-examination. People lost themselves in work, frantically trying to "fill" the "void" left by the fire. Their success in covering up what the flames revealed would haunt them into the century's final decades.

We will look next at this critical period of rebuilding in terms of its architecture to search for signs of the great modern work of John Root, Louis Sullivan, and Frank Lloyd Wright, remembering that theirs was an excruciatingly active investigation of reality, a demythologizing very much at odds with Chicago's stubborn will to forget or flatten uncomfortable and progress-delaying contradictions. Their work would prove to be quite a contrast to the earliest attempts to rebuild the city and very much at odds with Chicago's prevailing mood of forgetting, a civic amnesia characterized by A. A. Hayes when he wrote in 1880 a brief history of Chicago for *Harper's New Monthly Magazine*. "Strange to say, in the face of the heart-rending stories which have been told, the writer can not learn of a single life having been lost in the flames."[48]

The fire, after only nine years, was already confused with the rest of the city's past, its memory conveniently edited and polished. Consider the psychic price of all the void-filling, the rewriting of such a carefully documented event. Tell Frank Luzerne, who visited the morgue the night of the fire, that what he saw was no longer part of the record. He counted the bodies and reported: "The next was the body of a young man partially clad in common workingmen's attire. The hair was completely burned off his head and body; the features were blackened and distorted with pain; the swollen lips were wide apart, disclosing the glistening teeth, and imparting a horrid grin, such only as agonizing death can stamp upon the face. The flesh was bloated to an astonishing size. The poor wretch was roasted alive."[49] Seventy corpses, buried twice: once interred in the ground and finally erased from memory.[50] Chicago would have to come to terms with its obsessive need to build and its damaging will to forget.

Derrick Time
Architecture, Memory, and the Poetics of Ruin

Architecture in two forms was at the center of events after the fire. In ruin it provided the evangelists proof that the end was near, while in plans for new buildings it substantiated a vision of what the morning papers were already calling the "New Chicago." For architects the fire had created a radical condition in which the material past in the form of buildings was suddenly obliterated, leaving a context like the virgin land of two generations earlier. But this promise of invention was soon lost. By requiring immediate results, city leaders and builders concerned about their own survival and sensing the public mood for quick action limited architecture's inventiveness. Before too much self-examination delayed results, architects joined in the rebuilding to assure the city's most recent triumph over adversity and to offer new evidence for its "inevitable" progress.

Chicago architects desired respectability and found their new celebrity charming. Their marginal social position at the time and, more alarmingly, their actual part in the fire had made them uncharacteristically silent. In addition to destroying generations of work, the blaze had uncovered the shoddy way Chicago was built, a fact which posed a nagging problem for builders and boosters who wished to use architecture as a symbol of the city's rebirth. Hulks of blasted buildings undermined all such propaganda by suggesting a damning conclusion: that cheaply ornamented and hurried architecture had been the essential fuel of a fire that had nearly destroyed the entire city. This inalterable fact, seen everywhere in the mountains of building debris, would continue to shadow the city if nothing were done to offset it. At the moment of their greatest visibility and opportunity, Chicago architects avoided the more difficult lessons that the fire held for them and chose to join the general frenzy of rebuilding.

11. State Street in the 1890s, showing the Masonic Temple under construction.

By 1880, when *Harper's* reported that no one had died in the fire, enough of Chicago had been rebuilt to make the fire seem deeper in the past than it was in fact. Journalistic distortions of this sort were part of a widespread desire to put the disaster to rest. A process consistent with the city's demonstrated skill at transforming loss into gain was simply accelerated by the fire. Prominent new buildings began to tower above the ruins, and those commentators who paused to remind the city of its brush with tragedy were viewed as spoilers and their cautions ignored. The architect appeared in this climate to be the very model of the modern man who thought only long enough to determine a successful course of action.

Immediately a dialectic developed between the compulsion to move forward and the constant reminder of loss seen by the survivors in "the mass of ashes, stone-fragments, brick-bats, mortar-dust, slag, metallic debris, melted and agglomerated nails, spikes, horse-shoes, bars, bundles and other forms of iron, crockery, china and glass-ware and ten thousand other relics."[1] As late as 1892 a mound of iron debris, huge independent objects permanently forged together by the heat of the fire, still littered the site of Burnham and Root's new Masonic Temple. A contemporary report focused on architecture's particular burden: "If the fire had annihilated them all (buildings and the life they contained) it would have been well; but there they lay, the bones of the old Chicago to be buried out of the path of the new."[2] After twenty years, remnants of old buildings were still in the way, like open wounds. Even when recycled, they never seemed far enough removed. The old Lake Front Park, within the area of the Illinois Central breakwater, was requisitioned as a new landfill for millions of tons of rubble. Seemingly endless loads of debris provided substance for all the prior metaphors of renewal by becoming the actual foundations for the new city. Alert to the prevailing spirit, enterprising children salvaged pieces of the shattered Court House bell, renamed them "cinders," and sold them as good luck charms. Grotesquely twisted pieces of metal were transformed from worthless objects into popular icons celebrating the miracle of survival.

During the first hours of the fire, Chicago had been forced to witness in reverse its meteoric development. As if inspired by the unstoppable energy of the flames, the reconstruction seemed similarly possessed. A century-long process of settlement was restored in a matter of years, putting history on its head. The preachers were wrong; the city was not at time's end but amazingly seemed to be at its beginning, suddenly offered a blank slate, a radical freedom to begin again. It had only to select those aspects of the past that fit the present and improvise or invent the rest. The business district shifted toward the Loop, a new area more suited to the rebuilding.[3] To aid businessmen before the insurance claims could be settled and new structures built, the city allowed them to appropriate housing along Michigan Avenue for commercial purposes. Soon construction derricks rose above the scorched ground as an optimistic sign of recovery. New structures began to replace those which had failed to resist the fire, easing the trauma of survival, until one had to look deliberately for the physical signs of what he had just been through. The

12. Ruins of the Tribune Building, corner of Dearborn and Madison Streets.

recent past paled under the boosters' rhetoric and the architects' walls, until it threatened to disappear completely like the fire dead. Architects, who were embarrassed by what the massive destruction had revealed about their past work, made an alliance with the boosters that would come to haunt them. They looked past the present and joined forces with those who claimed only to see the future. The initial rebuilding favored speed and too often settled for elaborated recreations of what had stood before. But failure was all around, daily piled up and carted away to make way for the new city, and no amount of feverish activity could erase it all. The architectural failure could have been foreseen; it was inevitable.

Fires at the time were an accepted hazard of urban life, particularly for the western settlements that depended extensively on timber construction to sustain their accelerated pace of development. Given the prolonged drought of 1870–71 and the rash of summer fires in Wisconsin and Minnesota, both Chicago's fire department and its general civil preparedness had been completely inadequate.[4] Politicians who prided themselves on how much tax money they could save by keeping city services at a minimum were at a loss to rationalize the devastation of the city's main architecture. Quality or type of materials, expense, or style appeared to have had no effect on whether or not a building had survived. The Tribune Building was typical of the city's most durable building type. According to a contemporary account, "The Tribune was, by several hours, the last building in Chicago to survive the general destruction, and its magnificent fire-proof building was the last to succumb, although it had been surrounded by fire on two sides for about four hours." The report continues with the resigned tone of disbelief we associate with the loss of the Titanic or the Challenger: "The ceilings were of corrugated iron, resting upon wrought iron 'I' beams, while every partition wall in the entire structure was of brick. It was, in all respects, one of the most absolutely fire-proof buildings ever erected. That is, it was fire-proof up to the date of its destruction."[5] Here was a double loss: gone with the buildings was faith in a technology that was supposed to be free of failure.

Immediately, the city tried to soothe itself with moralistic tales and with explanations that were comfortably wide of the mark. They put blame on Chicago's poor and fueled renewed resentments against the city's newest immigrants and politically disenfranchised; and it temporarily shifted the focus of failure from the commercial center to the outlying southwest slums where it was less in view.[6] Yet whatever anecdotal explanations one might concoct for momentary relief from the facts, deep smoldering holes at the city center created horrifying images of vulnerability; one had only to remember that what was there hours before had suddenly evaporated. Images like these accumulated until they challenged the ability of language to compensate. In the midst of destruction, one's normal relation to things was radically altered.

Memory was strained; little was familiar. Chicago was transformed into a city of shock victims, where a kind of amnesia was not pathological but the logical consequence of experience. Church steeples, formerly the tallest points in every neighborhood, street signs, and other landmarks that defined a place were obliterated. "Buildings had been reduced to ashes, and the wind after scooping rubbish and all in a body, hurled it forward in a perfect blinding cloud. Division Street was swept clean, not a stone remained which could have pointed to the spot where stood some well-known building." [7] One's known world was altered irrevocably, as if by a bomb or volcanic eruption. Friends vanished without leaving a mark. Things thought solid and permanent melted and disappeared, leaving only their shadows in the undifferentiated rubble. An eyewitness confirms this horrifying feeling of being lost at home: "For three days after the fire we walked through the streets, covered everywhere with heaps of debris and parts of walls, and could not help comparing ourselves to ghosts. . . . All those magnificent streets, all those grand palaces, which but yesterday were the pride and glory of the chief Western metropolis, are today indeed, a mass of scattered shapeless ruins." [8]

What was the character of this architecture that failed to offer protection, and what did it, in ruin, imply about Chicago as a contending modern American city? J. M. Van Osdel's Court House more than any other single building represented prefire architecture in the city. Neither the tallest, largest, or most expensive to construct, the Court House was the building most clearly associated with the city's past and its desires for the future. Because it contained records of births and deaths, and particularly land deeds, all Chicagoans had some connection to the building. As they entered and saw the hodgepodge of neoclassical and continental styles they were reminded that the Court House was no merely practical structure but a deliberate if somewhat pretentious piece of architecture. "The round-headed windows with keystones, the heavy bracketed cornice, the curved pediments, and the huge stone urns proclaimed that Van Osdel had mounted the band wagon and was giving the city the last word in the French style, at least as he understood it. Even its contemporaries admitted 'it lacked unity'." [9] But for all its pretended elegance it was difficult not to notice how the building was forced to be practical at least in one matter. To accommodate Chicago's perpetual mud, an awkward story-high flight of stairs on a steep grade allowed the people to enter safe and dry at the second floor. This reluctant accommodation to reality made ridiculous any grandiose claims to European stylishness. The Court House was faulted for "lacking unity," but its basic architectural assumptions were left unquestioned. So completely out of balance were architectural priorities before the fire. Although fire safety and the problems for foundations caused by the water-saturated soil should have been primary

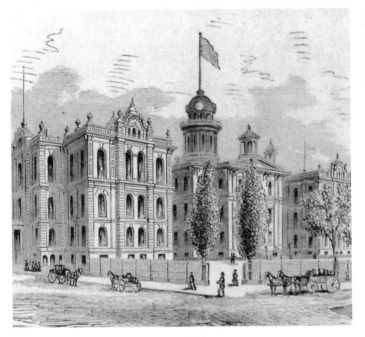

13. J. M. Van Osdel, Court House (1853, 1858). Reproduced from *The Lakeside Memorial of the Burning of Chicago* (1872).

considerations in the design of buildings, they were thought secondary to passing fashion. The solidity of architecture, arguably its most important feature given Chicago's hostile climate, became in fact a secondary consideration. This architecture proved a costly illusion.

Van Osdel came to the city in 1837, in the early days after incorporation. He was there at the very beginning of the first building boom and designed the Court House in 1853 to replace the modest Greek Revival building that was standing when he arrived. The site, bounded by Clark and LaSalle streets on the east and west and by Randolph and Washington on the north and south, was seen from the very beginning as requiring an important building. The choice of a prominent location and of the city's most celebrated architect, a man who had been chosen by William B. Ogden, Chicago's first mayor, to build him a house in the 1830s when the city was still a mudflat, supported the impression that the Court House was the city's finest architectural example. Originally two stories tall, done in a consistent Greek Revival style, the Court House had grown an additional story and east and west wings by the time of the fire. It was built of limestone from Lockport, New York, and from Cook County's Lemont quarries (the local stone was called "Athens marble" to give it class and distinguish it from its out-of-state competitors).

Atop the building Van Osdel had fitted a giant cupola which housed the municipality's fire bell and served as an observation platform to overlook the city after a Sunday stroll. The building's social and civic centrality had ensured Van Osdel's fame and had made architects in general more visible on the city scene. The failure of the Court House to resist the fire put into question architects as a group and challenged the city's notorious self-confidence.

There was no way to minimize what had occurred. The event was too public to cover up; something essential had been revealed by the fire that even Chicago's normally high level of rhetoric and mythologizing could not entirely obscure. The burning Court House figured prominently in eyewitness accounts and was the subject of a widely-circulated illustration in *Frank Leslie's Illustrated Newspaper* (October 28, 1871). A journalist sent by the Michigan News Company reported, " At 10 minutes past 2 o'clock the Court House tower was a glorious sight. It stood a glowing, almost dazzling trellis-work, around which was wrapped a sheet—a winding sheet—of flame." When he later returned to assess the damage to the building he observed how the native stone had fared: "The effect of the fire upon the Athens marble has been remarkable. In some places the stone has disappeared altogether. In others, such as the LaSalle street front of the Court House, it has been gnawed and eaten away, or fallen on the great flakes." [10]

While the facade of the Court House liquified or flaked, the bell in the great cupola let go and went crashing through the building's core. The skin of the building continued to blister and run as the inside imploded. Only the freestanding walls survived, in eerie self-parody. The architectural rubble fell into the basement and joined the city's accumulated records, which had been rendered into a fine gray ash by the intense heat. Land records, held in presumed safety in the now-destroyed Court House vaults, were burned beyond recovery. The destruction of land records put into question the ownership of even the ruins around which the stunned population moved. It was one thing for Roe and others to rhapsodize about the extraordinary mixing of classes during the fire, and quite another to endorse a permanent redistribution of land. Any building attempted without proof of clear title would be frustrated by the actuality of endless litigation. Chicago was spared this second disaster by the "abstract-men," who cleverly found a way to minimize the actuality of the loss.

John G. Shortall, whose instant rise to prominence was recalled twenty years later in novelist Joseph Kirkland's popular history of Chicago, was an unlikely hero in a city famed for powerful and reckless men. Shortall, who resembled a meek accountant more than a prairie titan, was a partner in one of the flourishing abstract businesses that had grown with the local real-estate trade. His firm prepared summaries (abstracts) and indexes of city land transfers. From his nearby office window he watched the Court House burn in a "perfect rain of fire." Aided by two prisoners who had been permitted to escape from the doomed Court House jail, Shortall, dressed in a velveteen housecoat, saved abstracted copies of city land deeds from his office, by loading ledger books onto wagons and carting them away. Acting with two other firms, Chase Brothers and Jones and Sellers, Shortall then reconstructed a reliable record of property transfers. This work became the basis for Illinois's Burnt Record Act (1872), which reestablished a legal basis for ownership that allowed banks to finance the rebuilding.

Looking back in 1891, Shortall recalled the times vividly: "The destructibility of all material, the instability of all substance, even the most impervious, shocked me. I saw those walls crumble with the heat, they seemed to melt, slowly, steadily; one could see them moving in the process of disintegration, and presently sink hopelessly down."[11] Shortall saw the walls move in a macabre parody of life, whereas others in an odd reversal of his view saw men in their deaths suddenly appear mechanical. A man trapped by the flames on a roof "vibrated like a pendulum from side to side" before he died.[12] The fire so consumed or radically distorted human beings caught directly in the flames that they became just another indistinguishable part of the larger spectacle of material collapse. A generalized abstracting of grief and loss accompanied and eventually overwhelmed the personal accounts seen earlier in letters, diaries, and intimate narratives. The horror is reflected in the following accounts: "Two men were also found in the neighborhood of a livery stable near the Pacific Hotel, burned and charred so as to render recognition an impossibility; only a part of their legs and trowsers remained to establish the fact that they were human beings."[13] More often than not there was nothing left to identify. "So intense was the heat, and so completely was every thing consumed that could be, that in many cases not even the bones of those who perished in buildings remain to tell the sad tale."[14]

Shortall's frantic activity during the fire was undertaken for no immediate profit; there were also plenty of schemers of a more entrepreneurial bent. Laborers with wagons made small fortunes moving people and their belongings away from the fire's path. Soon after, some discovered a good business digging out safes from the debris of collapsed and burned buildings, while others found an active trade in painting removal signs for those eager to advertise their temporary business quarters. Tales of the great real-estate baron Potter Palmer, who while sweeping the ruins of his own property was already planning in his head the new and improved State Street, provided an image of industry and optimism equal to that of young Ben Franklin entering Philadelphia. Such restless industry was consistent with the way William Bross and the city's other prominent boosters wished to characterize both the struggle against the fire and the seemingly instantaneous recovery. One of the hundreds of reporters sent to Chicago to cover the fire and its aftermath caught the mood: "It is Wednesday [October 11, 1871]. The people desired to blot out the past—rub the old reckoning off the slate and commence anew."[15] Chicagoans chose to look everywhere but down. But the past was all around, a shadow in the ruins.

The natural impulse to minimize loss and get on with everyday life was from the beginning threatened by the disaster's enormous scale. In the districts where buildings had been constructed of stone or brick, people could barely locate the outlines of where they had once lived or worked. In places where wooden structures predominated, "absolute desolation was the rule." The same eyewitness continued: "A stranger, ignorant of the occurrence of fire, might have travelled over acres without scarcely meeting a single thing to even suggest that the areas through which he was passing had ever been inhabited."[16] Another reported the city to be a place where human beings "were doubtless so consumed as to leave no trace of their existence."[17] As the shock wore off, the city was presented with a new problem. What would be the shape and character of the city after it was rebuilt, and in what way, if any, would it acknowledge the experience it had been through? The miraculous speed with which the abstractmen cheated total ruin created a seductive model of action. Architects, who because of the precision required by their work needed to take a long time to design and execute building plans correctly, became themselves addicted to the seductive prospects of instant recovery in a way that would seriously compromise their work.

At a time when "religious fanatics predicted the destruction of the world,"[18] architecture's demonstrated fragility questioned Chicago's secular claims on the future. Particularly at risk was the city's own version of manifest destiny, in which the city viewed itself as the beneficiary of uninterrupted development, on a vector of progress with only a forward force. In the communal desire for immediate reconstruction and the unprecedented opportunity to build, architects lost their natural desire, reinforced by their training, to pause and evaluate what had gone wrong. The situation was further complicated by the fact that the city's architects had only recently emerged from what Carlyle called the cultural period of the "inarticulate poet," in which good art is created only unconsciously or when purely utilitarian.[19] This "naive" work had been followed immediately by painfully self-conscious work, including the embarrassingly arriviste Court House.

Reasons for Chicago's social and cultural awkwardness seem to all derive from one source. In the view of a Chicago writer at the time, the city's "struggle with nature had to precede everything" before architecture or any other art could overcome the "dull philistinism of the American character."[20] The architecture exposed to the flames had liberally substituted style for character and structure, breaking only superficially from the early days of the city's settlement, when building without professional architects had been the rule. Given the rapid expansion of the city grid due to unregulated speculation, sheer mass had been thought more important than any considerations of form. The tendency toward rapid growth was reinforced by a crucial technological development which had occurred the year of Van Osdel's arrival.

George Washington Snow's balloon-frame construction technique forever changed the way buildings are made.[21] Snow, a Chicagoan from 1832, when he paddled a canoe north to the mouth of the Chicago River, shortly after his arrival made it possible for a group of laborers to do the work of master carpenters and tradesmen, at a fraction of the cost. This single innovation made wood construction cheaper and more efficient. Replacing the costly and time-consuming post-and-beam method, the balloon-frame technique created a building that was an interplay of ribs and skin, easily assembled and even prefabricated. Boards that were nailed were not structurally weakened by the many cuts required by mortise-and-tenon fabrication. (Building balloon frames with two-by-fours and two-by-tens made traditional methods all but obsolete.)

The widespread implementation of balloon framing initially threatened the small group of Chicago architects and put them on notice. They needed to find some way to distinguish themselves from the amateurs and tradesmen who

14. Home Insurance Building demolition, showing steel-frame construction.

threatened to replace them even before they had gotten a decent foothold on Chicago's muddy terrain.[22] By the 1850s, the city had established a fledgling literary journal, *Chicago Magazine*, credible daily newspapers, social clubs, and, in Juliette Kinzie, a novelist. But it was architecture that most stridently insinuated itself into Chicago's earliest experiments with culture. Chicago's claim to culture of any kind focused on its buildings, the visual proof of its social advancement.

To look at the buildings was, as a local writer declared, "to partake of the true Chicago spirit which effaced the foottracks of the Indian with brick and mortar, and reared a magnificent city upon the sides of a crooked creek and in the marshes of the prairie." Architects William W. Boyington, Otto Matz, Edward Burling, and August Bauer, along with John Van Osdel, were the city's prominent social and cultural arbiters. As business and labor drove Chicago's economy, architects transformed its appearance, prettied it up in the accepted manner of a major metropolis. The same commentator understood that architecture's primary role in Chicago was to make it appear as more than a town in which to make money. "It is actually not more than ten years since the higher evidences of culture began to show themselves. Within that time, they have attained a prominence that is wonderful, not alone because of the briefness of the intervening space, but because they have forced a recognition in a community that has been regarded as purely mercantile in spirit."[23] But these impressive changes unfortunately did not go very deep. The fire revealed that with remarkable efficiency, stripping the city's architecture of its illusions in the way a walk around a Hollywood backlot reveals a solid American Main Street to be a phony set of propped-up facades. An eyewitness observed, "Few dreamed that the exquisite creations of genius, the handsome, massive marble structures which had comprised the wealth, the hope, the pride of the mercantile community would prove but pasteboard obstacle in checking the advancing flames."[24] What began as sadly ironic commentary ended in fierce protest. There would be no easy architectural equivalent to the abstract-men.

On the night of January 15, 1872, a march organized by the politically active German community exposed Chicago architecture to a rare level of criticism. The protesters objected to proposed legislation aimed at setting new fire limits and regulating the kinds of buildings erected in the central city. The protest might appear strange given the city's recent brush with disaster, but the demonstrators accurately understood the mood of the moment. They perceived these proposed laws as favoring the commercial interests. Particularly at risk was the city's large stock of single-family homes. Chicago, unlike other large American cities, offered the opportunity for the poor to own their homes. Sprawling land to the west of the city center offered a cheap property base on which to homestead with modest wood structures.[25] Petitions were collected and demonstrations planned to convince the "Fire-Proof" aldermen to allow rebuilding in wood within carefully restricted areas. The petitioners correctly feared that aroused public sentiment would force them to abandon their long-standing right of home ownership. If the legislation passed, families who had lived in their own homes and improved their properties for, in some cases, as long as the city had been incorporated would be forced to rebuild using prohibitively expensive materials. In the absence of any sure means of fireproofing, brick and stone, thought more resistant than wood, were to be required, at a cost dramatically increased over that of familiar balloon-frame wood construction.

Burned-out homeowners faced the real prospect of being

herded into tenements. Particularly for those lacking insurance or any clear means of employment, the antifire laws seemed a great leap backwards, helpful only to the real estate interests, who, collecting in full from insurance companies or owing nothing on their land, would profit from the driven demand for new rental units. Predictably, public sentiment weighed against the working poor, who were lumped together with the notorious denizens of Conley's Patch and other vice districts. By the better-off, the fire was already being viewed philosophically as a necessary social hygiene or as a convenient redistributor of assets, which had happily attacked marginal residential areas and created more room for the city's growing commerce. This common attitude can be found in business discussions of the time. Typical were the views expressed in an article, "The Effect of the Fire upon Real Estate," that appeared anonymously in the same month as the protest demonstrations. "Those parties who suffered most severely by the fire, in the destruction of the noblest business edifices were certain well-known capitalists who had made immense purchases during the spring and summer of 1871, in the new Park and Boulevard region." Even suffering was denied the class that had borne the fire's main assault. In fact, the loss improved the city: "Chicago property now stands better classified, and its future more distinctly marked, than could have been possible before the fire."[26]

Anton Caspar Hesing, publisher of the German-language paper *Staats Zeitung*, argued his willingness to support sane new fire laws, but would not accept legislation that penalized a single class. He argued that it was self-serving of the political majority to blame the disaster on the poor. Focusing on the drunken O'Leary family simply reinforced established prejudice—that the root of the city's problems with unregulated growth could be isolated in its libertine slums. Hesing shifted attention precisely where the aldermen, deliberating at the temporary Court House, did not want it to go. He pointed out that new fire laws did not help rehabilitate existing properties but primarily aided speculators by forcing owners of lots where wood houses had formerly stood to sell their land at a loss. New brick and stone structures required capital that was not widely available in ethnic neighborhoods. Political reform burdened the social class least able to bear it.

Carefully directed political agitation revealed that cheap wooden construction was a sin not exclusively of Hesing's constituency. Circulated petitions alluded to the widespread architectural use of dangerous wood framing for unnecessary cornices, mansards, and other confectionary applications of "style" to otherwise utilitarian structures. Such ornamentation served as a form of advertising or individuation that was lacking in the structure as a whole. Just as Athens marble had provided an illusion of solidity, wood ornamentation was more like the city's ubiquitous plank sidewalks than the classical world to which it cheaply aspired. Chicago's proudest architecture was pasteboard fuel, a long wick for Mrs. O'Leary's overturned lantern.

Its geometric rise in population, increasing concentration of capital, and growing national reputation as a commercial and trading center overwhelmed Chicago's institutions after the Civil War.[27] Politicians and businessmen did not adapt quickly enough. Development or growth for its own sake was given a priority over all other considerations of public policy. Ideas of control and social equity were left to the invisible hand of opportunity. Given the facts of an ever-expanding economy and a population eager to supply necessary labor, this unregulated system worked surprisingly well. But the fire challenged the status quo, as Hesing and his followers were quick to understand. Rebuilding must not mean the disenfranchisement of those who had borne the hard labor of development and were only recently in a position to claim their rewards. The stalemate over an equitable and enforceable fire code in the months after the disaster only brought to the fore issues previously submerged in Chicago's euphoric prosperity and economic promise for all classes.

"Pasteboard" architecture was the glaring symbol of two generations of mostly hollow improvisation. "Marble" that was really inexpensive local stone, cornices made of stock two-by-fours to look like masonry, and Parisian mansards composed of the same material as a squatter's shanty gave a lie to the city's most public achievement. Architects were in league with the rest of the city's business community, providing a cosmopolitan veneer to frontier-like machinations. They were not distinct from the boosters but really their indispensable agents. John McGovern, in his novel of the fire, draws attention to the particularly close marriage of politician, businessman, and architect in prefire Chicago. "Ralph Errington was a man 'in thorough harmony with the people'. He was a 'popular idol'. He espied the fact that the people of Chicago wanted wooden houses, and he said at once that the voice of the people was the voice of God. Some of the capitalists were putting three-story mansard roofs on five-story buildings, making eight stories in all." Alderman Errington, the model of the urban populist of the day, understands that allowing such unnecessary additions would result in putting vulnerable wooden construction beyond the reach of the city's water hoses. But he still votes in favor of this dangerous building practice. "A strong attempt was made to stop this form of balloon building, but Alderman Errington was eloquent against any move that would 'harm the future of our glorious city'."[28] McGovern's book is the most completely dramatized account of the symbiotic relationship among architecture, business, and politics that made the fire an inevitability. For our purposes it helps to clarify architecture's complicity in an event that the rebuilding sought to bury in landfill and hastily forget.

Architects dressed their buildings up with ornaments and created an impression of permanence as a stopgap measure of consolidation. For decades, Chicago's working and upper classes had become increasingly segregated, with the enlarging middle class in an uneasy geographical middle ground. The poor migrated to the West Side, while the rich stayed close to the lake and later moved to the near-north suburb of Evanston and the near-south suburb of Hyde Park.[29] These changing residential patterns were accelerated after the fire. The ease of acquiring burned-out properties aided in the accumulation of commercial land packages, particularly along State and Lake streets, and the city was rebuilt along stricter class and ethnic lines. Before the fire these social and class distinctions were less a matter of location and gerrymandered districts. Architectural manipulation of facades, illusions of expansive space, and overall mannered design put architecture in the camp of the speculators and the aldermen. Chicago's prefire architects were happily gentrified frontier businessmen who aided unquestioningly the dangerous logic of unsupervised development, (not, as they liked to see themselves, independent professionals struggling against the crass encroachments of business).

John McGovern's *Daniel Trentworthy* connects the myth of Chicago's development with the events of October 7, 8, and 9, 1871. For McGovern, architecture is the hinge upon which pivots the city's mythic view of its progress and the reality of its inadequacies. McGovern, writing a generation after the events he dramatized, incorporated into his narrative Hesing's critique of large real-estate interests and sense of working-class exclusion. McGovern's biblical and sublime natural imagery—"torch of the destroying angel" and "viewless Niagara"—is not literal, as it was in earlier novels of the fire, but is a coded way of distancing a traumatic event. McGovern understood that simple moralisms were, by his time, stock metaphors that did not actively engage the mind, signs that the imagination was dulled and not actively engaging the experience. He chose not to challenge these conventions directly. If he had, the book might have had the realistic quality of Crane's best urban fiction and of *The Red Badge of Courage*. Instead, his book is a hybrid, partially at war with the same literary formulas that sustain it, sometimes extolling the myths it sets out to debunk. The novel is never under tight control. But it remains a good source of critical information on the prefire city, a tough view of early modern Chicago that challenges the survivors' fantasies of class harmony and unity, until it replaces them with its own.

Daniel Trentworthy is the scion of a wealthy family, a westerner like the novelist Frank Norris and not the typical luckless young man from the East. McGovern has slightly revised the Victorian paradigm of Ivy League Anglican values in opposition to the grasping, improvised morality of the new city. Daniel is educated at Harvard but is the son of a western entrepreneur. His father heads the El Dorado Bank in San Francisco; he lives in a "palace" and is considered the "greatest speculator in the history of finance." McGovern describes the feverish transfer of money in the same terms he uses for the fire: "A Niagara of molten gold was thundering over a precipice into an abyss of credit." The father drowns himself after he botches a deal and loses money. Bad speculation and evil living are equal reasons for instant retribution; the climactic scenes of the fire underscore this idea of retributive justice.

The melodrama is interesting because it is forced to double back on itself. It is not simply a conventional tale of a young man making his way in the big city; Daniel makes his way by reliving consciously his father's life, during a historic time. From his father's San Francisco palace he winds up in the "other Chicago" of rooming houses and seedy characters. "So, down at the end of the nastiest street this side of Erzeroum; down at the end of a double row of chicken crates nearly a mile long; down at the end of an avenue where green grocers' wagons, packed like sardines, carried away only a portion of the green things that must wither and mildew in a day; within a few feet of a sewage lagoon that had not yet been drained into the Mississippi River—to such an inn the boy was forced, by the force of one man over another, to go." Daniel's entry into Chicago, like Jane Addams's and Jacob Riis's excursions into the city's underworld, is a descent into hell. McGovern's imagination breaks with the fire-and-brimstone imagery of the evangelists. He calls the fire Phlegethon after the underworld river of flames in Hades and describes Chicago's fire world as a place where everything was unearthly dark and "men were black."

Daniel settles on DeKoven Street, center of the same unfortunate neighborhood forever linked with the fire. Befitting a visitor to the underworld, Daniel requires a guide. He finds his Virgil in an old friend from his San Francisco days, Christian Holebroke. Christian has changed his name from Harmon to reflect his new, pious ways, particularly his pledge of sobriety, which radically separates him from the dissolute poor. His poverty is politically motivated, not the result of failure. Christian is a vehicle of the conventional plot, but as guide serves the author's purposes in more imaginative ways. He introduces his friend to his sister, the novel's love interest, but also to the "good" workers of the Southwest Side. He is a member of the Chicago Printers' Co-operative Association, the kind of organization sponsored by Anton Hesing. Christian and later Daniel, who is a fireman until he is disabled by a falling wall, are opposed to slumlords and other nonlaboring profiteers like Errington and his dissolute wife. The poor are not patronized in *Daniel Trentworthy*; the novel makes its most interesting move when it connects Chicago avarice, the boosters' glorified engine of progress, with the fire.

Mary Holebroke, Christian's sister and Daniel's earliest love interest, has gone bad and married Alderman Errington. On the first day of the fire Daniel goes to the Errington mansion, where he finds Christian dead and discovers that Mary has murdered her husband. Mortally wounded by her own hand, she says in her death swoon, "The city is burning; I am glad of it." The deaths of Errington, Mary, and Christian Holebroke, who has contracted lead colic from working as a typesetter, are meant as correctives to the day's dominant business ethic. McGovern improvises on the familiar Christian melodrama in which a pilgrim is initially humbled but eventually is triumphant over the anti-Christ businessman and his pursuit of worldly riches. Errington's new business is the hellish smelting of metals. In McGovern's novel the fire has put together God and Satan in the same pagan underworld of Phlegethon. Extremes are equally rejected, including Errington's self-serving secularism, in which "respectability had become his god," and Christian's primitive communism. The fire reduces all to nothing. In McGovern's view renewal comes not through the traditional crusade of the pious against the infidel. The pagan fire is not a blaze of judgment but an unmoralized agent of change. He accurately portrays the mood of the rebuilding—parables of judgment or retribution simply did not fit the optimism of the moment. McGovern distinguishes between the anarchic experience of the moment and a hard-earned sense of control. "It was absolutely impossible for living witnesses to consider the destruction of Chicago in its entirety. They attended to the idea of the hour, not to the affair of the century." [30]

Daniel does not leave the city, nor is he humbled in the manner of one of Mrs. Lamb's or Roe's characters. The fire provides the opportunity to begin again. He marries Mary's sister and with a long-lost relative goes into the building business. One year after the disaster, Daniel is able to achieve the distance necessary to begin again. McGovern feels no obligation to explain Daniel's transformation from radical to entrepreneur. "Two places on Michigan Avenue stand side by side. There live the two brothers. And how comes this great wealth? It comes of invention. In the year 1872 the city was rebuilt. John Trentworthy perfected a machine to lift mortar. It came into instant use. He next made a machine to sandpaper wood. The firm of John, William & Daniel Trentworthy was established. It flourished."

McGovern's fictional recreation of events is close in tone and substance to Alfred Sewall's eyewitness account, published the year of the fire. Sewall considered the event a "special providence" and made the point that he was "not writing as a preacher but rather as an historian." For him, the fire's meaning was neither ordained nor teleological. Interpretation waited not on God but on the performance of survivors like Daniel Trentworthy. Chicago "was selected instead of some other, because of her prominence as a central figure in the world's habitations and commercial activities, so that the blow falling thus upon the very nervous center of the country, might have, as it certainly did have, the effect to startle, and thrill the entire financial, commercial and social fabric of Christendom." [31] Sewall accomplished two important things by arguing the centrality of the event to American life and mostly abstaining from evangelical rhetoric. To Sewall the fire's lessons were purely for "human instruction." He found a narrative that would allow people to order what they had been through without suffering further punishment or fear of judgment. Rebuilding, and not faith, was the new hope: "All the buildings are dotted with wooden buildings for temporary occupancy by residents and dealers; the ruins are being removed; brick walls are rising where they stood before; and the symptoms of convalescence and returning strength are only a little less perceptible here (North Division) than in the South Division, and that which a month ago was one great horrid waste, will not the less surely, before many months, again present the appearance of a great city scourged by fire but restored by the wondrous energy of a community of resolute men."[32] Reconstruction to Sewall was a value in itself, and he was careful not to criticize the extensive use of wood and unprotected brick that would inevitably lead to serious fires in the following years. The swiftness and surprise of destruction dominated his and others' thinking about the rebuilding.

Speed was thought more important than deliberation. It was as if the survivors had still to prove to themselves by the new buildings that rose around them that they had made it through. F. B. Wilkie, one of the first reporters to describe the destruction, understood their amazement and relief: "Already have the Ruins of Chicago become almost a thing of remembrance. Brick walls have risen like an exhalation from among their disorder, and whence the smoke struggled up sullenly and where the moon flung a pitying veil, there now are thronged the temporary structures which are the overture to Chicago's architectural resurrection."[33] Architectural quality was less important than the psychological function of allowing people to forget. The narrative of rebuilding seen in the activities of the abstract-men, reported and conceptualized by eyewitnesses, and fictionalized by McGovern, rested on the premise that Chicago might instantly rid itself of the memory of loss. In the first month of the new year 1872, Wilkie reported: "The grand, far-reaching ruins are narrowed into scars, and, in a little time, under the healthful operations of the circulation of Chicago blood, even these will be obliterated. Gone already is the first hideousness of the destruction; and scarcely before the world shall have recovered from the moral shock of the event, the Ruins of Chicago will exist only in the remembrance, or upon the canvas of the artist."[34]

Observing the heightened pace of rebuilding, Wilkie understood that the city was not likely to agonize over its misfortunes. What he could not have foreseen was how short the initial reconstruction period would be. By late summer of the following year the European financial downturn had spread to the United States. On September 8, 1873, a prominent New York bank, Jay Cooke and Company, failed, and New York Stock Exchange prices fell sharply, setting off a panic. Though hit hard, Chicago's economy survived the ensuing six-year depression better than most prominent American cities by paying cash from its cattle and grain businesses and by not expanding its public debt. Effects of the crisis were still dramatic; new building in the city essentially ceased.[35] Buildings completed immediately after the end of the panic, like Adler and Sullivan's Borden Block (1879–80), Burnham and Root's Grannis Block (1880–81) and Montauk Block (1881–82), where ornamentation and superficial issues of style were subordinated to the more essential architectural priorities of light, space, and form, had a different character from those buildings completed during the earlier frantic reconstruction. The intervention of financial panic and of political and labor disturbances put a lucky distance between the immediate architectural response to the fire and the more enduring one begun in the 1880s, now internationally recognized as the "Chicago School."[36]

The history of the first truncated rebuilding is too often neglected or simply subsumed by the larger and grander history of the city's later architecture.[37] But it was this brief period of building and the forced hiatus of the middle seventies that allowed architects to comprehend the fire. At that remove, the excessive speed of the reconstruction could be viewed as an understandable response to trauma and a desperate way to overcome a crisis. Ironically, the city's subsequent economic misfortunes, coming less than two years after its aborted destruction, provided a welcome corrective to the city's manic desire to put things right instantly. Chronic national social and economic conditions basically unresponsive to local manipulations, along with essential inventions that could not be immediately integrated into the new, larger buildings, made architects slow down and, in effect, rethink what the city had experienced, and then find appropriate forms to express it.[38]

What is considered modern architecture—stripped down, bold in mass and form—had its origins in a reimagining of the fire by a new group of architects lured to the city by the unprecedented opportunities to build, who had not directly witnessed the event but who were its beneficiaries. They stayed on through the difficult days with little to do but paper architecture and study of what others before them had done. John Root was conscious of the ironies. He gave up the promise of a good job in Washington to follow the exodus to Chicago. The depression took hold a short time after he had joined Daniel Burnham to form a new firm, and all his plans, including one for a Romanesque cathedral, were aborted. He wrote to his sister: "In my own case, I know that if I had been as successful in business as I expected to be when I started, I should have gone to the dickens as fast as my legs would carry me. Now I feel so doubtful of myself that I should very much dislike to be tried with much money. So I can see why I am kept back and thwarted in many schemes that have so fair a promise. There must be in this way some excellent reason for the condition in which we find ourselves." [39] He found that "excellent reason" in the boom-town architecture that seemed to be falling down almost daily in sight of his office on Washington Street. He viewed the new crop of designers as "green" and "buoyant" and the old guard who were there when he arrived as "fossils." In a letter dated March 17, 1873, he described the scene: "A very costly building of one of the old men is literally falling down of sheer bad construction; another one opposite our office was for several days in such a condition that no one would walk on the same side of the street. There are half a dozen costly buildings in this neighborhood held up by jack-screws, all because of the ineffi-cience [*sic*] of the architects, who appear daily in the news-papers with cards that talk nonsense about 'bad stone,' 'frost in the walls,' and what not." [40] The interruption of his ambi-tions turned into a blessing; it distinguished him and other talented outsiders from their incompetent colleagues. In ad-dition, he had the unusual opportunity to reflect at the height of his energies about what he might build. Unable to act im-mediately, he and the other new arrivals, like Louis Sullivan, were compelled to observe and imagine what they might one day do.

The very thing that appalled the "fossils" and the "green" young men was what compelled Root. Like Poe's purloined letter, the key to the new architecture was right in view, in the same ruins the builders tried so desperately to hide. A divi-sion developed between the architects who bore some re-sponsibility for the ruins and the talented newcomers like Root, Sullivan, Wright, Richardson, and Burnham, who were free to see them anew. The paradox is still powerful: Chicago's first modernists were successful in direct relation to their in-ability to build at once and without restraint. The inhibitions of the mid-seventies produced the creative conditions for the century's last two decades. Root sensed just this and sounded prophetic in a letter written during the nation's centennial year, when all the architectural action seemed to be taking place back east at the Philadelphia fair: "Our business contin-ues so dull that I have deliberately given myself up to a course of daylight reading. Perhaps it is a 'providence' that we thus have time to cultivate our minds, inasmuch as it saves us from doing much crude work that in after times we should be ashamed of. This compulsory idleness doesn't depress me very much, though it is tedious; for the ultimate success of a professional man is so dependent on his knowledge and industry and is acquiring the knowledge, he feels he can, if necessary, wait."[41]

Root's period of "compulsory idleness" followed what Joseph Kirkland called "derrick time," when the entire city seemed under construction. "A certain informality, comradeship, frankness, is the inevitable result of this state of things; shipwreck brings all passengers to a level of helpfulness, as their nature may be; whether they be first cabin, second cabin or steerage. The natural leaders go to the front and the natural workers follow them."[42] Kirkland's version of Roe's "barriers burned away" was itself a romantic fantasy in which unified action overwhelmed deeply-held social differences. In fact the postfire period proved the opposite to be true. "Steerage" was in revolt; August Hesing lobbied for a progressive fire law, modeled on a plan adopted in Cincinnati after a recent experience with a destructive fire, that would permit wood and other inexpensive construction techniques on a block-by-block basis. The "Cincinnati compromise" passed in Chicago after several violent street confrontations, but really was never an important factor. By the time Mayor Medill's "progressive" new government approved Hesing's plan, much of the city had already been rebuilt to the appalling standards observed above by Root. The use of wood in workers' housing was in effect more controlled than the more dangerous use of it in downtown commercial construction. Christine Rosen's sensitive study of the problem offers a useful summary: "One of the ironies of the struggle over the fire limits was that the proposed ban on wood construction was never, in any of its formulations, a particularly effective instrument for fireproofing the city. Although all of the proposals outlawed frame construction in at least some part of the city, even the strictest ones permitted flammable felt and tar roofs, wooden sheds and outhouses, wooden sidewalks, wooden cornices and window frames and other wooden exterior work, and various unsafe construction practices in the protected zones."[43] Only after the "Little Fire" of July 14, 1874, a multimillion dollar disaster, did the city extend prohibitions to include wooden awnings, cupolas, and cornices.[44]

Reform was not a priority of the politicians and builders; they endorsed a laissez-faire attitude in which results were all. An essayist, H. W. Thomas, looked back on the period and wrote appreciatively of the recovery: "The facts of the quick re-building of the city, and of the regaining of lost fortunes are evidences, not only of the unconquerable energy and persistency of the people of Chicago, but evidence also of the boundless resources and wealth of the growing country on whose great National highway the city stands." But there was a cost to the impressive speed. Thomas insisted that one had to forget to get on with the work: "Less than fifteen years have passed since the great fire, and yet it has become a thing of the past; is not often referred to, or even thought of by those who saw it." [45] Just as *Harper's* "forgot" that anyone had died, architects might profitably forget their own role in the calamity. Thomas insisted that "the feeling was soon common that the new city must be upon a plan far more substantial and elegant than had been the old. The result was, that only one building of any size,—that on the corner of Clark and Washington streets, was put up cheaply; and that has been torn down to give place to the new Chicago Opera-house block." [46] The facts, of course, were very different.

A. T. Andreas, in his comprehensive history of postfire Chicago, included Thomas's article as counterpoint to his own more critical attitude. By 1886, when he was writing his last volume, he could already see around him an architecture that answered to criteria different from quickness and manufactured elegance. With Jenney's First Leiter (1879) and Home Insurance (1884–85) buildings, Burnham and Root's Montauk and Grannis blocks and Adler and Sullivan's Troescher Building (1884), Andreas had other models. He incorporated Thomas's work as the first essay in his history's third volume to dramatize the difference between the old architecture and its apologists and the new. Andreas is blunt in his condemnation of the earlier architecture and the myths of progress that supported it. "It was not uncommon to see building, supposed to be of this class [fire-proof], surmounted by a Mansard roof, as inflammable as a pile of kindling wood." He notes critically the overwhelming need to erect "larger and grander" buildings. The "Chicago school" of architecture was first associated with a "morbid fondness" for cheap decoration: "As a characteristic of the architecture of this period (particularly with relation to private residences) may be mentioned diffuse ornamentation, which, in a number of instances, degenerated into vulgar if not gaudy—display." Designers compensated for the unnatural speed of the rebuilding with cheap tricks. "Architects found their resources taxed to the utmost to prepare plans, and in many cases, so eager was the desire to build, the interval of time between the maturing and the execution of the plans was inappreciable. A noticeable illustration is furnished by the

15. W. W. Boyington, Board of Trade Building (1882–85).

Grand Pacific Hotel, the re-building of which was commenced even before the plans had been completed. To this spirit of eagerness (not, perhaps, unmixed with that of emulation) may be attributed the erection of many structures, even in the business center of the city, of a character—architecturally speaking—which were discreditable alike to the owners who erected them and the municipal authorities who tolerated them." [47]

What happened during the "compulsory idleness" of Root and his colleagues that so radically transformed, within a generation, the character of Chicago architecture, from a "gaudy display" to a rational and aesthetic utilitarianism? Arriving architects like Root entered less a city than an enormous construction site. John Van Osdel prided himself on being able to replicate a lost building within months of its loss. His Tremont and Palmer hotels were bigger and grander than the originals. William Boyington quickly replanned his ornate Grand Pacific Hotel, the original having been burned to the ground before it had had time to open, to eclipse all others in size and pretension. In the hands of Chicago's resident designers, new buildings only departed slightly from what they had been before the fire. The insatiable appetite for more space produced an obvious architectural gigantism that made these designs appear even more out of scale than their prefire parents. It was growth by accretion and not by analysis. A totality or three-dimensional unity, in plan, section, and elevation, was abandoned to the overall impression of wealth.

Aboriginal postfire architecture was a mad scramble for attention. One building might have Italianate entrances, Versailles facades, and Empire cornices, mansards, and chimneys. A catalog of vanities was available, from which any architect might select a given detail of style. "The broad facades occupying important corners offered unlimited opportunity for architectural embellishment. The three orders, Doric, Ionic, Corinthian, with their respective entablatures were called upon for heavy duty: stone balconies at strategic points, sculptures and caryatids for opulent effects; and, crowning the roofs over the pavilions, domes in the approved Parisian mode."[48] Typical of the time were the Boyce and Superior buildings. Described as Gothic because of their pointed headings, they also had pronounced Norman details. The Boyce's second-story treatment was straight arched Norman, while the fifth floor was Renaissance Italian in appearance. Confused continental, classical, and vernacular styles were reassembled with no special hierarchy. Given the opportunity to build anything, the city's resident architects in the first years were content to recycle the old, with little attention to safety or meaning.

An inane battle of styles existed in place of any serious reconsideration or debate over what was being put up. Called "cosmopolitan" at the time was an anarchy of influences, free of a serious rationale or an articulate advocate. Architects were simply filling the holes made unexpectedly vacant by the more and more distant fire. A thoughtful review of the period later reported on the trend: "The American idea, or the French, combated with the Teutonic, or German and Dutch, so that it was not uncommon to see a gabled, or a severely plain square, facade acting neighbor to the Renaissance, or between a French and an Italian elevation. This form has come down to the present."[49] Buildings in progress at the time of the fire had ornamental details added, and it was not unusual to see elaborate new structures, like Edward Burling's Chamber of Commerce Building, which had been criticized in 1865 for its restrained and practical ornamentation, "improved" with the addition of unnecessary classical effects. With the benefit of insurance and federal and state aid, the city gave vent to its every fantasy of elegance and the good life. *Industrial Chicago* reviewed the situation with little sentimentality: "The necessity for a prompt rebuilding militated against art in a wonderful degree. The architect himself was as hurried as the owner and contractor; and the masons, bricklayer and carpenter were often at work before the draughtsman began the design. Thus, for some little time, after the great fire, Art suffered from haste and necessity. Men, sane in other affairs, tolerated the construction of wooden buildings to resemble stone and stone buildings to resemble wood. A wild mixture resulted. What the Apache is to civilized man, those buildings were to architecture."[50]

This period of "some little time" was an observation laboratory for the architects who would make Chicago over. Root, for one, came to understand that by turning frustration into patience he might avoid the failure of his contemporaries. The city still held clues to an architecture he might embrace. There were already a few buildings from which to draw inspiration, although the designers who felt liberated from a demand to replicate the former environment or to "gaudy-up" the new were in the minority. William Le Baron Jenney was one of these. An engineer educated in the East and in Paris, Jenney opened a practice in Chicago in 1868 and found he was more interested in the ways buildings were put together than in how they were finished ornamentally. His Portland Block (1872) shows an emphasis on directness in its transformation from cluttered beginnings on paper, particularly from its multidormered top to the plain roof and expressed horizontality of its final form.[51] The Portland's greater simplicity created a powerful impression for other architects and gave it a two-decades success as an office building. Jenney resisted extruded elements and emphasized the flat planes of wall surfaces made of pressed brick, a material whose widespread use he pioneered.[52] A masonry structure and asymmetrical V plan made the building look solid. The Portland gave the impression of rising out of the earth. It did not insinuate itself into a false association with "style" but sought, in appropriately urban materials, a clarity associated with the best functional architecture of the prairie. When Sullivan discov-

ered that it had been designed by a young draftsman in Jenney's firm, he was given hope that he too might have a turn at designing an important building after he began active work.

Otto Matz's Nixon Building (1871) was another prominent counterexample to the prevailing confectionary school of postfire architecture. The building was almost complete on the day of the fire. Built with an interior cast-iron frame and modest exterior, the Nixon was constructed of heavy masonry supported on narrowly-spaced piers. Its ceilings, clad with concrete and one-inch plaster of Paris, helped it survive the fire; exterior walls and interior frame survived and just required cleaning.[53] The reassembled building was a suggestion of what architecture might be in the future. Although no masterpiece itself, in no clear style, the Nixon's flat, practical facade, particularly between the awkward first stories and the incompletely classicized cornice, suggested elements that might be exploited later, once a unifying principle of design could be located. Burnham and Root's more tightly organized

17. William Le Baron Jenney, Portland Block (1872).

and severe Montauk Block mirrored design aspects of the Portland and the Nixon, including a Nixon-like flag waving ten stories on axis above the entrance.

Both in its failed opportunity and lack of imagination, the most telling example of postfire architecture was W. W. Boyington's Inter-State Industrial Exposition Building (1872–73), on a site now occupied by the Art Institute. It was expressly commissioned to memorialize the fire. A successful designer of hotels, Boyington intuitively interpreted his commission in the manner of the boosters and builders of the "New Chicago." The building commemorated progress since the recent fire; it avoided any further associations with the actual tragedy, although the land upon which it rested contained buried debris. Using chiefly iron and glass, Boyington ironically built an *opaque* building, suggestive of the popular Crystal Palace in London (1851) or similar transparent exposition space in Paris (1867) and Vienna (1873). By designing a conventional shingled roof and avoiding the inevitable sense of fragility of

18. W. W. Boyington, Inter-State Industrial Exposition Building (1872–73).

a glass building, Boyington acknowledged that he and the city were not ready for an audacious new building technology that emphasized transparency. An aestheticized engineering, in the later manner of the Brooklyn Bridge or Eiffel Tower, was not at that early moment sufficient.

Root and Sullivan, among the new breed that included Holabird and Roche and later Frank Lloyd Wright, who were excluded from early participation in the aborted rebuilding, were paradoxically both far from the fire, because they had no part in it, and closer to its meaning. They could learn from the few good buildings that stood and further investigate others that failed. Sullivan could sense the oddly pregnant state of the city when he first arrived. "The pavements were vile, because hastily laid; they erupted here and there and everywhere in ooze. Most of the buildings, too, were paltry. When Louis came to understand the vast area of disaster, he saw clearly and with applause that this new half-built city was a hasty improvisation made in dire need by men who did not falter. And again spread out in thought, the boundless prairie and the mighty lake, and what they meant for men of destiny, even as the city lay stretched out, unseemly as a Caliban."[54]

Touring the scene a day after the fire was like taking a walk through the underworld. Artists and photographers were sent from the national magazines like *Harper's* and *Scribner's* to record the sights. Next to the Civil War, the Chicago fire was one of America's first national media events. George N. Barnard, who had photographed the Confederate ruins in Columbia, South Carolina, photographed Chicago in the days after the fire for the Lakeside Publishing Company. His photographs accompany the text in *The Lakeside Memorial of the Burning of Chicago* (1872). The documenting of modern ruins was an established tradition in Europe; A. Liebert's 1871 shots of the Paris Commune destruction record a traumatic loss of life and property comparable to Chicago's. It is significant that the scene of conflict was relocated so naturally, even unconsciously, from the battlefield to the city center. Within weeks, Americans read about the terrible disaster and heroic resistance. Contemporary illustrations evoke the spectacle of the flames ripping through holes in the buildings, as tornado-like winds made tight spirals of the smoke. Others show refugees in the back of open wagons: women holding on to their children, the wounded laid out on their backs. The mix of

19. Ruins in Columbia, South Carolina.

20. Columbia, South
Carolina: View from
the capital.

21. Grand Façade, Hô-
tel de Ville, Paris
(1871).

22. (*Opposite*) Interior
of the Ballroom, Hôtel
de Ville, Paris (1871).

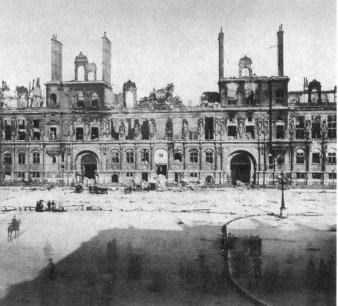

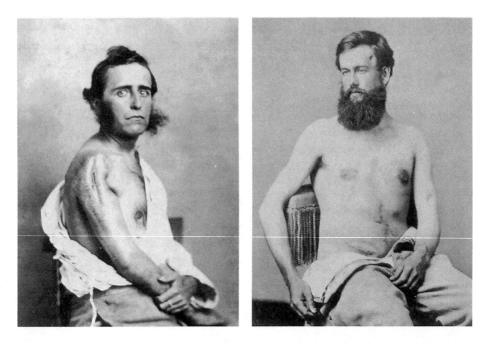

23. Successful intermediate excision of the head and three inches of shaft of right humerus for gunshot fracture (1864).

24. Case of Corporal Bemis, thrice severely wounded in three battles (1864).

spectacle and particularized human suffering satisfied the audience's desire for an understandable story to order what had happened. Prints of the raging fire alternated with melodramatic tableaux of families and neighbors in wide-eyed witness to the horror. High drama and domesticated scenes of survival became accepted ways to communicate the event, oddly comforting because they contained a closed narrative of trials and triumphs which insisted that things would be all right.

The photographs are another matter, as they bring us closer to the fire. Here the horror is unmitigated. Photographs of ruined buildings are not recreations of events by an artist who has drawn the flames in a choreographed way or made the victims look like pathetic souls from a serialized period novel. These black and white photographs are raw. Hiroshima, Dresden, Chicago, Mathew Brady's and Timothy O'Sullivan's battle pictures of the Civil War, or William Bell's pathology photographs of war wounded—the images are the same in the silence of mute forms. The grander or more heroic our pretensions, the more the shattered figures appear to mock us. The soldiers in Bell's photographs live as walking ruins. Consider some examples.[55] In one photo "marble" lions spring toward a bald eagle with wings unfurled. The big bird nestles in the keystone of the main entrance to nothing

(formerly the Insurance Exchange). In another, next to the
ruined Honore Block on Dearborn Street stands the four-
story facade of Bigelow House, held up by its own weight and
a row of skeleton columns. Under the burned cornice of the
entranceway is the date 1870 in chiseled numbers. Like ancient battlements built deep into the earth, foundations are
discovered in lines, while in other places Corinthian columns
rise in graceless weightlessness, as if out of an upside-down
world, *above* their broken pediment. Pictures are all that remain of these wasteland vistas, and it is only through the
imagination that we can reconstruct what must have seemed
the world's end. Poeticized by the distance of time like a walk

26. Ruins of Field, Leiter & Co. store, corner of State and Washington Streets.

in Ostia, Herculaneum, or Pompeii, the ruins hold a mystery for any of the living willing to consider them deeply.

These ruins are haunting because they are devoid of the same active lives they vividly suggest. Occasionally in the photographs there is a lone figure in black, staring in disbelief. If the photographer was close enough the figure's face can be seen to register paralyzed shock. At a distance, survivors are used only as scaling devices so we are able to measure the physical if not psychological size of the event. These are not the same people in the illustrations, who even in the midst of chaos appear animated and filled with purposeful action. Here in the photographs, souls wander an alien world

27. Ruins of Chamber
of Commerce, corner
of LaSalle and Wash-
ington Streets.

before it is reclaimed. These photographs record the earliest
moments of catastrophe, which were later denied or overwhelmed by language, explained away by talk of progress
and visions of the hero. For instance, while the blasted Grand
Pacific Hotel was still horrifying or simply compelling in its
titanic vulnerability, survivors walked amidst the ruins,
which smoldered and groaned as the site heaved with each
convulsive new crash of falling material.

Over a hundred years after the event, the photographs are
messages from the grave, existing between the trauma of the
fire and the special kind of forgetting represented by the initial rebuilding. They show us the moment when Root and

28. Ruins of the Court House, from corner of Clark and Washington Streets.

Sullivan arrived and "many ashes remained, and the scene of ruin was still blended with ambition of recovery."[56] Against their own immediate desires to get on with building, the economic slowdown allowed them to view the ruins not simply as an impediment to progress but as profound objects in themselves. For a longer period than they wished, they were caught like those mute black figures contemplating the awesome display of destruction. But because they were trained to see architecturally, they were also free to see through the ruins to something new that they might build, which relied on neither replication nor the tyranny of fashion. Chicago architecture of the eighties and nineties would not be grounded

29. Ruins on Clark Street, looking south from the Court House.

in a narrative of miraculous recovery alone but in a deepening acknowledgment of loss.

For the new architects the fire proved to be an exemplary architectural critic. Buildings were stripped of everything unessential. First to go was ornamentation applied to achieve an effect. As if in direct response to his earliest observations, Sullivan developed his later extensive system of ornamentation from the structure out, not placed on the surface. Profound in their isolation from other mediating forms of civilization, the ruins provided a model of what architecture was at its most basic before artists "improved" it. Sullivan's sense that "form follows function," Root's "architectural expres-

30. Ruins on LaSalle
Street, looking north
from Monroe Street.

sion," and Wright's "organic architecture" developed from
reimagining the ruins, not simply as rubble to eliminate but
as architectural elements on their own.

To the new architects, and to those few like Adler and Jenney who had had brief careers in Chicago before the catastrophe, the fire was not the challenge to development the older
settlers feared. The newcomers did not fear losing control
over a city in which they had not yet played a major role, with
the exception of Daniel Burnham, who at the World's Columbian Exposition and in his Chicago Plan would indulge his
own Faustian appetite for development.[57] Chicago architects
were appropriately slowed down by the fire, which permitted

31. Ruins on Clark
Street, looking north
from the Court House.
The flaked, melted
"Athens marble" can
be seen here.

them more time to accommodate the unprecedented pace of
invention that included development of the electric elevator
and George H. Johnson's perfection of fireproof cladding.
They did not necessarily associate speed with success. Even
Sullivan, who loved to use language, cautioned against its
promiscuous application to matters that required reflection
and calm: "It is wise to handle words with caution. Their content is so complex and explosive; and in combination they
may work beautiful or dreadful things."[58] Given this statement, his choice of words to describe the wasteland as a
touching or compelling monster—Caliban—is given additional weight. Sullivan was not appalled by the failure but

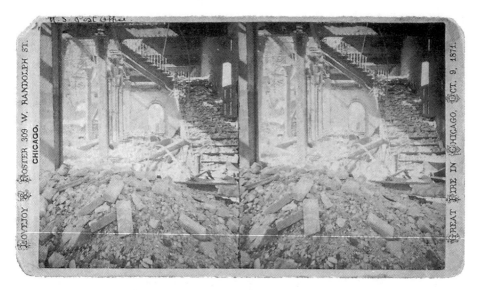

32. Ruins of the Post
Office, interior view
(1871–72).

33. Ruins of the Trib-
une Building, corner of
Madison and Dearborn
Streets (1871–72).

embraced the monster, the retarded part of progress, as his own. Like the fictional Daniel Trentworthy, Sullivan personified the fire with a pagan image to give it autonomy and to break the evangelical sense of judgment and egotistical need to control associated with the city's boosters and builders. For him and others of his generation the ruins were soulful, not a vision of their own defeated heroics, and they contained their own autonomous meaning. The fire, in this view, could be seen as a welling up against the city's monomaniacal compulsion to rule and order. The ruins, seen as oracular and not as judgmental or symbolic of guilt, encouraged a criticism of the city's single-minded myths of unity. In ruin all the city and its people were the same. O'Learys and Palmers were reduced to equivalent human material. As architecture the ruins provided an insight—to live with the monster, the chronic sense of our own Calibanic selves—to those who could patiently look without wanting to exterminate them. Stripped of all ornament and vanity by the leveling flames, the fallen buildings appeared as visions of the future. In a section of *Kindergarten Chats* entitled "Pathology," Sullivan explained the process of recovering compelling architecture. He arguably was thinking of the ruins from his youth when he wrote, "To perceive health, we must look through and beyond disease; to locate sanity, we must wander through the jungle, the swamps, the marshes and the arid places of confusion worse confounded." [59]

The Fire as Image
Architecture and the Problem of Loss

$F.B.$ *Wilkie surveyed* the city on October 9, 1871. Surprised by
the extent of the fire, he wondered how Chicago would recover. However, unlike other commentators who focused on
their own problems or on the immediate physical distress of
others, Wilkie concentrated on things. "So consuming was
the fire that, in many cases, it not only obliterated everything
constructed by man, but even licked clean the usual traces of
progress."[1] He instantly identified the health of the community with the buildings that now lay in ruins. A year later,
when Sullivan and Root arrived in Chicago, they found a city
excitedly expressing through new buildings its rejection of ill-
ness and any suggestion of death. As Wilkie had wanted, the
city now associated new architecture with Christian metaphors of rebirth and resurrection and saw proof of redemption in the buildings that quickly rose above scenes of the recent devastation.

Neither young architect was moved to see the rebuilding in
this way. They were outsiders who viewed the frantic and
dangerously inadequate new construction that was going on
in the name of the city's health as a "pathological" mirroring
of the fire itself. When he returned in 1875 from a year at the
Ecole des Beaux Arts, Sullivan found times slow and building
opportunities rare during the continuing depression of 1873–
78. He got some freelance work from John Edelmann but remained underemployed. Sullivan used the time to reflect on
a city that had come to resemble for him a jungle. The fire had
created the paradoxical condition of a wilderness at the heart
of a developed city. He rethought the event, not to redeem it,
like a booster, but to go deeper. Sullivan's addiction to what
he thought to be poetic language can be traced to this period,
when building alone was not enough to occupy him. Root,
haunted by the image of miles of burned buildings, took time

off to study and write about new methods of fireproofing. Initially inhibited from building because of poor economic conditions, Sullivan and Root were provided with an education by observing and absorbing the lessons of a city desperately at war with its own fate, the terrible fact of its loss. Their Chicago apprenticeships lasted nearly two decades, culminating for each in a representative building: the Auditorium (1887–89) and the Monadnock (1884–91).[2]

Sullivan's Auditorium is a prominent example of Richardsonian Romanesque.[3] (Even Richardson's first Chicago building, for the American Merchant's Union Express Company (1872), was in a neo-Gothic style, but it was well built and provided a strong professional image for the city's new architects.) Root's Monadnock is a bare-walled, brick modern composition, with only the most abstract allusion to an Egyptian pylon.[4] Upon completion, both buildings were viewed as having the very latest in modern conveniences and engineering. Sullivan and his partner Dankmar Adler introduced electrical lighting, mechanical air conditioning, and floating foundations to accommodate excessive loads. The Monadnock was the city's just expression for the dominant architectural form, the elevator building. It was as if, upon entering the century's last decade, Chicago was ready to complete its long reconstruction.

H. H. Richardson's influence on Sullivan and Root has been well documented, particularly in relation to the Marshall Field Wholesale Warehouse. Certainly, in the scope of its effect this was Richardson's critical Chicago work. But in terms of larger cultural issues, the Glessner House must be seriously considered as well.

The Glessner family lived only four blocks from where the Haymarket Riot took place. When J. J. Glessner commissioned Richardson to build a house for him on the already gentrified Prairie Avenue, he was concerned about security and fearful of the prospect of urban insurrection. Mrs. Glessner wrote in her journal on May 9, 1886: "Tuesday night we sat here quite late talking about our house plans when a terrible explosion occurred down on the corner of Des Plaines St. and Randolph—followed by a sharp volley of firing. In a little while the patrol wagon went by our house full of wounded men. The noise was from a shell thrown by socialists and rioters into a band of police who were there to disperse them. 68 were carried wounded to the hospital—no one knows how many more were hurt."[5] The Glessner House (1885–87) is different from the other grand homes on the avenue; they are more open and exposed, the products of a more

34. H. H. Richardson, Marshall Field Wholesale Warehouse (1885–87).

35. Louis Sullivan, Walker Warehouse (1888).

36. H. H. Richardson, Glessner House (c. 1888), Prairie Avenue elevation.

37. Glessner House courtyard.

optimistic time. Richardson built Glessner a domestic for-
tress. In elevation it communicates anxiety about the open-
ness of the American city. Root took Glessner House as a
model and exploded the scale in the First Regiment Armory
(1889–91) at Sixteenth and Michigan.

But there is also something revealing about the Auditorium
and the Monadnock which indicates that the city's final break
with a tragic past was more difficult than the boosters implied. These two great buildings were anachronistically constructed, the last two major masonry or load-bearing walled
constructions in the city. After them, Chicago buildings
would be constructed with some variation of a steel frame,
which had already been pioneered by William Le Baron Jenney's Home Insurance Building (1883–85) and perfected in
his Second Leiter Store (1889–91).[6] Adler and Sullivan were
familiar with this new technology and employed it in the cast-
iron columns for the Auditorium's interior walls.[7] Heralded as
the city's great celebration of the coming century, the Auditorium and the Monadnock also simultaneously spoke to the
past. Their very weightiness was a protest against the powerful contemporary aesthetic of steel and glass. It was as if
both architects wished to pause one last time and recapture

the moment when they were still young and entering the city for the first time, when the evidence of ruin was still around them and rebirth for a city and a people was not yet assured.

The Auditorium began with Ferdinand W. Peck's idea to restore Boyington's Inter-State Industrial Exposition Building which had been renovated once already in 1885 by Adler and Sullivan. The idea of a makeshift concert hall quickly grew under Peck's direction into an ambitious plan for a giant commercial and cultural center. Young Peck, who was from one of Chicago's oldest business families, sought out Adler and Sullivan because of Dankmar Adler's reputation as the city's best acoustical engineer. Two years before he entered into partnership with Louis Sullivan, Adler had designed the successful Central Music Hall (1879). Encouraged by his love of music and a good business opportunity, Peck organized the Chicago Auditorium Association in 1886. Culture underwritten by a profit-making hotel and business block was an attractive lure to the city's commercial and financial communities.

Sullivan understood the ambition of such a plan for Chicago. He characterized the promoter Fred Peck as a man "who declared himself a citizen, with firm belief in democracy—whatever he meant by that; seemingly he meant the—

'peepul'. At any rate, he wished to give birth to a great hall within which the multitude might gather for all sorts of purposes including grand opera; and there were to be a few boxes for the *haut monde*."[8] However strong his reservations about the developer's motives, Sullivan was not going to miss this chance to build.

A complex commission like the Auditorium, he felt, was the perfect artistic intervention for what was essentially a businessman's town. Here the architect might position himself between the commercial dynamo that physically rebuilt the city and the "living men" of Chicago, of the sort represented earlier by Hesing and the *Staats Zeitung*, who lacked the political power and money to effect their own will. By combining private and public, commercial and civic functions, the Auditorium belatedly addressed opportunity for mixed-use property previously presented in abundance but neglected by politicians and builders after the great fire's radical reorganization of the land.[9] Almost twenty years after the fact, Sullivan with the Auditorium dared to transform a city fueled and ruled by business into a place where art and commerce appeared to exist in perfect partnership.

Sullivan's declaration of parity between the artist and the businessman was premature. The Auditorium was a triumph of engineering and an enormous step forward in the unification of tall-building design, but it was not a great synthesizing cultural work. Although the conceptual base of Sullivan's writing was the putative relationship between language and architecture, "a living form of speech, a natural form of utterance,"[10] the Auditorium fell short, as any single structure would, of fulfilling such grandiose claims. Sullivan had miscalculated the moment. His civic aspirations for the building were dwarfed by the larger reality of its status as a predominantly profit-making venture. Peck knew his constituency better; he sold the project as a good advertisement for the city. G. W. Steevens, a visitor from England, caught the spirit of culture-vulturing in a town of "untutored millionaires": "Chicago is conscious that there is something in the world, some sense of form, of elegance of refinement, that with all her corn and railways, her hogs and by-products and dollars, she lacks. She does not quite know what it is, but she is determined to have it, cost what it may." By the time of the Auditorium's dedication the incorporation of the artist by the businessman was almost complete. Sullivan's idea of equal partnership was as antiquated as the building's load-bearing masonry construction. Steevens could have been describing the architect's more grandiose cultural aspirations: "The hog king, giving a picture to the gallery (The Art Institute) and his slaughter-house man painfully spelling out the description of it on a Sunday afternoon—there is something rather pathetic in this, and assuredly something very noble."[11]

William Morton Payne, a capable local novelist and editor of the influential *Dial*, was sympathetic to Sullivan's "noble/ pathetic" desires for the Auditorium but understood the difficulties. Payne correctly perceived that artists were led in Chicago by business, especially, he added, when, like Sullivan, they thought they were leading. Americans were content with "inarticulate poets," the carpenters and farmers who erected barns and other buildings that were beautiful because their form simply met necessity. They were suspicious of the self-conscious adaptation of the American folk idea of "form follows function" by a professional who claimed to have invented it.[12] More to the point, the architecture that Americans chose self-consciously (with the exception of the architecture of the Shakers and other ideal communities where design was fundamental to worship[13]) tended toward the cluttered and overadorned Europeanized fashions of the day and was not at all what the modernist Sullivan had in mind.

Art and architecture to the American were things to own; possessions that had no intrinsic value other than the price a buyer was willing to pay. Sullivan's pretense was that the "architect is a *product* of our civilization"; his role in buildings like the Auditorium was "the double one: to interpret and to initiate."[14] As sympathetic as this idea was, it was more a vestigial legacy of the short lived postfire euphoria about the Chicago spirit of rebirth than it was Sullivan's contemporary reality.

The ornamentation or "linguistic" aspect of Sullivan's program was discouraged by the client. His exotic elevations for the Auditorium were eventually turned inside out and used exclusively in the interiors. External marking or personifying of the building was something he had learned from Richardson's work, where ornamentation was not grafted on, as on the confections of prefire Chicago, but seemingly grown from within the building and extruded to the facade. To Sullivan, such ornamentations were the mediating figures that stimulated the public's imagination and allowed it to connect soulfully with what had become dwarfing structure since the integration of the electric elevator into the skyscraper. He attempted to mitigate this gigantism through ornamentation, classical tripartite vertical organization, and an increasingly accentuated horizontal axis, in even his tallest buildings. Per-

haps under the influence of Frank Lloyd Wright, a young
draftsman in his office who at the time claimed to despise skyscrapers, Sullivan began to balance further the obviously
striking verticality by paying more attention to the ornamentation and plane of spandrels and other horizontal members.[15] Progressively from the Wainwright (1890–91), through
the Guaranty (1894–95), to the Carson Pirie Scott (1899), Sullivan created the illusion of tall buildings that bore an increasing relationship to the street or ground plane. By the time of
the Auditorium he had gone some way in answering his own
central question: "How shall we impart to this sterile pile, this
crude, harsh, brutal agglomeration, this stark, staring excla-
mation of external strife, the graciousness of those higher
forms of sensibility and culture that rest on the lower and
fiercer passions?"[16] This language recalls directly his first im-

pression of Chicago in ruins as a Caliban, a compelling monster. Now at the peak of his career, he was still being thwarted in his attempts to infuse the primal energy of the imagination—the psychic energy engendered in the swamps and marshes—into Chicago's "sterile pile," its Brave New World of modern office buildings. His highly evocative architectural details were effectively removed from the street and given a lesser decorative role which only served to mock his broader intentions.

The Auditorium's ornamentation, some of it executed by Sullivan's "pencil," Frank Lloyd Wright, was intended as an idiosyncratic statement, inseparable from the mind that created it. While the structure was a combination of age-old masonry methods, inspired by Richardson's Marshall Field Wholesale Warehouse (1885–87), grafted on to a modern, evolving technique of metal interior support like that of the Rookery, the ornamentation was the architect's own. The use of endless variations on a single grain of wheat or another organic form, modeled in terra cotta or twisted in iron, was Sullivan's surest way of personally marking the buildings. If now these embellishments seem unnecessary to his characteristic architectural forms, it is because of our century-old familiarity with modern architecture. When built, Sullivan's Auditorium was on the line between the untempered masses and clutter of common nineteenth-century structures and the evolving spareness—design economy—of the contemporary steel-frame skyscrapers.

Sullivan's ornamentation reveals an anxiety about the modern, a reluctance to embrace it fully. Modernism in the shape of the tall building, stripped of the language of the past or of the memory suggested by extraarchitectural designs, seemed to him too hard, too cold. While praising the power of contemporary architecture, he also feared the universality or internationalizing of art that would fail to speak with an "American accent" or the "cult of a higher life."[17] Struggle to find an appropriate modern architecture continued throughout his life. It was the built equivalent to his writing, the same kind of Romantic anachronism that envisioned the artist, in this case the architect, as a Whitmanesque self-proclaimed priest, lecturing the people on a properly serious culture. Sullivan's "cult of a higher life" was his unsolicited warning to Chicagoans to look beyond business for fulfillment. The Auditorium's tripartite division—business block, hotel, and theater—was the integration of money and art that the architect desired for the city as a whole. This was the very same image of Chicago as a modern artistic center that was ridiculed by

Auditorium Building

ENTIRE STRUCTURE ABSOLUTELY FIRE-PROOF

COST OF BUILDING $3,200,000

BUILT AND OWNED BY
CHICAGO AUDITORIUM ASSOCIATION

The Auditorium Building includes

1 **The Auditorium** .. Permanent seating capacity over 4,000; for conventions, etc. (for which the stage will be utilized), about 8,000. Contains the most complete and costly *Stage* and *Organ* in the world.

2 **Recital Hall** .. Seats over 500.

3 **Business Portion** .. Consists of stores and 136 offices, part of which are in the tower.

4 **Tower Observatory** .. To which the public are admitted.   U. S. Signal Service occupies part of 17th, 18th, and 19th floors of tower.
Height of Auditorium Balcony, 260 feet.

(Above four departments of the Building are managed by Chicago Auditorium Association).

5 **Auditorium Hotel** .. Has 400 guest rooms. The Grand Dining Room (175 feet long) and the kitchen are on the top floor. The magnificent Banquet Hall is built of steel, on trusses, spanning 120 feet over the Auditorium.

[Leased to and managed by Auditorium Hotel Co.,
J. H. Breslin, of N. Y., President; R. H. Southgate, Vice-Pres. and Mgr.]

Ground was broken for the building January, 1887.
The Corner-Stone was laid October 6, 1887.
The Cope-Stone was laid on top of tower October 2, 1889
The Recital Hall was dedicated October 12, 1889.
The Auditorium was dedicated December 9, 1889.
The Hotel was dedicated January 30, 1890.
The building was completed February, 1890.

Area covered by building about one and one-half acres
Total street frontage (fronting Congress St., Michigan and Wabash Aves.)
710 feet.

Height of Main Building (10 stories)	145 feet
Height of Tower above main building (8 floors)	95 "
Height of Lantern Tower above main tower (2 floors)	30 "
Total height	270 feet

Size of Tower, 70 x 41 feet; the foundations cover about two and one-half times larger area.

Weight of entire building	110,000 tons
Weight of Tower	15,000 "

Exterior material: First and second stories, granite; balance of building, Bedford stone.

Interior material: Iron, brick, terra cotta, marble, hard wood finish, etc.
Iron work cost about $600,000.

No. of brick in building	17,000,000
" square feet of Italian Marble Mosaic floors	50,000
(Containing about 50,000,000 pieces of marble, each put in by hand.)	
" square feet of terra cotta (arches and partitions)	800,000
" " " wire lath	175,000
" " " plate glass	60,000
" miles of gas and water pipes	25
" " electric wire and cable	230
" " steel cable for moving scenes on stage	11
" electric lights	10,000
" dynamos	11
" electric motors for driving ventilating apparatus and other machinery	13
" hydraulic motors for driving machinery	4
" boilers	11
" pumping engines	21
" elevators	13
" hydraulic lifts for moving stage platforms	26

COMPLIMENTS OF
MESSRS. ADLER & SULLIVAN

41. Notice of the completion of the Auditorium Building.

contemporary novelists like Henry B. Fuller, who compared postfire Chicago ironically to "the Florence of the Medici after the dispersal of the Greek scholars from Constantinople by the Turks." Sullivan must have appeared just as foreign when he first arrived after the fire along with the other "learned exiles," flocking to the city to "instruct."[18]

The Auditorium Building was Sullivan's most sophisticated statement of the meaning of Chicago's reconstruction. In this singularly complex building plan, he argued, as had earlier radicals like Hesing, for a culture of inclusion. Rather awful murals of native Americans and pioneers in primal scenes were his attempt to encode the building with the very past that was so quickly and completely receding from the city streets, and an effort to project not simply his recollections but what he saw as a national memory.

When the theater was dedicated on December 9, 1889, the ceremonies included a recital by the reigning diva Adelina Patti, as well as a visit by President Benjamin Harrison. Still, the night belonged to the developer, who narrated a tale of how the building's original idea was transformed into reality. Though Peck acknowledged the architects, he was sure to

make it his triumph.[19] How appropriate to the city's real identity that the last great public masonry structure after the fire—the largest and costliest privately financed building in America—was seen as a monument to development. For it showed that the developer's money and not the architect's art was for most Chicagoans the source of the city's rise from oblivion. The architects, Adler and Sullivan, were presented at the glorious dedication only as the willing instruments of the developer. Although letters to Chicago newspaper editors attempted to correct this slight, and the perfunctory mention of the designers was excused as a confusion caused by the moment's excitement, there was a truth revealed by Peck's omission.

Chicago was celebrating itself in a familiar personification. The city was comfortable with developers and still ill at ease with artists. Sullivan's glorification of architecture as democracy's higher language was not what Chicagoans saw in the Auditorium Building. It was simply their biggest and newest building, the equivalent of the frontier opera house on a gargantuan scale.[20] The supremacy of Peck, who presented even a grander figure than the president of the United States at the

42. Louis Sullivan, Auditorium Theater stage, Auditorium Building (1889).

dedication, played out in microcosm a drama of development fueled by the fire. Visiting Chicago, Paul Bourget put it simply: the city had "frankly accepted the conditions imposed by the spectacular."[21] Sullivan's presumption that architecture would lead and instruct was an alien idea that he continued to pursue in his writing for almost thirty years after his last Chicago building. The Auditorium's elephantine massing seemed increasingly to be from another time, as more and more steel-frame, curtain-wall buildings were erected. Mme. Patti sang "Home Sweet Home" and the "Swiss Echo Song" at the Auditorium's dedication, as a classicist's acknowledgment to the moment's kitsch populism, but Fred Peck's aria to self and to the "Chicago Spirit" of development was the song of the hour.

Contrary to Sullivan's naive hopes, the art represented by the Auditorium's theater did not encourage class and social harmony. Combining commercial and civic functions like a modern, urban village green, the building instead accentuated class and gender differences. It quickly became the place for the rich to show off their finery and to relieve themselves of the tedium and insecurity of ceaseless upward mobility. If the men had to spend their days in the Loop creating fortunes, then at night the women, in the sullen company of their men, would in a sense launder that money, through their exotic cultural pretensions. Frank Norris captured the energy and conflict in his novel *The Pit* (1902). As initially seen through the eyes of twenty-two-year-old Laura Dearborn, the Auditorium is a place of almost pagan excess. "The women were, almost without exception, in light-colored gowns, white, pale blue, Nile green, and pink, while over these costumes were thrown opera cloaks and capes of astonishing complexity and elaborateness. Nearly all were bareheaded, and nearly all wore aigrettes; a score of these, a hundred of them, nodded and vibrated with an incessant agitation over the heads of the crowd and flashed like mica flakes as the wearers moved. Everywhere the eye was arrested by the luxury of stuffs, the brilliance and delicacy of fabrics, laces as white and soft as froth, crisp, shining silks, suave satins, heavy gleaming velvets, and brocades and plushes, nearly all of them white—violently so—dazzling and splendid under the blaze of the electrics."[22]

Laura, a neophyte in the city who has an aboriginal Chicago name, later surprises herself when she begins to prefer the "Battle of the Streets"—LaSalle Street's financial wars—to the "calm" of art.[23] She herself is caught in the city's double appeal. During her first visit to the Auditorium, overwhelmed by the hall's "electric" materiality, she has no patience for the two Chicagos under one roof and wonders, "Why could not men leave their business outside, why must the jar of commerce spoil all the harmony of a moment?"[24] In a scene recalling Emma Bovary at the agricultural fair, she reacts violently to two men reviewing out loud the daily trade in bushels and carloads of grain. Only when the lights are dimmed and the music is of sufficient volume to drown out the persistent talk of business does the Auditorium challenge the primacy of LaSalle Street. But even this interval in the Auditorium is not long enough to distract Laura completely from the "vast cruel machinery of the city's life."[25]

The Auditorium Building incorporated two dominant nineteenth-century notions, the Romantic ideas that artists should inform and then teach culture and that art should mediate between the world experienced day-to-day and the world of ideas. From Norris's perspective the Auditorium never mediated but provided the same kind of convulsive collision of interests first experienced in the fire and, within his memory, in the equally violent setting of the Haymarket Riot (1886). Sullivan's attempt to load the architecture with meaning, to stimulate individuals through a direct appeal to their senses, was his desperate way of further capturing the attention of those ever-distracted businessmen whom Laura Dearborn complains about. He loaded the Auditorium with meaning to create associational memories of a lost time before the fire when money, he thought, did not yet compel all human behavior. Had Sullivan been given the original commission for the Inter-State Industrial Exposition Building, rather than Boyington, the Auditorium would have been an ideal structure to build above the ruins. But the economy, the still-developing state of essential technology—principally the elevator, fireproofing, and floating foundations—and Sullivan's lack of reputation would not have allowed for such a building at the time.

Sullivan's specific context for the building was of a city projected out of the country, recalling Chicago's motto, Urbs in Horto. This vision, generated during his boyhood summers in New England, was grafted romantically onto the virginal architectural environment in Chicago after the fire, in which he had been prevented from playing an immediate part. When he returned to this recollection in 1924 he elaborated its importance in an odd mix of pastoral and urban images. He sensed the city as a power: "A power new-risen above his horizon; a power that extended the range and amplified the content of his own child-dream of power as he had seen manifested in the town within the splendid rhythm of the march of the seasons."[26] The energy and invention of the Auditorium's interior, and the later ornamental explosion on the two-floor iron screen of the Carson Pirie Scott State Street entrance, were part of Sullivan's attempt to make the building's skin erupt, to suggest that all was not well within.

The Carson Pirie Scott Building was a modern steel-frame and glass building, almost perversely clad with a seemingly organic growth of iron at its entry. Alluding to the organic forms displaced by State Street, Sullivan tried to recall not simply the architectural past, in the manner of the white neoclassicism of the Court of Honor at the World's Columbian Exposition, but America's past, lost forever in the flames of the Chicago fire. The Auditorium's elevations seemed to express a certain tension where the Minnesota granite—rough-cut and rusticated—was met beyond the fourth floor by lighter smooth-cut Indiana ashlar. The bottom stories alluded to what Henry B. Fuller called the "Black City" of the Loop and the top, a light grey associated in Fuller's *With the Procession* (1895) with the soaring towers of churches, which were replaced after the fire by office buildings as the city's tallest and most prominent buildings.[27]

There has been much written about Sullivan's aesthetic theories. His first biographer, Hugh Morrison, and his latest, Robert Twombly, have both had trouble reconciling the architect's statements about functionalism with the built work. They have rightly decided they cannot be reconciled. Sullivan's theoretical writing, sentimental agonizing about a long-lost America and later outright complaining, were really only the overflow that he could not fit into the architecture. Conflict over choice of material, the tension between a building's horizontal and vertical elements, and the problem of ornamentation are to some degree or another present in the Auditorium Building. The incompleteness of the solutions, most poignantly expressed by the awkward relationship of the tower to the main block, gives a unique status to the building. Sullivan's architectural syntax would be clarified in later work. By abandoning masonry construction, subordinating ornament to structure (with the exception of Carson Pirie Scott), and adapting to the rules if not the fickle stylistic fashions of international modernism, Sullivan would never again build as awkwardly or with as rich a grammar as he did in the Auditorium.

The Auditorium remains a confused and perhaps vainglorious attempt to combine a precocious architecture with an abiding sense of loss. Sullivan wished to employ architecture

43. Louis Sullivan, Carson, Pirie, Scott Building (1899).

to remember the immediate postfire mix of classes and the heady feeling of possibility before Chicago was transformed, before the popular culture associated with making money completely took over. In his architecture, Sullivan attempted to remember the "crudest, rawest, most savagely ambitious dreamers" as well as the new-money gentry who remained remote but proclaimed their ambition behind walled mansions and intimidating skyscrapers. He wanted ideally for his Auditorium to be a piece of history: the same common ground for Chicago as the fire, before the experience had all been conveniently forgotten or sanitized into a comfortable legend.

It was John Root, and not Louis Sullivan, who broke radically with the past. Sullivan had the revolutionary language, but it was John Root, along with his partner Daniel Burnham, who made the revolution. Root understood that architecture would not be supported in America if it was thought antagonistic to the client class that paid the bills. Pretensions of high

art would not serve the particular Chicago situation that required efficient and sound buildings after the debacle of the early postfire period. Rather, Root, with the encouragement of his shrewd partner, saw that architects were meant to be the servants of commerce. In this view, only after business was efficiently served could architects worry about their image. Root concentrated on Chicago's office towers, like the Monadnock Building, "because no class of buildings is more expressive of modern life in its complexity, its luxury, its intense vitality."[28] Almost completely unornamented and as large as a masonry structure could be, the Monadnock represented a fully rationalized architectural solution for the urban life of the time, when business was king. Although a contemporary image of a machine to work in, it still ironically acknowledged the fire with its fortresslike appearance of invulnerability.

Root, born January 10, 1850 in Lumpkin, Georgia, educated in England and New York, came to Chicago in 1872 and joined the architectural firm of Carter, Drake, and Wight. Peter Wight himself had only recently left the East to establish a business to profit from Chicago's rebuilding. New firms like his offered young architects a chance to design and supervise construction at relatively early points in their careers. Although in Boston, Philadelphia, or New York it might take a generation for an architect to develop, in Chicago the initial pace of reconstruction promised to accelerate the process of maturation. From the time Root entered into partnership with Burnham to the time of his death in 1891 on the eve of the World's Columbian Exposition, Burnham and Root was Chicago's most successful and influential firm. Epitomized by the Monadnock, completed before his death, and the posthumous Mills Building in San Francisco (1890–92), and Reliance Building in Chicago (1889–91 and 1894–95), the work of the principal design partner created a full aesthetic out of Chicago's pressing necessity to rebuild quickly.[29] At the time, Montgomery Schuyler wrote, "The business buildings of Burnham & Root were the first tall buildings in which the conditions both of commercial architecture in general and of elevator architecture in particular were recognized and expressed."[30]

While Burnham attended to the administrative side of the business, Root was free to pursue the artistic.[31] Like Sullivan's, his mature work was initially extrapolated Richardsonian Romanesque, a historical style employing local materials that allowed him to organize the huge massings required by tall buildings and announce a clear break with the more eclec-

44. (*Opposite*) Burnham and Root, Reliance Building (1889–91, 1894–95), principal architect Charles B. Atwood.

tic and haphazard historicism of the early reconstruction. But Root in his last buildings attempted an aesthetic of his own. The Mills's arched entrance, the Reliance's vestigial bronze and granite details, and the Monadnock's dark color bore only the shadow of their Richardsonian origins.[32] Root's signature was clearly evident in the Chicago architecture that the Boston architect Henry Van Brunt wrote "is based on a sleepless inventiveness in structure; on an honest and vigorous recognition of the part which structure should play in making a building fitting and beautiful. . . . Any architect of education and accomplishments is fortunate who finds himself a part of a young community so ambitious, enterprising, and restless in the pursuit of wealth and power,—doubly fortunate if he can make his art keep step with a progress so vigorous without losing the finer and more delicate artistic sense."[33]

Van Brunt understood that something new had happened in Chicago, a culmination of the postfire building boom. Root was the only one of Sullivan's contemporaries who possessed his design skills and opportunities to build.[34] Although Root also wrote semiphilosophical articles for *The Inland Architect* in which he discussed issues of style, originality, and appropriateness, he was never conflicted about his role as a commercial architect.[35] He and Burnham endorsed wholeheartedly the city's belief in a doctrine of the inevitability of progress, the urban-technological version of manifest destiny. Common wisdom had it that business had raised Chicago out of a condition of charity to one of self-sufficiency. Root thought the tall office building was the modern Greek temple or Gothic cathedral, a proper evocation of the age.[36] With this extraordinary declaration, he made a radical point. Through two decades of built work that included the aestheticized fireproofing of the Montauk Block (1881–82) and the distinctive terra cotta and brick of Burnham and Root's first major downtown commission, the Grannis Block (1880–81), to the precocious modernity of the Reliance Building, Root raised and rationalized the privately-owned commercial office tower to the status once held only by large public structures and churches.

Burnham and Root were the natural successors to the aboriginal generation represented by the Kinzies and the fire generation exemplified by William Bross. The sophisticated and optimistic urbanism of Burnham and Root perfectly fit their time. While their contemporary Sullivan railed against the philistine businessman the way Sinclair Lewis and H. L. Mencken would a generation later, Burnham calmly calculated the firm's next lucrative commission and Root drew it in

45. Burnham and
Root, Montauk Block
(1881–82).

plan, section, and elevation. They invented a form to accommodate the city's sporelike multiplication to its storied pace of development.[37] Root suggested that all one had to do was to look in the streets: "Even a slight appreciation of these would seem to make it evident to every thoughtful man in Chicago that all conditions, climatic, atmospheric, commercial and social, demand for this external aspect the simplest and most straightforward expression."[38]

Root did not view the scene as a moralist or with an abiding sense of what had gone before; he attempted objectivity.

46. Burnham and
Root, Monadnock
Building (1889–91),
with Holabird and
Roche south addition
(1893).

He thought himself a social scientist, interested not in asserting what should be but in portraying what was. The refreshing bluntness of commercial architecture required no rationale; its raw immediacy was its art. "These buildings, standing in the midst of hurrying, busy thousands of men, may not appeal to them through the more subtle means of architectural expression, for such an expression would not be heeded; and the appeal which is constantly made to unheeding eyes loses in time its power to attract."[39] In his view, buildings should not lecture or set themselves apart, but should ideally appear as if they had always been there, growing almost unconsciously to meet the present. "They inevitably become an integral part of the machinery of business," he argued. "In them there should be carried out the ideas of modern business life: Simplicity, stability, breadth, dignity."[40] His work was prosaic in the best sense: directly communicative, utilitarian, but still architectonic. Montgomery Schuyler called the Monadnock "the thing itself."[41] Earlier, in a more critical vein, Henry B. Fuller called this class of building "complete within itself." [42]

Although the Rookery is more typical of Burnham and Root's mature work in its ornamentation and planning, with its bold inner court and interpolated classical detail, the Monadnock as an unintentional monument to modernism fits more dramatically into the reigning dualisms in Chicago of the time. Sullivan's ornamental scheme was compromised by financial considerations, but much of it survived; Root's was radically transformed by these same conditions. He had been working with a varied program for the Monadnock that resembles more Holabird and Roche's elaborate addition built in the 1890s than the final abstraction. [43] But such compromises with economic realities were critical to the time. What we now view as the modern arose from powerful contradictions in Chicago, contained in the tension between the Monadnock's stripped elevations and its retro–load-bearing construction, or between its denomination as a New England mountain and its powerful Egyptian forms. Whether as sublime nature or imperial metaphor for the mundane city's Egypt-like habit of flooding, the building was made to bear powerful associations. Root's last great work in Chicago was in the end shaped by a dialectic of forces that existed between pure artistic intent, which in the Monadnock like the Auditorium was played out in a not completely coherent sequence of themes and variations, and a ferocious market economy that eroded, sometimes even, as in this case, for the improvement of the design, any serious claim to a pure romantic artistry. The Monadnock's marginal site and the evident complexities that contributed to its final stripped form make it inadvertently an appropriate monument to Chicago's reluctant modernism.

From the first days after it was completed, the Monadnock compelled attention as much for what it was thought to be as for what it was. Progressive critics were drawn to the building's seemingly bold assertion of identity, viewing it as architecture unconflicted about its role. Originally it was designed as an iron-frame skyscraper, but the developers persuaded the architect to build using masonry-wall construction. Evidently the developers, Peter and Shepherd Brooks, were nervous enough that the building appear extremely solid to convince Burnham and Root to revert to the older method. [44] Ostensibly, the Brookses' fear was founded on uncertainty about the Monadnock's tangential location to the city's main business district. Afraid that the building was too far west to guarantee complete tenancy, they wanted there to be no anxiety about its safety. Ruins from the 1871 fire were still frequently unearthed at construction sites, and they wished to do nothing that would further associate the modern buildings they financed with the old ruins. Questions of style were secondary; a Chicago building must first of all appear solid and permanent.

The Monadnock succeeded in just this way. Its walls were six feet thick at the base and a foot and a half on top, insuring the expression "of perfect stability." [45] In addition, the building was almost totally unornamented, in a radical break with the existing practice of other architects and even with Root's earlier work. A highly abstract Egyptian motif was the only detail to place the Monadnock in any other time than its own. Harriet Monroe, Root's adoring sister-in-law and first biographer, blamed the stripped-down modernism of the elevation on Daniel Burnham. She argued that while Root was away on vacation, his partner unclad the facade. Donald Hoffmann has argued convincingly that this was not completely the case and that Root had gladly accepted the developers' demands years before. [46] He had already integrated the original plan's more extroverted ornamental scheme for the Jackson Street elevation (1885), which included large panels on the tenth-story piers representing Egyptian lotus blossoms, into the building's monumental massing.

Root's eventual compromise with the ornamentation recalls Sullivan's trials with the Auditorium. In both cases the compromise finally improved the final design. In each case, the issue of ornamentation is a key to understanding the architect's larger ambitions for his work. Sullivan's references to pastoral America tried to counter what he feared to be the growing anonymity of cities—Chicago would, he believed, one day become indistinguishable from downtown Caracas. [47] Root's concerns were more abstract and aesthetic. The Egyptian associations were meant as metaphoric reminders of the Upper Nile's similarity to Lake Michigan's soft alluvial shore. In addition, associating Chicago's ambitions with imperial Egypt could not have failed to amuse Daniel Burnham. Both the Auditorium and the Monadnock were brought to reality through the efforts of prominent entrepreneurs. Where Sullivan had Fred Peck, Root had the Brooks brothers. Peter Brooks, the Boston financier, and his brother Shepherd were throwbacks to the immediate postfire days when Eastern capital, principally from New England, had been used in the city's reconstruction. The Brooks family, using Owen Aldis as their local agent, were representative of the kind of partnerships that rebuilt the city. Boosters might have boasted that

Chicago was responsible for its own phoenixlike resurrection,
but until well after the Columbian Exposition the great majority of the city's real estate was financed from outside.

Building the Monadnock like a rock and naming it after
one of New Hampshire's great White Mountains implied that
somehow it had always been there. Ornaments were unnecessary for mountains, and they only got dirty.[48] Because of the
Brookses' practical concerns, Root executed a far more sophisticated final scheme that pointed directly to the refinements of the Mills and Reliance buildings. The architect's
closeness to the developer, as contrasted with Sullivan's more
adversarial relationship with Peck, was prompted by his own
vivid memories of his arrival in the city. Root had learned
from Wight a lesson, confirmed by other architects who had
witnessed the fire, that ornamentation was the first thing to
burn.[49] For the more sophisticated and knowledgeable Chi-

cagoans of the eighties, ornamentation, like that which had adorned the huge Court House cupola and the mansards of the fashionable hotels, held a remnant of the fire's horrors long thought repressed. The developers intuited, and Root gladly endorsed, the idea that architectural embellishments, unless they were built of the strongest materials, would only remind Chicagoans of a less secure time when style was gerry-built and dangerous.

When Henry B. Fuller titled his new novel *The Cliff-Dwellers*, he was responding to just this anxiety. His main character is not a person but a skyscraper, the Monadnock-like Clifton. These buildings rivaled creation; they answered to their own natural necessity. Fuller writes at the start: "During the course of the last fifty years, the rushing streams of commerce have worn many a deep and rugged chasm. These great canyons—conduits, in fact for the leaping volume of an ever-increasing prosperity—cross each other with a sort of systematic rectangularity, and in deference to the practical directness of local requirements they are in general called simply—streets. Each of these canyons is closed in by a long frontage of towering cliffs, and these soaring walls of brick and limestone and granite rise higher and higher with each succeeding year."[50] In Chicago, the novelist's description suggests, the manmade has completely supplanted nature. For the sense of the change he has witnessed, Fuller adapts an existing natural vocabulary: the tall buildings are like cliffs; the concrete valleys between them are canyons; the crowds of businessmen, rushing streams.

The buildings that the Brooks brothers financed and Fuller observed received their power not through a system of ornamentation that linked them to important structures of the past or to current fashion. Although he did not morally endorse it, Fuller recognized exactly that quality the developers commissioned Burnham and Root to produce. The Chicago business block through its "systematic rectangularity" implied a new order, a new nature equal to the old. Where nature was irregular and organic, Chicago was mathematically regular and orthogonal. The skyscraper viewed ideally was the vertical extrapolation of the same horizontal grid that had in the 1830s rationalized land transfer and developed the city.

Root saw the tall office building as culminating a process that adapted form and available materials to the needs of the western expansion. Unlike Sullivan, he did not see architecture as a mediating force between competing constituencies. Rather, for John Root, "the machinery of business" was the day-to-day working out of American democracy. Such a dynamic process required buildings like the Monadnock that would through "their mass and proportion convey in some large elemental sense an idea of the great, stable, conserving forces of modern civilization."[51] The Monadnock was a sixteen-story blank wall with only a perfectly proportioned rectangular cut, like a door to Pharaoh's tomb, to mark its entrance. Yet the elegantly chamfered corners of the Jackson Street elevation and the heliotropic bay windows that claimed all the available north light made the building rich in essential detail. Root's last great work was an unabashed testimonial to the forces that raised Chicago from the ruins, a temple to business. And it was properly unadorned because there was as yet no agreed-upon iconography to mark Chicago's special faith in the process of making money.

Not simply the result of technological innovations and the necessity of constructing tall buildings to exploit limited real estate in the central city, John Root's Monadnock Building was undeniably elegant. Like the earlier Rookery, which gave a squat impression of burrowing deep into the earth, it provided the Chicago businessman with an image equal to his own sense of self-importance. Only a story shorter than the huge Auditorium tower, the Monadnock conferred high status on buildings used exclusively for business, and in turn enhanced the reputation of incorporated artists like Root in relation to that of the visionaries Sullivan and Wright.

"*We drew up beside* a skyscraper under construction, a headless trunk swooping up, swarming with lights. Below the early darkness now closing with December speed over the glistening west, the sun like a bristling fox jumped beneath the horizon. Nothing but a scarlet afterglow remained. I saw it between the El pillars. As the tremendous trusses of the unfinished skyscraper turned black, the hollow interior filled with thousands of electric points resembling champagne bubbles. The completed building would never be so beautiful as this."[52] Over a hundred years after the fire, Saul Bellow was drawn to Chicago architecture in its stripped form: unclad, technologically advanced, but primitive in the immediacy of its image. He does not welcome the completed building; Bellow knows the future. In fact, he waits for darkness until the structure is "turned black." He forces the image of the building back into the night, to reclaim it dreamlike from the builders for his imagination. He senses the ruin beneath the new and understands that when the slick skin is hung on

48. Burnham and Root, Rookery Building, interior court.

the skyscraper only the memory of its dark bones will remain.

In the final two decades of the last century, Chicago architecture was a search for the "thing itself." It was not to be like the great towers of New York, historicist and desperately evocative of something grander.[53] Beginning around the time of Jenney's Fair Store (1890–91) and Manhattan Building (1889–91), Holabird and Roche's Tacoma Building (1887–89) and their refinement of the office block in the Marquette Building (1893–94), through the office block's most elegant manifestation in Burnham's Railway Exchange Building (1903–4), the struggle over a proper commercial style was resolved in the form of modern hybrids that appeared effortlessly to satisfy the popular inclination towards classical detail stimulated by the recent fair, without any obvious compromise of form. Its implementation by inspired designers had made large-scale urban architecture routine. Gone were the kinds of dualities that marked a single building like the Rookery, whose light, steel-framed inner court contrasted sharply with its ponderous, dark masonry exterior. Frank Lloyd Wright mediated brilliantly between the two in his renovation of the inner court. Debates over a proper or "organic" ornamentation were viewed as amusing sectarian battles of the past. The triumph of an often improvisational commercial style through efficient entrepreneurship and invention, combining innovations as diverse as George H. Johnson's system of covering structural members with fireproof hollow tile of clay, brick, or terra cotta, the elevator, poured concrete, steel floating-raft foundations, and electric lights for excavating sites at night, enabled almost an instantaneous transformation of idea into act.[54]

Because it grew out of tragedy, the development of Chicago architecture adds a profound dimension to the cyclical story of American success. Arriving architects were deeply inhibited by the shock of disaster: "A stranger, ignorant of the occurrence of the fire, might have travelled over acres with scarcely meeting a single thing to even suggest that the areas through which he was passing had ever been inhabited."[55] He was also slowed down by economic depression. The unavoidable drag of events acted as a powerful counterweight to the American compulsion to move forward. Root credits the time to reflect, Sullivan the "pathologyzing" of a city recently in ruin, with their success and originality. The developer's habitual premium on speed was replaced with a deepening of the senses. In part, it was as if they all had to wait for invention to break with the "fossils" who had made a mess of the early reconstruction.[56] But in the waiting, the inactivity they first cursed, they were able to see in the ruins the present as well as the glorious future that their fellow citizens claimed to see even more clearly.

The ruins demanded attention like the fire dead. "About one hundred and ten bodies have thus far been found, some scarcely scorched, and some charred and blackened and roasted into horrible, unrecognizable fragments of humanity."[57] The grief and melancholy associated with the fire, suggested by the grotesque forms of the victims and the tortured shapes of buildings suddenly reduced to basic structure, fragmented the city's controlling vision of unity. The period of forced idleness or reflection allowed people to reclaim the experience through delayed mourning. In grief, they could directly encounter the "unrecognizable fragments of humanity," the healthy turned grotesque and pathological, made safe by the relative distance of time. Finally, artists were able to reimagine the experience in their work. For Frank Lloyd Wright it meant he could radically reorganize the office type, although not in Chicago. The Larkin Company Administration Building (1904) in Buffalo relinquished the central lighted space to the workers and put their bosses off to the side.

49. Frank Lloyd
Wright, Larkin Build-
ing, (Buffalo, N.Y.,
1904), Light Court.

50. Frank Lloyd
Wright, Larkin Build-
ing, view across the
Light Court at fifth-
floor level.

51. Frank Lloyd
Wright, Larkin Build-
ing, Seneca Street ele-
vation.

52. Frank Lloyd
Wright, Larkin Build-
ing, intaglio relief and
fountain.

Wright transformed a conventional place of business into a
cathedral for work. A motto engraved in stone at the main
entrance overwhelmed any corporate identity: "Honest Labor
Needs No Master / Simple Justice Needs No Slaves." Sullivan's last commissions, his Midwest banks, would be in-scale
explosions of his tombs for industrialists commissioned at the
time of the Auditorium. "Although grief involves grave de-
partures from the normal attitude to life, it never occurs to us
to regard it as a morbid condition and hand the mourner over
to medical treatment. We rest assured that after a lapse of
time it will be overcome, and we look upon any interference
with it as inadvisable or even harmful."[58]

The Shanty and the Skyscraper

The wasteland created by the Great Fire came at a fortunate historical moment when essential new technologies were just at the point of development or already complete and immediately available from the outside. Out of necessity, the city was compelled to welcome experimentation. Chicago was burned out of an earlier and relatively primitive form of industrialism into the most modern. In this environment, techniques that might have remained dormant under normal conditions of urban growth were perfected and then rigorously tested. Locally, George H. Johnson and Peter B. Wight conducted separate successful studies of fireproofing. Burnham and Root developed foundations capable of supporting great loads on the unstable subsoil. Adler and Sullivan perfected a "floating foundation" of reinforced concrete and brought several acoustical and electrical refinements to the interiors of their large buildings. Chicago was the first major city to experience what is now a more common phenomenon, associated with the reconstruction of Berlin and Tokyo after World War II. Regardless of tradition, those things thought useless and retrograde are abandoned; necessities are first improvised and eventually refined to operate at higher standards than in the past.

The fire further liberated Chicago from its own borders. More than ever it was a crossroads for businessmen, financiers, artists, architects, and later, for intellectuals (drawn to the new University of Chicago). Men and women from all over were attracted to this former western outpost. For the remainder of the century, American culture shifted west. Chicago became the testing ground for its own and imported ideas. A general cultural hybridization was in effect; ideas from all over were transformed to meet the city's special conditions. Parochial local myths that had sustained Chicago in its first periods of growth were now exposed to outside influences. Like a provincial city on the old China silk route, Chicago was the beneficiary of a more sophisticated world brought daily to its doors.

The practical application of the electric passenger elevator demonstrates the point. New York's Equitable Building, designed by Arthur Gilman and Edward Kimball with George B. Post as associate engineer, had the first electric elevator at the time of its completion in 1871. The Haughwout Building (1857) in New York earlier employed a steam-driven device, followed shortly in Chicago (1864) by the Farwell Store. A hydraulic lift was also used briefly for tall buildings until the development of a dependable electric model.[1] Remarkable for its very high bulk, the Equitable in the accepted Second Empire fashion was a squat structure that hogged every inch of its square block. The elevator was simply a utilitarian device incorporated into the original plan to utilize fully every inch of rentable space. Later New York buildings—George Post's Western Union (1873–75) and Richard Morris Hunt's Tribune (1873–75) buildings—were clad with heavy French ornamentation and featured clumsy European clock towers at unnatural heights. These first attempts at skyscrapers, or "elevator buildings" as they were more accurately called, failed. Spurred by heated real-estate speculation and the necessity for efficient vertical multiplication of the existing grid, these buildings still never achieved a satisfactory form. They remained awkward imitations that simply exploded the scale of their European models. A good designer could make a correct Beaux Arts classicism work for a conventional four- or five-story public or commercial building. Such an application worked best when applied to the enormous townhouses then being commissioned by Philadelphia, Boston, and New York robber barons. The method ultimately collapsed when it was hurriedly made to accommodate the buildings of unprecedented heights made possible by electric passenger elevators. New technology without an equally inventive architectural response proved to be the most effective critic of mindless neoclassicism, which did not work at the enormous new scale technically possible. Architecture at this scale required full integration of style into the massing of the building. The best modern/classical composites, like the Marquette in Chicago or the Flatiron in New York, became originals mostly independent of their neoclassical sources. In the worst instances, as the scale increased so did the possibility for awkward or sometimes comical effects in the elevations.

Fly-by-night methods and superficial stylistic manipulation of elevations began to look ridiculous when the elevator was added and masonry structures could be as tall as sixteen stories. No longer was the most rentable and desirable space on the more accessible bottom floors, but on the top. Building height was no longer determined by human limits. For the first time in history, the willingness or capacity to walk stairs ceased to determine urban scale. Montgomery Schuyler observed at the time that the elevator would eventually change the way architecture communicated. "The structure cannot be expressed in terms of historical architecture, and for that reason the attempt to express it has been foregone."[2] Schuyler was thinking of Chicago. Although the habit remained for years, Chicago, by losing its major buildings in the fire, was freed from the necessity of historicist expression. Elevator technology, lightweight fireproof cladding, stronger foundations, and new metal framing provided practical disincentives, as Schuyler suggested, against reviving the old design formulas. Reborn Chicago required a new architectural type.

Ironically, the city's relative cultural backwardness and rawness produced exactly the situation required to assimilate the crush of the new. Today's American architects and critics generally agree about Chicago's unique position after the fire, but they still tend to judge it harshly against the standards developed in Boston and New York. Henry-Russel Hitchcock has observed, "If the Chicago architectural scene had any virtues around 1880 they were largely negative ones: no established traditions, no real professional leaders, and ignorance of all architectural styles past or present." He describes an environment with "no hampering traditions." But he also offers a less critical assessment. "The maturing of an original sort of skyscraper design around 1890 is a Mid-Western, and almost specifically a Chicago story to which New Yorkers made little or no contribution. Boston's architectural leadership had ended with the death of Richardson; despite the prominence of McKim, Mead & White and their large Eastern following, leadership on this field passed almost at once to Chicago."[3] William Jordy adds, "For those who would take an overly provincial view of Chicago achievement, for instance how puzzling that two of the principal clients for Chicago commercial buildings were the Boston financiers, Peter and Shepherd Brooks, who seem to have been exceptionally forceful in instructing their architects (through their Chicago real estate agent Owen Aldis) on the virtues of architectural austerity . . . Yet the Brooks' exhortations seem to have been powerless to effect anything in Boston comparable to the Chicago achievement." This "Chicago" point of view, according to

Jordy, had its roots in a "scantily explored decade of preparation, from the Great Fire to the building of the Montauk and Home Insurance at the beginning of the eighties."[4]

Why was Chicago so available to the new architecture? Hitchcock is critical of the city's inchoate culture, but it is precisely the absence of a high culture that allowed the innovations of markets and engineering to occur. Eastern cities were paralyzed by the idea of the correct way to build, to write, to think. Jordy is closer to the mark: there was something in the postfire city that allowed innovations, both imported and home-grown, to take root. In fact, its blasted condition and its relative freedom from traditions except its own powerful self-mythologized belief in itself, allowed the city to reimagine itself completely. The city's violent dislocation from its physical past, its passionate commitment to rebuild, and the emergence in the city of a radical working-class counterculture all made the city a dynamic environment for change. With a new capital base, borrowed from established Eastern banks but collateralized by the city's geographic centrality and record of production, a practical group of merchants and industrialists could remake the place relatively free from interference by any aristocratic pretensions which might be inefficient or needlessly costly. These were midwestern Croesuses, who arose out of the ashes either to reclaim their wealth or to replace those who could not. It was a new game. In the image of the fire ruins, the stripped buildings that went up in the eighties were part of an ongoing transition to a new, modern iconography fully expressive of contemporary life.

New players and old made the city work; so completely did they combine Chicago's acquisitive and creative sides that architecture was the first of the city's arts to develop. In the decade after the fire, the city approached the condition James Jackson Jarves described as ideal: "Not before we appreciate the possibilities of architecture in a grand combination of the intellectual and spiritual faculties, aroused to action by the deepest emotions, can we expect to create work to rival that of olden time."[5] The process Jarves recommended developed against the background of the fire, which surprisingly remained a daily reality of Chicago life through the turn of the century.

In the eighties and nineties, reports on the city's contemporary condition returned obsessively to the subject of the fire. "There are still [in 1881] many vacant lots where the moldering walls of old buildings, burnt in the fire, stand as reminders of the event; but no great length of time can now transpire till the increasing demand for more stores and offices, as well as demand beyond the present supply for private dwellings, will not only fill up vacant lots in the burnt district, but enlarge the area of the city."[6] Architecture was the city's measure of how far it had travelled from tragedy and a key to its present health. Discouragingly, however, the remaining ruins continued to prevent the ultimate hygiene, when the new Chicago would completely supplant the old. As late as the opening of the world's fair (1892), the new city was still incomplete, the wounds still open. An English visitor observed that Chicago looked "half baked." He concluded, "It is in many respects a large cluster of incongruities. The rectangular regularity which so severely rules the lines of the streets is balanced by the most startling irregularity of architecture. The 'sky-scraper' and the shanty stand side by side."[7] Chicago's incongruous condition became its modern identity. Despite all efforts at reinterpretation that might render the catastrophe a positive agent of change, the fire's enduring presence stubbornly resisted any complete transformation and provided a perverse source of authenticity to a city bewitched by its particular version of manifest destiny. While boosters preferred optimistic images of the phoenix rising, to the reality of steel-frame business block and wooden slum sharing adjoining lots, the shadow of Chicago's frontier origins reappeared during the entire rebuilding period, to stimulate survivors' vivid memories almost a generation after the fire.

New and old Chicago existed side by side, a double reality present on the street. The primeval mud reerupted in a surreal contrast to the new buildings and gentrified manners of Potter Palmer's "improved" State Street. City pretensions were mocked as soon as they were proclaimed. As in the first years of settlement, sidewalks were improvised, imitating the vagaries of the shifting subsoil underneath. Some walkways were solid and made of perfectly graded concrete; others dropped suddenly a few inches or a foot, and rose again without warning. New and "better than ever," the city was still relentlessly confronted with its chronic state of disorder: "The same genius for contrast presents you with great patches of raw prairie within a few yards of some of the finest boulevards in the world. Nay, in the very heart of the city, at the corner of one of the busiest blocks, where the whirl of traffic is at its fiercest, and all the appliances of the latest modern civilization are in full swing, close to sky-soaring 'temples,' elevators, telephones, electric light, almost grazed by the cable cars, I found a veritable unmistakable tree stump. It was of course, cut down to the level of the road, but there it stood,

53. Rebuilding: View from Court House looking southeast (c. 1872–73).

54. Rebuilding: View from Water Tower looking south (c. 1872–77).

an eloquent reminder of the wilds which reigned around it
sixty years ago."[8] In the fire's long aftermath the city's crude
past reasserted itself. A frontier crudeness, long thought
mastered in the abbreviated development from outpost to international city, threatened to reassert itself as an unwelcome
counterpart to the pathetic state of the roads and sidewalks.
The spontaneous expression of freedom and license witnessed during the conflagration and later seen in the streets
of the Haymarket and Pullman was linked to the city's chaotic
condition during the rebuilding; no rhetoric or exhortation to
progress could completely obscure it. The fire had a direct effect upon the way architects viewed themselves and the way
they came to be seen. In the words of one of Henry B. Fuller's
characters, architecture was useful in a city recently burned
back to a primitive time suggestive of its earliest days, "to tell
who we are."[9]

The arrival of an army of young architects into Chicago offered the temptation to recover immediately more in image
than in fact. The opportunity to build quickly also came at a

56. Rebuilding: View
from Water Tower
looking west (c. 1872–
77).

good moment for an infant profession desiring national attention and greater prestige. The timing of the fire was perfect
for architects, whose professional identities were insecure
and the market for their work, small. Firms became larger and
more specialized, and their power solidified as a system of
general contracts began to replace the policy of negotiating
separately with individual trades. Outside capital and the accelerated demand for building instantly put the Chicago architect at the profession's vanguard, consolidating professional gains achieved over decades,[10] and shifting national
attention away from the Eastern firms of McKim, Mead, and
White, Richard Morris Hunt, and Ware and Van Brunt. In
New York, Boston, and Philadelphia, architecture was more
or less a society game, remote from most people, but in Chicago it was associated with the question of survival. In postfire Chicago the architect was a key social type, appearing frequently in literature and social criticism. Architecture became
the most direct way to know the city, relatively free of Chicago's self-serving rhetoric and posturings.

Paul Bourget first exposed the city's commercial architecture as being a marvelously well-built scrim crowding the lake and hiding the other Chicago. Looking west from the Auditorium tower he was in fact looking back into the city's past, which was still an open wound. To him the new buildings' unprecedented heights seemed to encourage the city's tendency to abstract its condition, to see it simply as the accomplishment of a bold new skyline. From almost two hundred feet above the ground it was easy to dream away the twenty years that separated the new White City of the fair from Chicago's last attempt at rebirth. Down on the street Bourget found the reality decidedly more complex. "You go down to look more closely into the details of this exuberant life, this exhaustless stream of activity. You walk along the sidewalks of streets which bear marks of haste—here flagstones, there asphalt, yonder a mere line of planks crossing a miry swamp. This want of continuity in road material is repeated in the buildings."[11] One of a procession of distinguished visiting Europeans that included Anthony Trollope, Rudyard Kipling, Oscar Wilde, and G. W. Steevens, Bourget did not moralize about what he saw. That approach would find its apotheosis in William T. Stead's surprisingly insightful *If Christ Came to Chicago* (1894). Rather, Bourget reported the city not purely as it wished to be seen, but complete with its shadow. Of his arrival in the city during a storm, he reported that he "could see nothing but the outlines of gigantic buildings hanging, as it were, from a dark sky streaked with lightning, and between them small wooden houses, so frail that it seemed as if the furious wind must scatter their ruins to the four quarters of the tempest-tossed city."[12] Looking out from the Auditorium tower, he compared official Chicago, where buildings reached a height of twenty stories, to the towering islands of the Cyclades seen from Negroponte, while the buildings of the "unimproved" city he could barely distinguish from the pavement below. Bourget pictured a city divided from itself; he saw the fire not unifying the city, as the accepted Chicago mythology had it, but as disrupting it as much as war. Only a war from the same period could equal the fire in the imagination of a European: "In 1871, that is to say, later than the Franco-Prussian War, there was fire writhing around this very place. . . . That month of October, 1871, was more than near to me; it seemed as if I could touch it, as if I were still in it."[13]

To visitors to the city years later, the fire still seemed present, suggesting something essential about Chicago. Europeans figured time in distance from the last war; Chicago's real progress could be measured by reference to its remaining links to the fire. "I realized with an almost physical accuracy the length of the years since that date—twenty-two. How few hours that makes after all!"[14] Time to Bourget was revealed in Chicago as "physical." Particularly to the outside observer, free from the rhetoric of booster or evangelist, the architectural contrast between the city's striving for a unified monumentality and the chronic presence of wooden slums is Chicago's essence. Like Balzac's Parisian whore, Chicago was not a unified whole but a dynamic of equal opposites, a city high and low. Trollope caught the spirit of the place when he wrote about the bigness of the shops, hotels, and public buildings for a "new Corn-Exchange nobility."[15] He also observed that Chicago had large theaters but at least on the day he attended, no audience.

G. W. Steevens, who wrote an Englishman's version of *Outre-Mer* in *The Land of the Dollar* (1897) reported the same apocalyptic split of opposing forces. Even a parade organized by the city to commemorate the fire's twenty-fifth anniversary could not present a consensus. The grand procession became two separate marches. The first, sponsored by the city's elite, was the official Republican version emphasizing the way the city wanted to be known. "By their untamable energy they have built her up from a heap of ashes in their own lifetime to be great and wealthy and pulsing with virility."[16] Marchers included millionaires with their workers waving corporate flags as if enacting a medieval pagent. This was the official version of survival, with rich and poor united—as full of itself as William Bross's first official narrative of reconstruction. An elite that once self-servingly viewed the fire as a great leveler when it served the rhetoric of reconstruction now presented myth as a reality a quarter-century old. Steevens sensed the pretension and saw it more in feudal than democratic terms. "The great drapery establishment of Marshall Field & Company led the way—six partners of the firm riding abreast, and after them shop-workers, salesmen, cashiers, porters, office boys, all in rank and file, and all in step with the music. Firm followed firm, club followed club. . . . All kept their formation and marched in step."[17]

Steevens saw the fantasy of a unified city where haves and have-nots accepted economic differences as naturally as nineteenth-century Indians accepted caste differences. The actual example of the fire as a time when social differences had melted—the rich and poor were made equal in an instant—was resurrected for this sanctioned occasion with all the actual conflict edited out. The Republican parade was a pastoral reordering of anarchy. Like the sanitized accounts of the fire, the official parade, by suggesting new partnerships of owners and workers tramping together under the same banner, suppressed the city's permanent class conflict.

But this was still just image-making. Around the edges before the parade got underway the restlessness of the crowd reinacted the chaos of the day being commemorated. The "dense phalanxes of people crushed on to the pavements." That night the Democrats held a counterdemonstration to complete the city's remembrance of the single most dramatic event of its past. The night procession of men and women with torches accentuated the ghostly symbolism of the scene. Steevens described the second parade as seen from his hotel window: "On the horizon the red and white lights shine steadily over the black solemnity of the Lake. Nearer in is the abroad belt of muddy waste that Chicago is going to make into a park when the City Council gives back the money it has embezzled. And right below us is Michigan Avenue, dark with heaving masses of men, flickering with gold and silver and red fire, and volleying cheers, hoarse and shrill, far over the solemn water, and up to unanswering heaven. All poor men these. No two hundred million dollars here."[18] Screaming labor slogans and jeers, this was the fire mob reincarnated, left to march together at night in a ghostly parody of official Chicago. These marchers seemed to come out of the mud (not yet a park) as if to animate Bourget's intuition of the past's physical presence. Steevens reported that workers had been ordered to join the morning's parade out of fear that they might be fired if they disobeyed their bosses. In contrast, at night they exhibited real enthusiasm for a free-form march of their own. Steevens drew his own conclusions: "There is more life, more sincerity, more devil in this muster than in the other. . . . The affair goes in a whirlwind of cheers from start to finish. It may be smaller, it is more exuberant. It may be less overwhelming, but it is more inspiriting. I am getting enthusiastic myself."[19] There was no "one Chicago." Taken together in direct opposition to each other, the two parades accurately reflected the condition of the city on October 8, 1871 as well as twenty-five years later. Chicago was still divided and uncertain about its past; the problem of how to remember the fire put the city at perpetual war with itself.

Although architecture in ruin most poignantly commemorated the disaster, architects were approached, as the recovery progressed, to remember the event in a formal way. Like Christopher Wren after the Fire of London (1666), William Le Baron Jenney was asked to design a monument. The Chicago

57. William Le Baron
Jenney, first proposal
for a fire monument,
to be built of safes and
columns taken from
the ruins.

architect and engineer presented two schemes. In the initial
plan Jenney struggled to find a suitable iconography free of
tired literary and religious imagery, already worn out by the
city's journalists, politicians, and preachers.[20] His immediate
source of imagery was the fire itself. He chose not to impose
a mythology but raked the ruins for a particular language immediately suggestive of the event. He discovered that the
city's materiality—its ceaseless quest for things and property—transformed by fire was ultimately its own proper
monument.

Jenney's first proposal was for a tower of litter salvaged
from the city's failed buildings. Out of his own loss and direct
experience, Jenney made a populist architecture in the same
vein as the children's "cinders," fragments of twisted metal
which had been sold as instant relics. He planned to stack

partially deformed objects one on top of another to form a surprisingly graceful series of setbacks. Neither mawkishly sentimental nor striving after false effect, the odd tower of metallic debris, which was to include deformed building parts and surviving safes from office vaults, all tested by the fire and allowed to find their own forms, was unselfconscious, a poetic gesture that reshaped the fire's destruction into a permanent ruin. Jenney's initial instinct was to reject a high-art expression for what a city of mixed class and ethnicity had experienced, but his efforts at folk realism were not appreciated by the "reformed" city government that wanted a monument less dissonant with the dominant religion of reincarnation.

Jenney's permanent ruin was never built. In its place the city asked him to design a monument of "sufficient dignity."[21] The cornerstone for this more conventional fire monument was laid on October 30, 1872. To satisfy the West Chicago park commissioners and their high notion of refined public taste, Jenney made a radical conceptual change that completely overthrew his primary idea. No longer a monument to the irrational or pagan process of disorder and destruction imagined by John McGovern (in *Daniel Trentworthy*) and others, the revised scheme was consistent with the city's elaborate fantasy of rebirth. In the place of the contorted debris were "cut stones obtained from destroyed buildings." To replace a collection of actual objects to be remembered and then reconsidered, the revised plan substituted the abstraction of destruction into what was thought to be a high-art composition. The second scheme imbedded "surviving" slabs of indistinct masonry into a hackneyed Gothic tower, complete with a "spire surmounted by a quadruple Gothic column on which stand a female figure holding aloft in both hands a flaming torch, emblematic of destruction by fire."[22]

Jenney retreated into an accepted Christian image of resurrection to replace the image of loss. Here spirit, in the form of a female with flaming torch, triumphs over adversity. The fire is not remembered as an uncontrollable force capable of warping and transforming the most solid forms, but is instantly resigned to the past through comforting conventional imagery. There is nothing here specifically to engage the imagination. The second monument, with its revivalist base and generic heroic statuary, incorporated the boosterism explicitly resisted by Jenney's haunting first idea. As endorsed by the park commission, the reformed monument was to serve as a civic recognition not of the community's own suffering but of national charity. The focus was permanently shifted from a singular disquieting event to one of shared experience. "One of the remarkable facts connected with our great fire was the unprecedented generosity of the entire civilized world in contributing to the relief of the needy sufferers. As a slight token of recognition, we would inscribe upon the monument the names of the cities contributing and the amounts of their most liberal donations."[23] The city's first attempt at memorializing the fire was compromised into an innocuous piece of public relations.

In time even this inoffensive pile proved unacceptable. Money to build the memorial dried up, and a general lack of interest in any reminder of failure, no matter how classical or upbeat, ultimately doomed the project. Pictures of the unfinished monument show it haunting fifty-nine acres of pastureland south of West Madison Street until it, too, was razed in 1882, leaving the city free to develop another parcel of land free of any inhibiting memory. The city would take almost one hundred years to commission another memorial. In 1956, Mayor Richard J. Daley decided to build the Chicago Fire Academy to mark the location of Mrs. O'Leary's barn on DeKoven Street. In the Academy's courtyard stands Egon Weiner's banal metal sculpture in the shape of a flame, invisible to all except the immediate neighborhood or the odd tourist.

Chicago's rejection of Jenney's first memorial scheme reflected an uneasiness with professional architects that already had a long history. The city longed for the impossible—an available American classicism, secure in its own traditions with agreed-upon rules. The architect would only be marginally free to invent, so that his work would never be overly critical or disquieting. Jenney's encounter with the canons of public taste was only the most recent instance of a larger national problem that Chicago had inherited, a question of identity with origins in the earliest architectural discussions of Thomas Jefferson and Benjamin Latrobe. Was American architecture to be, as Latrobe wished, simply an adaptation of English neoclassicism, correct in its unities? Or could it be—at least potentially—more romantic and less predictable? A New World Palladianism might be architecturally "correct" but lack the necessary invention to accommodate the nation's perpetual experience with urban and natural frontiers.

To deal with America's almost daily experience of reinvention, Jefferson's classicism was modern in intention with

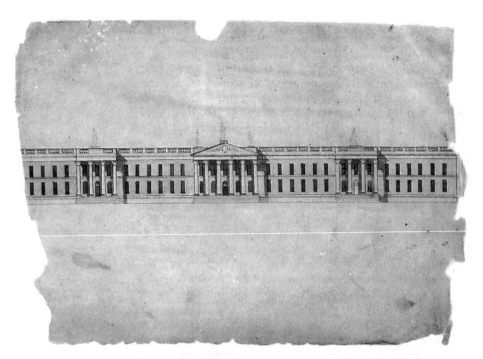

58. William Thornton, study of University of Virginia dormitories (1817).

pragmatic goals. He was unhappy with some associations implied by his selective historicism, and content with others. The overall result was abstruse. His architecture was radical in plan and section and conservative in elevation, as can be observed in his overall conception of the University of Virginia. He rejected the typical medieval cloister plan of the country's oldest educational institutions and their theologically inspired curricula. In his university's most radical incarnation, seen in an early perspective, Jefferson left the main north-south axis open at both ends. When asked for his professional advice, Latrobe strenuously argued that the former president's open scheme violated all established rules of closure, and he urged Jefferson to include the Rotunda at the north end. In a letter of July 24, 1817, Latrobe stressed his concern with decorum: "Center building which ought to exhibit in Mass and details as perfect a specimen of good architectural taste as can be devised."[24] Jefferson agreed with the change but refused, as he was instructed, to shift the orientation of the principal rooms to face south rather than, symbolically, the east and west. At the same time he resisted Latrobe's pressure to use the Rotunda conventionally as a central chapel, rather than as a library. The controversy was important beyond its particulars. Latrobe was right in a strictly formal sense, but Jefferson was most interested in the *idea* of the architecture. In the end, Jefferson proved to be meeker than he needed to be.

After a five-year tenure in Paris in the 1780s, Jefferson was aware of radical treatments of architecture's established grammar.[25] Although he never made wholesale application of what he observed when he was in Europe, he gained a certain audacity by using elements of what he had observed to break the order of his contemporaries' more doctrinaire classicism. The university's exclusion of a central chapel recalls Ledoux's project for the model town of Chaux, where the village church is relocated outside the city's primary ring plan. Monticello, Jefferson's most personal work, is in elevation a beautifully detailed neoclassical facade that masks the sophisticated play of plan and section. This is not the literal Greek Revival style that followed the nationalistic attack on things British after the War of 1812 but a thoroughly-worked classicism in three dimensions, always threatening to break, warping the elevations like the serpentine walls that trail off the university's main plan. Resisting literalism, he also avoided an obvious academic classicism of the sort suggested by Dr. William Thornton, one of the professional architects the "amateur" Jefferson consulted. Dismissing the low-art solecisms of populist design while incorporating their spirit of play, Jefferson employed high, Europeanized classicism as a container.

Like Jenney, caught in the middle between high and low, Jefferson tried to tailor the conventions to his own purposes. To preserve order and high purpose, invention was highly controlled in elevation or deferred to the interior through

59. Thomas Jefferson, Bird's-eye-view of the University of Virginia, shaded by Cornelia Jefferson Randolph (1820?).

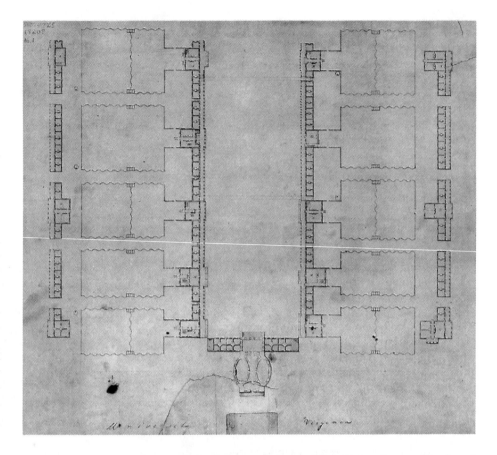

60. John Neilson (d. 1827), study for 1822 engraving by Peter Maverick of the University of Virginia campus.

clever manipulations of plan and fanciful gadgetry. He played with the eye of the informed observer. But the inventions were reserved and almost puritanical in their modesty, hidden like the dumbwaiter in the walls. In France, Boullée and Ledoux looked to Jefferson and his generation for a revolutionary politics, but they were much closer to an architecture free of the old iconography of class than their American contemporaries. Boullée's Newton cenotaph and royal library, Ledoux's houses for the woodcutter, the agricultural guards at Maupertuis, and the directors of the River Loue, are all conceptual projects that attempted to look beyond historicism to express the originality of the revolution's "new man."[26]

Ultimately Jefferson chose what he thought to be a stable form of architectural language over a more problematic kind of experimentation in practice. He underplayed the revolutionary aspects of his work, subtly subverting neoclassical planning while preserving its solid impression. Jefferson's

61. Claude-Nicolas Ledoux, Director's house, saltworks at Chaux (1775–78).

radical conservatism, so appropriate to his tentative stance as amateur artist, the aesthetic counterpart to his yeoman farmer in politics, had an unwelcome and long-lasting result; it helped stigmatize invention as something to be hidden away, more appropriate to the tinkering engineer than to the public maker of form. His fondness for a conservative image and instinctive deference to professional authority over imagination initiated a confusion over the role of the architect in American life.

At the time of the Chicago fire the confusion was still evident. In November 1870, a Unitarian clergyman, William Henry Furness, was invited to give the closing address to the fourth annual convention of the American Institute of Architects. Furness had only a tangential interest in architecture, but as a former abolitionist he had a nose for political controversy, particularly in those issues relatively remote from his own constituency. The actual connection he claimed was familial and not professional. His son Frank was an established Philadelphia architect and an early mentor to Louis Sullivan. Another son, W. H. Furness, Jr., was a portrait painter influenced by the transcendentalists. A friend of Emerson, Furness was a living link between the earliest philosophizing about American artists and their current attempts at professional acceptance. His talk was modeled on the American Scholar Address (1837) in which Emerson had lectured a group of select Harvard upperclassmen about their duty to reject book learning and preachings in favor of a more activist stance. Furness wanted the architects of the AIA to feel that they could be the new models for Emerson's engaged intellectual, once they freed themselves from foreign influence and received opinion. It flattered the AIA members to think that the architect was the perfect American hybrid—a successful artist who could be trusted with other people's money.

But Furness, the old guard intellectual, was not there to flatter. His talk had an edge as he raised issues not usually welcomed by struggling organizations. Furness in his short talk revived all the old issues that historically had questioned the identity of the American artist. He challenged the assembled delegates, already drugged by days of formal presentations on problems of structure and siting, and strategies for billing clients, to a passionate self-appraisal. Were they American originals like Thoreau and Whitman, or dandies dressing up European styles? He brought a revivalist message into the private precincts of a newly respectable business, challenging the delegates, "Certain it is that no man ever achieves anything great, anything beyond keeping body and soul together for a few years, unless he is possessed of a certain divine fanaticism for his art, or pursuit, whatever it may be."[27] Hired to give an old man's blessing, Furness disappointed the AIA in tone and substance. His talk of fanaticism and passion upset the crowd, which had been basking in blissful self-satisfaction. He raised the old problem of the country's aesthetic bankruptcy. The chant was first taken up by Emerson and was echoed by others, like the sculptor Horatio Greenough, who complained: "The mind of this country has never been seriously applied to the subject of building. Intently engaged in matters of more pressing importance, we have been content to receive our notions of architecture as we have received the fashion of our garments and the form of our entertainments, from Europe,"[28] and Calvert Vaux, Olmsted's partner on Central Park, who asked rhetorically, "There are the buildings, but where is the architecture?"[29]

Unique to Furness's presentation was his audacity as a declared nonmember in carrying an insular academic and literary debate to a group of practitioners capable of acting upon his conclusions. Architects as professionals were ideally neither simply thoughtless builders nor pompous orators, but could be effectual by bridging the strictly practical or mechanical trades and the high classical arts. He argued that these two often conflicting aspects of architecture must be kept together, with each preserving its own identity—what Whitman called "opposite equals." "The consequence of this confounding of artists with mere mechanics is that your art is not only defrauded of its dignity, it is without its rightful authority; and you have incessantly to submit to the humiliation of discussing as questions of taste what are no questions of taste at all, but matters of knowledge, of fact, with persons who, so far from having studied them, have never given a thought to them before—with persons who, if they knew what makes for their salvation (architecturally speaking) would sit silently at your feet, and listen and learn." [30] At the start of a decade that would see unprecedented demand for architects, he argued that architects must not be incorporated by business or distorted by the desire for instant espectability and warned that such determination might not always make for smooth professional development and advancement. At times the architect could find himself outside social conventions and possibly at odds with a clientele that "know nothing of architecture."

There was more agreement about the nature of the profession than Furness imagined. His strong message of cultural engagement was alien to a group that had evolved slowly from a loose guild of handymen to the higher status it was only beginning to enjoy. The AIA was reluctant to risk hard-won changes in perception in favor of a more problematic position of maintaining architecture as a vehicle of social criticism. The direction Furness supported had already been rejected in the most successful East Coast practices, as architects there defined themselves more conservatively to accommodate the new rich. Despite all these efforts, the architect remained a double with two insecure identities: the first was conventionally professional and was dominant in practice, the second was poetic and philosophical. Chicago's protracted rebuilding would show these two to be intertwined. The architect as stolid man of business closeted a romantic shadow. Increasingly, in self-presentation and in practice, as reflected in literature and by architects' own writing, these two formerly distinct identities became confused, and were simply treated in practice as interchangeable social roles that could be used and discarded at will. The problem of identity was also exacerbated by outsiders with little knowledge of the slow internal development of architecture as a profession, who sought to define the architect for their own polemical purposes.

Writers and critics saw the architect as an educable primitive, a noble savage with the gift of invention, at his best when responding to necessity, as with the prairie balloon frame, the urban cast-iron front, or the clipper ship. Their hope was that he might temper the increasingly brutal process of development, what the painter J. F. Cropsey called the "axe of civilization." To romantics, the architect represented a uniquely American type, an artist in the rough, as Whitman mythologized himself. Praised for his technical skills and motivated by an interest in beauty, the American architect could meet the material needs of a developing country without adding to its incipient philistinism. Lacking the rawness of those who actually settled the nation in sharklike moves west, yet free of courtly Europeanized sentiments or complementary garret bohemianism, the architect at least in theory was the nation's model of a hands-on artist. However, if one actually observed architecture in the rough, the conclusions were not as comforting. The reigning nineteenth-century art critic, James Jackson Jarves, observed: "Strictly speaking we have no architecture. . . . The one intense barren fact which stares us fixedly in the face is, that, were we annihilated tomorrow, nothing could be learned of us, as a distinctive race, from our architecture."[31] Jarves recognized that Americans had comfortably settled on three forms of architectural expression: the high-minded rationalism of Victorian Gothic, the reassuring domesticity and historicism of Colonial Revival, and eclecticism, if the other two proved too rigorous.[32]

Between theory and practice, the American architect was for the first time taken seriously when the time came to build after the Chicago fire. As an army of builders struggled with the realities of a city in ruin, the architects who crowded Chicago caused theory and practice to collide. Conservative notions of profession, defined at leisure by an elite mimicking similar societies of doctors and lawyers, were threatened by more romantic theorizing from outside, with which educated young architects were generally familiar. The professional architect, hired to do the work responsibly, quickly, and within budget, liked to think of himself in private as worthy of Emerson's and Thoreau's attention. When Louis Sullivan and

Frank Lloyd Wright proclaimed themselves visionaries, they were not so much anomalous as simply substituting the architect's private for his public role. Sullivan's heroic brooding and Wright's dandyism were the formerly closeted role, the shadow personality, of American architecture now openly proclaimed.

Against the background of the profession's recent development these romantic excesses can be seen as the formerly repressed side of an art made to conform to business. They suggest that something important remained sublimated. Lost in the fire's premature burial, important matters were still left unexpressed. Bourget thought that Chicago had devoured individuals in its fantasy of complete recovery, like the uncounted fire dead. "Its aspect reveals so little of the personal will, so little caprice and individuality, in its streets and buildings, that it seems like the work of some impersonal power, irresistible, unconscious, like a force of nature, in whose service man was merely a passive instrument." In light of contemporary observations, can we better understand Sullivan's and Wright's primal markings on their buildings? Their ornamentation was an act of reclamation from that "impersonal power" that seemed to remake the city, where architects "ruthlessly accepted the speculator's inspired conditions,— to multiply as much as possible the value of the bit of earth at the base by multiplying the superimposed 'offices.'" For Bourget, business had replaced the elemental power of fire. "This power is nothing else than that business fever which here throbs at will, with an unbridled violence like that of an uncontrollable element. It rushes along these streets, as once before the devouring flame of fire; it quivers; it makes itself visible with an intensity which lends something tragical to this city, and makes it seem like a poem to me."[33] The florid writings, posturings, and ultimately the architecture of Sullivan and Wright responded to real problems. Chicago could be rebuilt but never fully reimagined until it incorporated its "tragical" origins, which somehow frustrated all demolition, new construction, and landfill. As late as the last Chicago buildings of Sullivan and Wright, the existential questions raised by the fire were still being subordinated to the machinery of myth and the self-generated necessities of business.

Jarves had only recently warned of the problem. Architecture no longer embraced "in its erection and purposes an entire community," as it had in the building of the great cathedrals. "Architecture dwindled to the business of a class. What had been the care and joy of a people was delegated to a professional one. . . . Architecture delegated to a professional priesthood had lost its power of growth. It had but one step lower to fall. Having ceased to be practiced to develop beauty, it passed into the keeping of tasteless, superficial professors, who, having enslaved art to vulgar sentiments, in turn easily became the slaves of ignorant patrons, in whose minds utilitarian or egotistical considerations reigned paramount."[34] Architecture, now in the hands of a few privileged practitioners, had lost contact with its natural constituency. In its practitioners' desire for acceptance and success, American architecture had become remote from its natural sources. It was in danger of becoming academic and irrelevant.

Architects were tested at a sufficiently grand scale in Chicago; they had scarcely a decade to habituate themselves to the seductive glimmer of high status and their new respectability. The experience of the rebuilding further refined in strictly American terms techniques imported from abroad. Less than a generation had passed since architects first began to charge on a percentage-of-commission basis, which first established them as serious professionals. Until then they were like any other tradesmen, working at low compensation on an hourly wage. These internal charges went basically unnoticed until architects began to play a visible public role during the final stages of New York's and Boston's extensive rebuilding in the 1850s. These extended opportunities to work provided relief for architects from the country's cyclical boom-or-bust economy. The improved professional climate led to the successful organization of the American Institute of Architects (AIA) in 1857, which in part was established to diminish the negative effect of future market fluctuations. Able to boast only a single chapter, on the East Coast, for its entire first decade, the AIA became a success; it stood in marked contrast to earlier attempts at organization like Ithiel Town's abortive Academy of Fine Arts in New York (1836–37). The AIA's Chicago chapter was founded on December 13, 1869.

More than an improved economic climate allowed the architect to develop a professional identity. The American architect was no longer from the lower classes that the midcentury critics had found so remarkable and full of romantic potential. The professional architect typically came from a more elevated background than the traditional craftsman glorified by Thoreau and Whitman. Relatively well-off, he was less vulnerable to wide economic swings and could accept the romance of artistic mendicancy without having to suffer it in fact. Led by Richard Morris Hunt, a new breed of practitioner emerged, concerned as much with image as with design. President of the AIA's inaugural meeting, Hunt was the first

American to study successfully at the French Ecole des Beaux Arts. Hunt was from a wealthy family, and he enjoyed sufficient distance from the gritty making of money in America to be at ease with the stylish Parisian role of artist-professional. When he returned to the States he imported a tested European manner as well as an architectural system.

The French atelier system was dedicated to the study and production of neoclassical architecture; each architect had his own designers as well as clients. Parisian Beaux Arts style was a postrevolutionary accommodation to the making of money, in which one's bourgeois appetite for material advancement was sheltered safely behind an aristocratic noblesse. Hunt, who could personally afford this conveniently high-minded view of art, also had the foresight to understand that this pose might effectively separate him from the clamoring mob of developers he had left behind in America and was now about to rejoin. He knew that cash in America was not something disdained. In the fever of contemporary deal-making, money in America had attained an independent reality of its own. Great business families were the first popular aristocracies, and the "business blocks" later refined on the streets of Chicago were the new palazzi.

When Hunt returned to New York, he developed his own version of the Parisian independent artist and quickly established a highly profitable atelier. He offered his designers a rigorous architectural apprenticeship combined with professional education which was not yet within the exclusive domain of the universities. Soon he was followed by Henry Hobson Richardson, the second prominent American architect to study at the Beaux Arts. Richardson settled in Boston, where he successfully practiced, stressing the virtues of collaboration. These American adaptations of European practices proved immediately successful, and collaborations like those of William Ware and Henry Van Brunt were founded on similar principles. Prosperous firms in New York, Boston, and Philadelphia were soon established precedents. The same period saw the founding of the first American architectural schools—at the Massachusetts Institute of Technology (1865), Cornell University (1871), and the University of Illinois (1873)—each modeled on European institutions. This desire for professional acceptance culminated in Charles F. McKim's organization of the American Academy in Rome (1897). Americans, like the French, now even had their own Prix de Rome.

Along with these organizational changes came an unwelcome fidelity to easily replicated neoclassical styles. At the time of the fire, the new generation of educated architects was more or less ignorant of native American discussions of an indigenous national architecture. Richardson was the first to break from a strict academic Beaux Arts classicism. His use of the Romanesque employed native rusticated materials and eventually led to thoughtful experiments with massing and space. For Chicago's first generation of professional architects, "modern" meant some contemporary interpretation of Beaux Arts and did not at first imply a rigorous method of its own drawn from the actual on-site conditions. At its best, the permanent reordering of professional architecture in America shattered its stultifying parochialism. In theory it profited by assuming an international character. But in practice, the internationalizing of architecture obscured the particular condition of the American city—more half-baked and chaotic than master-planned Haussmann Paris or any other available European model. By incorporating style, American architects might have temporarily solved their identity crisis, but there was something absurd about it all. Images that comforted the architect bore no relation to the job at hand of permanently rebuilding a city like Chicago.

Provincial architects, sometimes no more than prairie builders, in Benjamin Latrobe's terms, were given a prominence never before imagined. John Van Osdel, William W. Boyington, and Otto Matz were the best of the group that supervised the initial work. Yet the enormous scale of the project guaranteed that Chicago's relative insularity would not continue. Daniel Burnham and John Root joined Peter Wight's new firm; Sullivan, fresh from Frank Furness's office in Philadelphia, went to work for William Le Baron Jenney. The hundreds of others who followed, along with the new immigrant labor, provided Chicago with a raw cosmopolitanism. Architects immediately profited from the attention that contact with an instantly mythic event could bring. The fire provided the situation that encouraged a native architectural practice, which transformed Europeanized affectation into a distinctly American form. A short time after the financial panic ended, in the 1880s when the rebuilding began again in earnest, the necessities of the job overwhelmed the niceties of a "correct style."

*W*ork *at the pace* demanded in Chicago could not be met by individual practitioners or small, informally organized firms. The fire's aftermath supplied all the necessary evidence that the modern practice of architecture must be highly structured. Whatever romantic notions of practice they still retained, Chicago architects to be successful in an atmosphere of uncommon competition had to be businessmen. New York's McKim, Mead, and White, originally modeled on an atelier plan, transferred its partnership to a tripartite organization: an outside man to meet with clients, a production supervisor to oversee the completion of projects, and a principal designer, in whom all of architecture's art and excess were tolerantly left to reside. In Chicago, for economy and ease of decision-making, the tripartite division was characteristically trimmed to two, as in the prominent firms of Adler and Sullivan, Holabird and Roche, and Burnham and Root, which after Root's death was the first architectural firm to be run on a strict corporate model.[35]

Principles of consolidation and specialization were fixed. Significantly, these seemingly necessary organizational divisions of labor between business and art fed the confusion about the nature of American architecture. Given this split between business—the selling and servicing of clients—and production—design and application—architecture could be perceived as a schizophrenic profession with its identity suspended or afloat. While in fact these organizational divisions were often abridged, notably in the active design contributions of Daniel Burnham and Dankmar Adler, their establishment pointed to a strained interdependence of business and art.

More than any other architect who experienced and profited from the fire, Daniel Burnham understood and exploited the American uneasiness with high art. Eventually ensconced in the Rookery, the firm's own commercial palazzo, the office of Burnham and Root came to epitomize modern architectural practice. A contemporary observed: "Here for the first time we saw a large, thoroughly equipped office. It impressed like a large manufacturing plant."[36] This comment was made around the time the Rookery (1886–87), Monadnock (1890–91), and Reliance buildings were being constructed, as Burnham began the preliminary plans for the World's Columbian Exposition. Burnham and Root, later D. H. Burnham and Company, did for the modern office block what the dominant East Coast firms did for public and domestic architecture. Burnham managed a great business and orchestrated his partner's considerable design skills to promote a positive image for his primary client, the American businessman. In turn, close identification with business and businessmen determined the image of architects. Sullivan noted the fact:

"During this period (late 1880s and 1890s) there was well underway the formation of mergers, combinations, and trusts in the industrial world. The only architect in Chicago to recognize the significance of this movement was Daniel Burnham, for in its tendency towards bigness, organization, delegation, and intense commercialism, he sensed the reciprocal workings in his own mind."[37] With the success of his firm, Burnham had completed a process begun by Hunt upon his return from Paris.

With the commercial buildings of the Loop and the White City on the lake, Burnham was able to combine the appealing single-mindedness of a Louis Sullivan with the mock-aristocratic hauteur of a Stanford White. White, who built stylish establishment architecture primarily in the East, was in the words of a contemporary: "Full of whims and flashes, and [he] expected his client to accept them as signs of genius. He could build a building half-way up, decide it didn't please him, tear it down, build it differently, make the owner pay the bills and like it."[38] Unlike White's, Burnham's improvisation on the professional model rarely involved such bluster. Paul Starrett, a builder who had his start as a copyist and later a draftsman in "Uncle Dan's" shop, was in a unique position to judge his technique. He called Burnham the salesman of the team. "He had a magnetic personality. That, combined with his magnificent physique, was a big factor in his success. It was easy to see how he got commissions. His very bearing and looks were half the battle. He had only to assert the most commonplace thing and it sounded important and convincing."[39] Whereas Sullivan's and Wright's intellectual adventures were associated with a radical strain of highbrow populism,[40] Burnham's version of the modern architect existed outside any particular ideology, so as not to disturb the equanimity of potential clients.

Two widely circulated period photographs illustrate role-playing within the profession. The first is a portrait of Richard M. Hunt costumed in an embroidered smock, hooded cape, and leggings. He is posed heavily, flipping through canvases at an easel. Oblivious to self-parody, he is dressed as the early Renaissance painter Cimabue, who to the Beaux Arts architects of the day was seen as the first great neoclassicist. The second is of Daniel Burnham and John Root, sitting across from each other in the library of their offices at the Rookery. Like two buffaloes they sit in front of a large corner fireplace. On the mantle is a reproduction of the Venus de Milo. In these photographs and others, like a later one of Wright with a beret on his head and an overcoat placed rakishly over his

62. H. H. Richardson
in monk's robes
(c. 1888).

shoulders, standing tall in the foreground of a panoramic prairie, the architect desires to dissociate himself from other successful bourgeois. In addition to this often comically self-conscious image-making, distance from any obvious convention was thought to be gained through grafting onto their natural, sturdy conservatism the legends of the few legitimate heroes of the profession and other romantic figures liberally drawn from the history of art. H. H. Richardson gave his Chicago clients as a gift a photograph of himself dressed in a monk's robe, with a faraway look.[41] The earliest instance of this "dressing-up" in Chicago is a portrait photograph in 1872 of stolid P. B. Wight seated next to an open window with a shaft of light illuminating his bearded face. He is dressed in an Eton-style formal jacket and holds a pair of rolled gloves in his right hand. Wearing riding boots and a Tolstoyan hat, he looks ready for the hunt.[42] Fullblown, this grafting or legendizing became a standard operating procedure. A useful myth of the hero developed as a clever countermyth to the profession's real subservience to the marketplace. The fire offered a credible heroic narrative, providing a well-publicized center of activities.

But the memory of the fire and of the city's "intoxicating rawness" in the years that followed had another side that was more unsettling and not necessarily good for business. This was the Chicago that Sullivan and Wright addressed in talks, lectures, and articles, as well as in their architecture. For Sullivan and for Wright, who glorified his liebermeister in *Genius and the Mobocracy*, architecture was not about social acceptance but was about leadership and, inevitably, about cultural criticism. They did not look to the Renaissance for their models, but to the midcentury American intellectuals. In architecture, Sullivan looked no further back than Frank Furness and H. H. Richardson. He saw in the Marshall Field Warehouse a direct and pragmatic building type that was an architectonic transformation of a historic (Romanesque) type. In the work of Jenney and Root, Sullivan also found contemporary support. The importance of these contemporary references was not only architectural; psychologically, they freed him, and later Wright, from the tyranny of the past. Sullivan and Wright could begin to argue convincingly that the heroic generation was not in the time of the Kinzies or earlier, but in the present. They were ultimately freed to become their own authorities. Their poetic ambitions were different versions of Burnham's more traditional path to success. Their translations of literary romantic jargon into architecture must be judged independently of their writings and intentions. However in the end, Hunt's ludicrous posturing as Cimabue and Sullivan's and Wright's gassy rhetoric were not all that different. All reveal an anxiety, almost a panic, over being thought successful in the conventional terms for which the AIA fought. In their minds, architecture was a calling and only secondly a business that they practiced successfully.

The AIA could do the hard, dull work of building up fees and protecting practices, but it could not answer the larger cultural ambitions of a few of its more celebrated members. In effect, two versions of the architect came to maturity after the fire. The most radical was maintained by Wright, who insisted that his success or failure, and that of the small circle he respected, were not to be judged using accepted professional criteria. There is something perverse about Wright's studied imprecision. Architectural language is by definition precise, especially in the working drawings necessary for complex buildings. Wright, habituated to this kind of technical precision, chose to be vague in describing what he and Sullivan did. Wright saw his former employer experimenting with an audacious professional identity that to him seemed infinitely more poetic and rich than the usual talk of his trade. The more accepted professional compromise was associated at the time with Daniel Burnham, who with a nod to the high art on his mantle made the necessary deals to get his projects built. Although formidable and justly celebrated, Burnham made himself easily available to the business community. Capable of executing or sponsoring great work himself, he did not set himself off from the group that sustained him. The key was that he was not so different from the businessmen he served. He was not conflicted about their version of American success. On May 11, 1868, before he settled permanently in Chicago, he wrote in a letter to his mother: "But I shall try to become the greatest architect in the city or country, nothing else will be near the mark I have set for myself. And I am not afraid but that I can become so. There needs but one thing. A determined and persistent effort."[43] There is no discussion here of the kind of architect he wanted to be. He wishes only to succeed, to find a large audience. His attitude was directly contradicted by Wright's idea that architects were first of all artists who could never be fully known. Always, at least in part, their work remained larger than life and removed from life. Wright saw Sullivan as a martyr to these principles and suggested that he was so great because he was ineffable. "In the heart of him he was of infinite value to the countrymen who wasted him not because they would: but because *they could not know him.*"[44]

When architects finally received the national attention they craved, they were divided over the nature of their profession, caught between the lure of great commissions and the ideologues who consistently argued against professional expediency. These conflicting aspects were exemplified by two major Chicago practitioners: Burnham, who was accessible and matter-of-fact; and Sullivan, who represented all that was excluded from traditional practice and was so advanced that he was naturally obscure and difficult to understand. Sullivan liked to believe that although businessmen commissioned his buildings he was building for the anonymous and disenfranchised general population dramatically made visible during the fire. But they too, now relatively prosperous themselves, abandoned the Loop to the new homeless and indigent and flocked to Burnham's White City or to the Midway to seek their architectural "emanation." Sullivan's own contribution to the fair was his Transportation Building. Its great polychrome plaster doorway, in an exuberant Moorish-Romanesque style, ornamented a conventional shed located off the main Court of Honor. The deliberately retrograde structure abandoned the Crystal Palace-type use of steel and glass that he and Adler had successfully employed years earlier, in an exposition space (1885). The tarted-up entry to a functional loft was Sullivan's enervated protest of the fair's dominant neoclassicism. He employed his own commission to remind Burnham and the others of the old Chicago eclecti-

63. Louis Sullivan, Transportation Building Golden Doorway. World's Columbian Exposition.

cism—which had dominated the city before and immediately after the fire—and of how easy it was to fall back again into pastiche. His *Autobiography of an Idea* and Wright's *Genius and the Mobocracy* are ironic settlings of blame not only on the architectural establishment but on the people of Chicago, who chose surface flash over the oracular obscurities of Sullivan's and Wright's predominantly nonhistoricist modern design. Wright understood that the problem went deep when one was an artist in fact and not only in affect. "I am branded as an 'Artist' architect, and so under suspicion by my countrymen—and especially since I have been an 'insurgent' in private life as well as in my work; and my hair is not short nor my clothes so utterly conventional as to inspire confidence in the breast of the good American Business Man that I am a good 'business proposition'." [45]

Burnham's point of view and style of practice prevailed. Any aggrandizing myth was fine as long as it did not interfere with business. Hunt's form of dressing up was acceptable because it was in private. Sullivan and Wright's exaggerated sense of theater was more troubling. They did it all the time; their posturings were fundamental to their imagination. They were finally radicals who risked their own careers to challenge the smug alliance between commerce and art. By the turn of the century both were in exile from working in Chicago. Their versions of Furness's "divine fanaticism," combined with uncompromising personalities, landed them outside the relatively enlightened cultural consensus of Chicago and Oak Park.

In the winter of 1885, at the first meeting of the Illinois State Association of Architects (ISAA), Dankmar Adler sounded more practical than his impetuous partner. He agitated for state licensing and reform of the federal contract system for hiring architects. At this same inaugural session, Burnham urged code changes and alterations in the rules governing competitions. Both he and Adler were adhering to the national AIA line; they were concerned first with maintaining a proper commercial persona and aspired to nothing more dramatic than being considered reliable by their clients. Adler declared, "I believe in a business community like this; it is a body that appears to have money that is respected."[46] There is no suggestion here of his partner Sullivan's spiritual invocation of a people and culture seeking architectural expression. Adler's concerns were more fundamental. He knew that architects would not significantly share in American prosperity until they demonstrated a desire and "ability to earn money."[47] The turn towards conservatism, predictably championed by Burnham and more surprisingly by Adler, was enthusiastically endorsed by the convention delegates. Once independent and radical, the ISAA joined the federated AIA in 1887, a year after Chicago's Haymarket Riot.

The struggle for a unique professional identity ended in compromise. Most working architects settled for broad public acceptance. This brief period of self-examination had a natural conclusion in Burnham's architectural organization of the world's fair. He managed a playful recreation of the frantic building that had followed the fire. Architects, again mostly imported from the outside, could show off their skills in buildings that were not meant to stand once the fair was over. Like Burnham's later grandiose Chicago Plan of 1909, the fair was a huge stage set hugging the lake. People would live in neither of these fantasized cities; they were dreamscapes. One was never built, and the other burned down like the confectionary architecture of 1871.

The intense building activity around the time of the fair also made a few think back to that less happy time. Sullivan linked the contemporary professional conservatism to the difficulty of finding an appropriate form to express anything less affirmative than the secular religion of progress. Was his position so different from Jenney's when he was first approached with the task of memorializing the fire? Sullivan attempted a summation: "We are at that dramatic moment in our national life wherein we tremble between decay and evolution, and our architecture, with strange fidelity, reflects this equipoise."[48] The architect was caught in the middle, the nearest link between the remote fine arts and America's action art, business. A period that began in 1871 with Chicago as a self-promoting western metropolis ended with the century, with its architects at the center of the architectural world.

Wright's Piano
Imagining the New Chicago

Gary Cooper, as Howard Roark in the movie version of *The Fountainhead*, played the American architect as he wished to be known. Ayn Rand manipulated real professional quarrels into a modern morality play in which the artist's will is raised above every idea of the common good. The novel provided an often unglamorous business with a kitsch identity. While visionaries like Sullivan and Wright are widely thought to be Ayn Rand's models, it was in Daniel Burnham's dominance that she found support for her oddball theories of the effectual creative man. The uneasy mix of petulance and entrepreneurial savvy in Howard Roark's character was an acknowledgment of the Burnham-like professional style that she had observed personally, on a smaller scale, as a secretary in the New York office of Ely Jacques Kahn. To her mind, the career of a great architect had two distinct phases: a youthful rebellious stage followed in early maturity by professional dominance. It is a formula for "genius." After great conflict, the "true" artist gets his way. She appropriated the frustrated heroics of Sullivan and Wright for Roark, who at novel's end designs the world's tallest building (like Wright's mile-high skyscraper). Roark gets the girl, his criminality in blowing up his own building is forgotten, and his power in the city is assured. In Ayn Rand's world, artistic excess is cleverly separated from its usual accompaniment of social scorn and is given grudging universal acclaim. In reality, Burnham developed a far more efficient and less conflicted approach to practice.

Unable to pass the entrance exams for Harvard or Yale, Daniel Burnham came to Chicago lacking the establishment architectural education common to his generation. Burnham's school was Chicago. He was not so different by reason of formal education or style from the city's original settlers; he had had his own flirtation with pioneering in Nevada. Peter Wight described the young Burnham when he came to work for him during the winter of 1872–73: "He was then twenty-six years of age. He was introduced to our firm by his father, the late Edwin Burnham, one of the early settlers of Chicago, who had retired from the wholesale drug trade at the time of the Fire and was very desirous that Dan should be cured of his roving disposition and continue the study of architecture. . . . We were busy trying to rebuild the burned city."[1] His first biographer, Charles Moore, said of him: "He was never so much a businessman that he was not also an artist. He felt as an artist, thought as an artist, and when he came up against his limitations in knowledge or as a creator, he never failed to recognize those qualities in others."[2] Wright had a different point of view. He thought of Burnham as a dictator whose genius resided in organization and not in the formal discipline of architecture. Wright complained in letters that Burnham "dominates everything that he has to do with . . . he is willing to take your ideas with no credit to you."[3] Knowledgeable in the ways of the city, Burnham demonstrated the qualities that made the working artist socially acceptable. He reassured those with money who were interested in investing in Chicago that architects could work with businessmen. He and John Root, as principal designer, raised the social status of the utilitarian business block, which had been formulated and meticulously executed by Jenney as early as the Portland Block (1872), itself a refinement in elevation and plan of Otto Matz's prefire Nixon Building (1871). In time, using all available technologies, Burnham and Root further refined several of their own efforts, notably in the Montauk (1881–82), a dramatic explosion of scale with more sensitive and ordered massing than the Nixon Building. The Rookery demonstrates that the collection of these refinements created its own form. A spacious light court, an open lobby, the modern tracery of the swooping staircases (later renovated by Wright)—all give the impression of something grand, but always as a working part of the city's daily life. It is a French department store in plan, dedicated to work.[4] In Chicago, the culmination of all this lavish attention to business can be seen in the elegant public space of the old Railway Exchange Building (1903–4), which was flooded with light from a huge central atrium and the moonlight white skin of the cladding. Holabird and Roche's work followed this lead, particularly in the Marquette Building (1893–94) with its historical murals in the entry hall that inevitably link the earlier romantic period of western exploration to the workaday world of business.

Burnham's success in containing the opposing tendencies of architecture produced immediate results. He perfected commercial architecture and provided developers an Americanized version of French master planning, which he employed successfully across the country from Washington, D.C., to San Francisco. With his ability to fuse his own organizational skills and keen eye for design, with extraordinary designers like Root and later Charles Atwood, he created a new social type. The incorporated artist was Burnham's special improvisation. His appetite for influence extended to offering to pay Wright's way to Paris so he could study at the Ecole des Beaux Arts. Burnham viewed the young architect, newly estranged from his apoplectic mentor and seemingly content in Oak Park, to be a good investment risk. Wright made a point of mentioning this offer in his autobiography and drew the expected moral. Three years in Paris and two in Rome for Wright and his family, to study classical architecture at the source, might convert him not simply to a form of academic architecture which Burnham was certainly years away from himself, but to a style of practice. Reflecting later on Burnham's offer, Wright remembered: "I felt the weight of the occasion. I saw myself influential, prosperous, safe; saw myself a competent leader of the majority rule. That much faith I had in it all. There would be no doubt about that, with Daniel H. Burnham's power behind me. . . . It was all so definitely set, too easy and unexciting as I saw it."[5] At least in later years, Wright inherited Sullivan's contempt for the fair's neoclassicism and viewed Burnham as betraying the new Chicago, represented by the best of the Loop and by Wright's own work in the suburbs. At the same time he acknowledged "Uncle Dan's" central place in the profession and sensed that he had defined the most successful route to practice.

While Wright's later polemics are instructive, his architectural response to Burnham's suggested incorporation was even more dramatic. In 1893, Wright built an addition to his own house in Oak Park, a playroom to accommodate his growing family. The barrel-vaulted room opens up off a severely compressed entrance from a short stairway. A romantic mural on the far wall by Giannini, a local artist, portrays an Egyptian youth seated in the sand, looking out to the sea. In the sky, a god hovers with wings spread wider than the picture plane, looking at a distance like an abstract rendering of one of the architect's pieces of furniture. The pagan scene

64. Playroom of Frank
Lloyd Wright House,
Oak Park (1893).

65. Bedroom of Frank
Lloyd Wright House,
Oak Park. Note the
half-circular, romantic
mural, like that of the
playroom.

offering the promise of future flight or escape dominates the rooted security of the hearth. This end of the room provides a graphic representation of the sort of contradiction asserted by the architect's manipulation of Victorian space in his domestic architecture: he blew out interior walls but kept the central hearth as a primal reminder of architecture's ultimate appeal to stability. These open spaces and the bookcase-framed hearth are surviving emblems of Wright's truncated Oak Park period. In his own home, Wright, the domesticated artist, worked in a small downstairs room until he completed a separate studio in 1895. As he worked, the children played under the supervision of his domineering mother. Wright's tenure as suburban pater familias ended for good when he took off to Europe with one of his client's wives in 1909, living out the very conflict suggested by the art on his wall.

Frank Lloyd Wright's skill at scandalizing society extended to his architecture. In a single gesture, over a decade before he left respectable Oak Park forever, Wright demonstrated his contempt for artistic niceties. While the mural in the playroom that terminates the axis can be thought of as overly romantic or excessive, it was only a slightly idiosyncratic ver-

66. Frank Lloyd Wright Studio, Oak Park.

sion of the kind of kitsch narrative art found in the city at the time. Yet on the near side of the tunnellike room, in an intensely focused architectural move, Wright took a baby grand piano and pushed it through the wall, making the instrument's underside a surreal canopy for the staircase underneath. The room, ostensibly designed as a child's place to play, reveals the inherent tensions of modern family life and the sometimes violent struggles of the artist. Even a room designed by his own hand cannot discipline all the contradictions. Here the imagination literally breaks through the wall. It is not monumental and used to glorify power, but wild and in advance of any appropriate form to contain it.

Wright's act of defiance, along with his refusal of Burnham's patronage, are part of the first-generation drama that helped define the architect as a major social player in Chicago after the fire. Burnham's model of accommodation to business and Sullivan's and Wright's histrionic rejections created a general interest in architects that went beyond narrower professional conflicts. The architect and the businessman, along with the city they were seen to shape, became the subjects of a new urban literature. Caught between the practical necessity to build Chicago's empire of ego and his own conflicted sense of profession, the architect was a convenient vehicle for any modern critique of the city.

Architects found themselves in a mad scramble to build big and tall, to create a permanent style legendizing their commercial patrons. Even a "pure" artist like Louis Sullivan appreciated the irony: "I see the realities. I am of the new generation. . . . there is only one thing any pair of eyes can see with absolute certainty nowadays, and that is the DOLLAR. To deny its reality, to refuse to worship, means ruin." [6] The "father of the skyscraper" unwillingly confesses: "It is not my purpose to discuss the social conditions. I accept them as fact." [7]

Thomas Cole's five-panel allegory *The Course of Empire* (1836), painted around the time of Chicago's incorporation, contains a powerful notion that applied to events later in the century. Cole linked the idea of ruin to America's obsession with progress. Less than three generations old, America already bore a stronger resemblance to Imperial Rome than to Winthrop's righteous "city upon a hill." Influenced by Italian and French period paintings, Cole took the subject of rise and fall popularized by Gibbon not as sentimental reflection but as prophecy. He was concerned with the moral and environmental effects of the ceaseless push west. *The Course of Empire*

moralizes the American relation to the land the way later urban melodramas would criticize the city for its corruption of youth and the misuse of capital. The first painting romanticizes "The Savage State." The second, "The Pastoral State," states the land is to be valued as a thing in itself, and not as a product. In "The Consummation of Empire," the third painting, a hedonistic scene goes on against a background of stately Roman buildings. Using Gibbon's formula, Cole follows this allegory of success (the architecture of which is remarkably close to Daniel Burnham's neoclassical Court of Honor) with "Destruction," which presents a battlefield version of the previous perspective. "Desolation," the final painting, shows these same noble buildings further in ruin.

Painting ruins was something of a cult raised to a fine art in Italy and France, and practiced most notably by Piranesi and Volney. But European painted ruins were fundamentally different from the subject Cole offered his American audience. For Europeans, old buildings in decay were safe objects of curiosity fit for romantic painting or poetic meditation, like Wordsworth's "Lines Written Above Tintern Abbey" (1798). Cole was imagining ruins where none existed, incorporating a European subject, like many a contemporary, while understanding that for Americans ruins were not comfortably in the past, but if anything foreshadowed a tragic future. Look again at "Destruction" and "Desolation," keeping in mind the Civil War photographs by George N. Barnard, Mathew Brady

67. Thomas Cole, *The Course of Empire*, 1: "The Savage State."

or Timothy O'Sullivan, or those anonymous images of Chicago after the fire. The American ruin did not produce a delicious melancholy but a specter of approaching failure.

Conflicts implied by architecture were further explored in period fiction. For a city that had witnessed its own destruction, every new building, sitting on a formerly charred site, harbored the suggestion of its own ruin. In detailed descriptions of these buildings, impersonal melodramatic plots meet perfunctorily the novel's inner narrative. The best of the genre, Henry Blake Fuller's *The Cliff-Dwellers* (1893), begins as a profile of a new kind of building, the modern business block, that replaced the church after the fire as Chicago's most prominent type of structure. Buildings like the Clifton displaced nature in the new America; a language still full of natural imagery describes how fundamental this displacement was. An orthogonal or right-angled geometry replaces organic nature. "Each of the canyons is closed in by a long frontage of towering cliffs, and these soaring walls of brick and limestone and granite rise higher with each succeeding year, according as the work of erosion at their bases goes onward. . . ."[8] Fuller registers the daunting human effect of these radical changes of scale, of the increasing height of buildings, by measuring them against their shadow, the deformation or canyon they create at street level. William Dean Howells praised this aspect of Chicago literature by recalling its "wonderful directness," where the common "level struck

69. Thomas Cole, *The Course of Empire*, 3: "The Consummation of Empire."

is low: the level of the street."[9]

Fuller's ambition was to write a whole novel about a building like the Clifton, in all of its aspects, "complete within itself."[10] He wanted to escape the conventions of contemporary popular fiction by letting only the conditions he directly observed determine the narrative. His plan works for the initial chapters, until the fiction is overwhelmed by the kind of automatic writing he had done in his first two books. Unable to sustain the larger analysis, he was still able in bursts to suggest the kind of book he might have written had he a greater gift. He presented a compelling idea, intuiting that the true contemporary novel had to be set in the city and needed to provide a countermyth to the Whig politics of blissful progress.

Ruin in the new American city need not arrive again in sudden cataclysmic events, but is the ubiquitous condition of daily life. The American city is continuously "eroding." Fuller reflects: "Modern man marks the earth with ruin in a thorough-going fashion that the poet, who wrote before the invention of the locomotive, could hardly have dreamed of. We take our pleasures as brutally as we satisfy our needs."[11] The relentless building cycle of demolition and construction makes time and place tentative, a sometimes shocking world of endless digging, dark canyons, and skyscraper-eclipsed light. The same buildings that glorify the skyline are set in holes the size of meteor craters. Fuller wished to write a

70. Thomas Cole, *The Course of Empire,* 4: "Destruction."

history of the "four-thousand souls" who daily inhabit the eighteen-story skyscraper—a history of the new urban America, a "heterogeneous tribe." The building is a microcosm of the country. "It includes bankers, capitalists, lawyers, 'promoters'; brokers in bonds, stocks, pork, oil, mortgages; real-estate people and railroad people and insurance people—life, fire, marine, accident; a host of principals, agents, middlemen, clerks, cashiers, stenographers, and errand-boys; and the necessary force of engineers, janitors, scrub-women, and elevator hands."[12] It is as if the Clifton were the last stop west, and thousands of pioneers had all to settle on a single hundred-by-hundred square of the grid. Despite their evident success, this heterogeneous group of settlers has landed in an oddly inhospitable, dry, and increasingly dark place: "This country is a treeless country—if we overlook the 'forest of chimneys' comprised in a bird's-eye view of any great city, and if we are unable to detect any botanical analogies in the lofty articulated iron funnels whose ramifying cables reach out wherever they can, to fasten whatever they can, to fasten whatever they may. . . . It is a shrubless country . . . an arid country . . . an airless country. . . . For here the medium of sight, sound, light, and life becomes largely carbonaceous, and the remoter peaks of this mighty yet unprepossessing landscape loom up grandly, but vaguely, through swathing mists of coal-smoke."[13] Fuller's Chicago is

the model for Fitzgerald's "valley of ashes," a place where nothing grows.

71. Thomas Cole, *The Course of Empire*, 5: "Desolation."

In Robert Herrick's *The Common Lot* (1904), Cole's promise of ruin is tied to a specific example of jerry-built architecture, a firetrap built from two sets of plans. The one filed with the building department meets all specifications, while the other, given to the contractors, cuts corners for quick profits. It resembles the buildings John Root saw self-destruct during his first years in Chicago. "There wasn't any steel in the bloody box, it was rotten cheese."[14] Herrick's *The Web of Life* (1900) also ties the city's fate to the fragility of architecture, corruptibility of architects, and inevitability of disaster. The story is set around the time an arsonist successfully set fire to the few standing buildings on the grounds of the Columbian Exposition, July 5, 1894—the Great Fire redux. This time the primary victims were some of the city's army of homeless, who were forced out of makeshift homes in the fair's ticket booths and the shells of other "temporary" buildings. But the event was quickly adopted as a more general tragedy that once again might be turned to advantage. "The fire—that was the one great thing—the fire was life itself."[15] In Will Payne's *Mr. Salt* (1904), a character views the fire at the fair site as a necessary part of Chicago's development: "It was splendid whatever it was . . . (a splendid) picture of destruction . . . the end of the old order."[16] Before 1894 was out, H. H. Van Meter published an illustrated commemorative poem, *The Vanishing Fair*. He, too, recalls the 1871 disaster:

> When the world beheld with pity,
> As the fiery cyclones flame,
> Swept across our smitten city—
> Then began its greater fame—
> So now may it swept by sorrow
> Rise to greater grander good.

In this populist vein, the poet recalls the violence of the Great Fire, which momentarily at least interrupted prevailing oligarchies and provided the formerly excluded with brief opportunities of their own. The fire, along with the raging Pullman strike, would make us begin "cursing those who count their millions." Ruin in Chicago, seen in the city's great tests and in its daily "erosion," was still firmly linked in the popular imagination with recovery, not with Cole's brooding. In the words of the poet:

> As we stand above the ashes
> of the fairest scenes of time
> May each fiery flame that flashes
> Light to visions more sublime.[17]

The architect raises a monument to ambition, only to have nature or greed reclaim the work, in a constant reflexive drama of glory and defeat. Employing the architect as a stock character whose actions are set against the background of Chicago's actual experience with such cycles, the novelist imagines the city. In these early naturalistic urban novels, building takes the place of sod-busting in the literature of the open prairie. The architect carries some of the same ambivalent associations that the gentleman pioneer held for Cooper, and he is tested by the city like those before him were by the wilderness. Entering modern Chicago for the first time is a challenge for a young adventurer. In Will Payne's *The Money Captain* (1895), the city looms in the distance as "an enormous blotch of smoke."[18] Despite its attempt to redeem, even the new architecture seems to add to the city's primal condition. Even the great Monadnock affects the neophyte as a "gigantic projection of a mud fence."[19] The new post office under construction is a Dantesque scene of digging: "Far below the street level, in the enormous clayey pit, steam engines hissed and pile drivers struck grunting blows. There floated faintly up to the clatter and clangor of the street the cries of teamsters and overseers as a hundred men toiled at the muddy beginnings of the great structure."[20] Architecture in the making or prematurely aging, encrusted with "imperial dirt and decay," is contrasted with the shining surfaces of a building on La-Salle Street with "glistening granite walls."[21] The architect is critical to this process, since he designed and fit on the city's skin. He entered American fiction in Chicago not as Ayn Rand's effectual hero but as a dandy, radical mostly in rhetoric. Caught between business and art, his very ambivalence was a key to survival in the new city.

The architect in this literature represents a larger urban type. Like Henry James's new woman, he is a direct beneficiary of the new American city. Not an aristocrat in background, he is most commonly a second-generation scion of an already successful family who views his professional success as a logical next step in the family's economic development. His soul is at risk in the late nineteenth-century morality play featuring the aspiring professional as pilgrim. It is a modification of the Puritan "captivity narrative," in which a young white woman, taken prisoner by the Indians and exposed to paganism, is ever-resistant; upon payment of a ransom, she returns to civilization, but never acknowledges any loss of "purity." Wright alluded to this age-old American tension between piety and the imagination in the Oak Park playroom. He finally yielded to it when he eloped with Mrs. Cheney, and then spent a good part of his early career in Europe, Japan, and the wilds of Los Angeles. The difference was that Wright never effectively returned from "captivity." His fictional counterparts always do. In the Chicago variation on this traditional narrative form, the reprobate is not captured by the Indians but by bohemian notions of art and license. He lives together in happy squalor with others of the tribe in places known as the "Warren Block" or the "hutch," only to return, not to Christian piety, but to fiscal responsibility and the "Temple of Art," where once again he can put his faith in the demonstrated grace of progress and good social connections.

In two novellas, "The Downfall of Abner Joyce" and "Little O'Grady vs. the Grindstone," collected in *Under the Skylights* (1901), Fuller observed the architect as the most visible of midwestern artists. As Robert Herrick also noted, he is at home in the new city because his "roots rarely go deep"; he appears undistracted by "men and women . . . (who) are somewhat hard and metallic in their nature." In the city, where an "American of almost any type stands like an alien," he has a traditional education, but must be able to improvise from his education on the streets.[22] Fuller studied his contemporaries but he knew the difficulties, as did Herrick, who complained, "Modern life, especially in our America, is too immediate, too confusing for us adequately to judge the material."[23]

Given these conditions, men and women who try to accommodate themselves to the city use sanctified ideas of art and culture as ballast against the unknown. Stephen Giles is Fuller's principal example of the artist on the make. He views his work as a commodity, holding a "middle ground between the 'artist-architects' on the one hand and the painters on the other and with this advantageous footing he was gradually drawing a strong cordon round 'society'."[24] Giles's willingness to please is seen in contrast to Abner Joyce's pious desire to be a pure artist; Joyce, modeled on Hamlin Garland, is the one who fails. Giles, not Joyce, understands the city, where one's success is measured in physical terms by progress on the grid from the seedy lofts of the Warren Block to the rarified salons at the Temple of Art. While the Temple signifies power and money, the Warren Block is the object of considerable affection, a place transformed, given character, by the poor artists who work there. The "bunnies" in their "warren" work in an authentic middle ground where the architecture exists in conformity with the lives it shelters rather than as an intimidating object set apart. But precisely its gritty authenticity allows it to assume a value that can be traded; the Warren is a target for cultural poaching of the kind that many years later transformed Soho in New York City from a legitimate place for the production of art to a trendy place for its sale.

Stephen Giles is busy designing a house for Mrs. Potter Pence, after she found him at the "hutch." A wife of a robber baron, she went there to find someone authentically bohemian but not hostile, who could build a properly dignified setting for her things. For her and her niece, Clytie Summers, artists are spiritual, like missionaries, but easier to seduce. Giles, who began his career after reading Emerson, ends it as a builder like Clytie's father. Giles is a midwestern Heraclitus who sees the world in constant change; "even the neighborhoods get spoiled before they are half put together."[25] He is endlessly adaptable, always fitting in between, not resisting like Abner, whose process of "ruralizing" prevents him from accepting Chicago's dominance over the countryside. Abner's sort of visionary artist gets it all wrong and is comically out of touch. He moralizes pathetically: "Oh, the cities. . . . They are passing. . . . They are disintegrating by their own bulk like a big snowball. And by their own badness. People are rolling back to the country—the country they came from."[26]

Consolidations and trusts were the city's most sophisticated art. Sensing this, Fuller followed the rise and fall of a typical Chicago cartel. Chicagoans view painters, writers, and "artist-architects" the way John Kinzie viewed Juliette, sensing that an arranged marriage between business and art is the only way to soften the former and toughen the latter. For their part, through their growing associations with the rich, artists of the Warren Block find glamour and success dazzling. "The pomp and luxury of plutocracy inwrapped him."[27] A city struggling to achieve a prosperous image for itself requires an architect, a "moderately old young man" to make it over.[28]

"O'Grady" opens with a declaration by Andrew Hill, vice president of the Grindstone Bank, that he needs someone to design a new building. He soon reviews the plans of an ambitious designer competing for the commission: "The new Grindstone of all the Temples of Finance within the town, was to be the most impressive, the most imposing, the most unmitigatedly monumental. The bold young architect had loftily renounced all economies of space, time, material, and had imagined a grandiose facade with a long colonnade of polished blue-granite pillars, a pompous attic story above, and a wide flight of marble steps below. The inside was to be quite as overbearingly classical as the outside. There was to be a sort of arched and columned court under a vast prismatic skylight; lunettes, spandrels, friezes, and the like were to abound; and the opportunities for interior decoration were to be lavish, limitless."[29] This delectation of things adheres to Burnham's new classical style but pointedly excludes a specific rendering of the city's achievements and failures, a way to relate its own story. A larger subject needs to be found to fit within the modish classical frame that is a "real achievement for our city."[30]

The bankers go off to the "hutch" in search of an artist to tell their story. Fuller's tiresome plot reveals two factions competing for the commission. The first is led by Daffingdon Dill, the chief artist of the high salon, the Temple of Art. He and a rich patron arrive at a scheme that they call Hymns to Progress, the main aim of which is to celebrate the great city while avoiding any reference to the "odious architecture of the primitive prairie town."[31] In fact, like Jenney's second scheme, their proposal avoids all specific references to Chicago. Set in white neoclassical architecture it, too, means to be timeless and universal. Dill chooses a neutral display of colors—shades of purple and olive—to decorate the twelve large lunettes without being "pictorial" or making his work "mere literature."[32] However, he finds it impossible to be completely disengaged. To these abstractions he begins to append evocative titles but soon gets bored, naming his blobs of color "The Genius of the City" and something called "Emerging . . . ," but never completing the thought. Fuller is aware of the problem of developing an iconography for modern Chicago without allowing for its actual history. Dill gives it one last try, "The Triumphal March of Progress Through our . . ." and is defeated again by vagueness. His patron (and lover) Virginia mercifully, if blandly and without inspiration, finishes the thought with "Our Midst."[33] But even these airy allegorical subjects are not sufficiently distant from the city. Her final suggestion is for a "history of banking" beginning with the Lombards of Italy.

O'Grady, a marginal artist, and his cohorts do not do much better. He and the "brilliant" immigrant painter Ignace Prochow are vague in their own way when they propose another abstract parable of progress. Theirs is a hymn to science and democracy. Both sides consider themselves modern, or more accurately, in fashion, because they avoid the Queen Anne solecisms of the prefire city. While Prochow wants to work with new forms and heave "history, tradition, legend into the furnace" he is as unsuccessful as Dill in satisfying the commission.[34] After looking at both proposals Andrew Hill declares, "To hell with art . . . what I wanted to do was advertise my business."[35] The artist in this sort of urban art does not even own his canvas.

Ironically, Chicago's artists were all left with the same dilemma. As "O'Grady" suggests, they were driven into abstraction by the lack of consensus over an appropriate narrative. The architect was simply asked to erect a billboard or a frame to advertise his patron. His patrons required a Roman history of the kind perfected by the first Caesar, in which all the negatives are safely edited out so that the story of triumph can proceed. Chicago had a moment of such manic clarity when Bross and others wrote those instant histories of the city immediately after the fire. However, the great unifying cataclysm receded and a usable social consensus evaporated until it became impossible to find a perfectly edited narrative to display on the walls of the city's great buildings. Modern architecture's fall into severe abstraction and its abandonment of ornamentation had its roots in Chicago of the last two decades of the nineteenth century. O'Grady returns to the Grindstone "to see the fatal placard [declaring bank failure] fastened on one of the Grindstone's great polished columns, and then tramped on down the avenue of ruin with the step and

progress is once again confronted by the reality of cyclical
ruin, the one narrative that no artist yet feels free to paint.

Neither artistically independent nor able to please his patrons,
the architect, initially portrayed as a sophisticated outsider, is
quickly compromised in the literature of the period. Through
him, uncertain urban realists could begin to write about aspects of the new urban culture they had trouble fully drama-
tizing. The architect is useful to register Chicago's effect on
the most conscious members of the old elites. A strong sense
of the dislocation experienced by the old families can be
found in Henry James's *The American Scene*. Returning from
his prolonged expatriation in 1904, James wrote defensively
about his "dispossession." A city of immigrants and unnatur-
alized new arrivals, of the kind championed by Jacob Riis and
Jane Addams, holds only terror for him. He longs for his own
kind of White City as he "tumbles back into the streets in appalled reaction from them, that the art of beguiling or duping
it became an art to be cultivated—though the fond alternative
vision was never long to be obscured, the imagination, exas-
perated to envy, of the ideal, in the order in question; of the
luxury of some such close and sweet and whole national consciousness as that of the Switzer and the Scot."[37] James remembered the "luxury" of a recent time when the faces were
all white and the only language on the street was English.

A small group of Chicago writers attempted something the
master disdained. Dissatisfied with viewing the American
city only from a distance, they took it with all its foreignness
as a given, using the architect as a white adventurer, an urbanaut launched into the unknown. In their novels, he is the
wandering WASP, "an alert, modern American," who has
traveled the world only to settle in Chicago for the adven-
ture.[38] Returning home from Florence, a Chicagoan recalled
the shock and exhilaration: "I came back to Chicago, of all
places you say. Yes, to Chicago, to see this brutal whirlpool as
it spins and spins. It has fascinated me I admit, and I stay
on—to live among the chimneys, hanging out over the cornice of a twelve-story building; to soak myself in the steam
and smoke of the prairie and in the noises of a city's commerce."[39] The device of the returning grand tourer provides
the writer with a brief opportunity to observe and record
without immediately moralizing about what he sees. Like a
nineteenth-century Englishman in India or Burma, the reac-

culturated midwesterner quickly moves from amused or titillated observation to considerable involvement in a culture he had come to instruct. He is a foreigner at home; his class privilege and armored sensibility prove useless as his soul is taken over. Soon he is trading in the local currency where his art is "only good when it succeeds. It doesn't live unless it can succeed in pleasing people, in making money." [40] Henry Blake Fuller's Tom Bingham in *With the Procession* and Mr. Atwater in *The Cliff-Dwellers,* Jackson Hart in Robert Herrick's *The Common Lot,* and Sidney Bane in Will Payne's *Jerry the Dreamer* (1896) are all architects with high pedigrees.

After ten years in Europe, five studying architecture, Sidney Bane returns rich and polished to Chicago. His high opinion of himself is echoed by others, and he is viewed by the aboriginal generation as least likely to disturb the progress made by the "knotty-fisted, hard-headed" yankees who settled the city before the recent "anarchist time" of labor strikes and immigrant agitation. [41] Also he appears to be like them because he too can make "something out of nothing—a good deal out of nothing." [42] Judge House, one of the city's established social climbers, considers him an agreeable mate for his beautiful daughter Georgia, through whom he hopes to continue his little dynasty. Secure in his office at the Rookery, Bane practices his hauteur as he prepares "to undertake that serious pretence of being an architect of warehouses and skyscrapers." [43] But the refined social skin that the judge and his daughter find so appealing has already been shed. Bane comes to Chicago to try a place where he too can be a hustler, even if it is hustling "of a graceful and dignified sort." [44] The architect is caught in a conflict of expectations. To the dying old settlers he is the avatar of high culture come to give the city some class and tame the "hideous monster" of the Loop. [45] To Sidney Bane, the city offers a compelling liberation from the conventions of high art in which he had been trained, a place to be bad and go native, using his considerable education and charm as commodities. This he accomplishes with mixed results.

Bane's education is just beginning in Chicago. A white, native-born American, he is increasingly the outsider. The Chicago that spreads out before him is impossible to euphemize or reclaim without creating another "whiter" version of itself, like the one that had recently glorified Jackson Park. To Georgia House, the city is a nightmare where the "unfinished skeletons" of buildings under construction "overwhelmed the lake." She is lost in a place that changes faster than her ability to adapt. Henry Adams noted the problem when he visited the city on his way to the fair. He could discover no unity in the chaos. These were not people he recognized or understood, with their annoying accents and strange appearance. Payne describes: "Scores of workmen scrawled, sat, ran, climbed, hammered, soldered over the great bare steel beams, careless of the hundred feet sheer down to the pavement. Over the whole bird's-eye prospect here and there vast buildings—fifteen, eighteen stories high—shouldered up above the common pack."[46] Strange people are everywhere, building this great mechanical city on the lake. Payne wanted to write about the "common pack," but could only observe it from above; the architect who built the city and was sometimes down in the pack was as close as he could get.

Robert Herrick's *The Common Lot* was the first novel to feature an architect as the central character. It is *The Fountainhead* free of the heroic myth. Where Howard Roark implausibly resists convention, does things his own way, and is vindicated in the end, Herrick's Jackson Hart moves deeper into compromise, remaining sufficiently corrupt to stay afloat in a foul town. In *The Common Lot* the architect is neither superior to the culture nor a critic of it. Those who separate themselves by way of class or sensibility are eventually leveled. Hart is never triumphant; he has to slink back to his first employer, a large firm led by a man like himself "who had fallen upon a commercial age and not been large enough to sway it."[47] Far from leading, the architect is caught in the scramble for quick gain. "The professions have been commercialized," and a young man like Hart can only succeed by following those with money.[48]

Jackson Hart's disappointing experience with Chicago is played against the legacy of the first generation, which had had raw energy but little polish. Understanding the deficiency, Powers Jackson, a patriarch in the style of Judge House, leaves part of his estate to his nephew Hart. His expectations are that the young architect, who has studied at Cornell and MIT, would have the proper tools and style to be a pioneer in the new city, as he was in the old city. Safely resting in his "ugly tomb, in the American Greek style, with heavy capitals and squat pillars,"[49] Jackson has left the younger man to fight the second-generation battle to "make our strong young cities memorable."[50] Hart's first impressions of Chicago are of a "dull, dirty city."[51] He views his job as a fight to halt Chicago's slide away from received opinions of taste. He argues that the Loop's stripped tall buildings are already superannuated, the "hills of the new world," but part of only a "first chapter," a brief period of raw invention before a sober return to neoclassicism.[52] Hart applauds Burnham's Court of Honor and views it as the architecture of the future.

However, after two years in the city, having been cheated out of most of his inheritance because of his uncle's late bequest to a workingman's charity, Hart begins to drown. His effete education is useless when he is forced to share the common lot. From his club, high above the crowd, Hart looks down at Chicago like a condemned man dangling over the pit: "Below, from the busy street, rose the piercing note of the city,—rattle, roar, and clang,—scarcely less shrill at eight of an evening than at noon. From the bulkheads on the roof of the next building soared a drab-colored cloud of steam, eddying upwards." Hart tries to remain aloof but is finally affected, drawn by the force outside. The city he chose to lead and shape instead shapes him. "The noise, the smell, the reek of the city touched the man, folded him in, swayed him like a subtle opiate. The thirst of the terrible game of living, the desire of things, the brute love of triumph, filled his veins."[53] Hart succumbs to the call until he becomes, by his own account, a "figure of deformity."[54] The urbanaut in Chicago's murky atmosphere cannot resist the game.

He gets involved with typical Chicago types who make money by building cheap and fast. Hart helps them by filing false sets of plans to cover up the dangerously flawed buildings that are marketed under his name. Herrick, trying to locate an explicit Chicago theme on which to moor his involuted narrative, requires an authentic image to enliven the ponderous realism. He connects a tragic fire once again to the imagination. Hart only becomes an insider, part of the common lot, in a disaster that mimics the original scenes of class harmony in October 1871. A "cheesy" hotel that he had designed goes up in flames. The fire "deforms" him like its real victims as he stands outside it. It is a powerful countermyth to the exultant tales of the phoenix that had lured him back. An often artless recapitulation of the city's great defining event is the closest Herrick can get to Chicago as a real place. His hero is forced to abandon Roarkian hopes of dominance. Through him Herrick can begin to observe and relate imaginatively his real subject, the underside of Chicago's prosperity. In specific detail linked to Chicago's history, not in a generic antiurbanism, Herrick begins to function as an artist. Hart is forced to testify at a coroner's inquest about how buildings in the city were often constructed. "He described the use of the old walls and foundations, the reduction in the thickness of the bearing-walls and partitions, the chief substitutions of wood for steel in the upper stories, the omitting of

72. World's Columbian Exposition: A fire at the Cold Storage Warehouse became an instant spectacle. Note the man jumping from the flame-engulfed tower.

fireproof partitions and fire-escapes, etc.,—in short, all the methods of 'skinning' the construction."[55] Buried within the general melodramatic fluff—boy meets girl, avarice is punished, and faith restored—is the Chicago subject. Locating it even in fragment offers Herrick a way to imagine the city.

Herrick narrows the essential Chicago narrative to a single hotel fire. His accounts of the dead and missing mimic the eyewitness reports of October 8, 1871. Moments before he sees the flames glow in the distance like the "great blast furnaces," Hart has complained that he finds little in common with those who live on the avenues of "monotonous small houses."[56] But the violent action is large enough to claim him, too. He gets "borne along in the current" by the crowd running toward the blaze. "The crowd grew denser every moment, and surged again and again nearer the building, packing solidly about the fire lines."[57] Herrick manufactures a new tragedy to benefit from the memory of the original. Only here the melodrama distorts the real event into a comfortable fiction of justice. The "real" is a new veil slipped over an old subject. Herrick relied also on the more recent memory of a brutal fire at a cold-storage warehouse on the fairground on July 10, 1893. Like the architect's own cheesy building, this one seemed to evaporate as firemen tried unsuccessfully to contain flames fed by the building's structurally useless ornamental towers. Viewing the fire as another of the fair's attractions, tens of thousands put off their day's sightseeing to watch the building fail. Seventeen lives were lost. While this sort of malpractice typically went unpunished, Hart's criminal involvement with his building instantly exiles him again from the crowd "rooted in horror, stupefied."[58] On the spot, he confesses, "It's a terrible thing to kill so many people, all at once like flies, like flies!"[59] In *The Common Lot*, a Chicago writer again, following Roe, Lamb, and McGovern, locates architecture and the fire as keys to the new city, without quite knowing how to reimagine it. Through it all, the architect is always lurking around the edges, a perplexing figure of the times drawn inevitably into the action.

Fuller's Atwater and Bingham are both Chicago products who register the shock of a raw city growing so fast that it does not disguise the "bare scaffoldings of materialism."[60] Buildings reveal their structure like a wound. Atwater longs for a more genteel past. He recalls a pastoral time when "local architecture was still in such exact accord with local society," but now finds architecture alienating and too often a thing apart.[61] "All a building is nowadays—one mass of pipes, pulleys, wires, tubes, shafts, chutes, and what not, running through an iron cage of fourteen to twenty stages. Then the artist comes along and is asked to apply the architecture by festooning on a lot of tile, brick and terra-cotta."[62] He misses the need for a basic commitment to structure in a city that was cheated in the fire by buildings that appeared solid only to melt in the heat. His first impulse is to try to make a building something it is not. Atwater again: "Don't go on believing that architecture nowadays has any great place for the artist."[63] Because the architect cannot bear to see the city undisguised, he feels he must dress it up to make it less intimidating. He ends up, as do the artists in *Under the Skylights*, as a grandiose interior decorator, flirting and ingratiating himself with his wealthy female clients. "Atwater was accustomed to people who didn't know their own minds too well . . . to people who had so much money they didn't need to have any mind."[64] Phobic about the conditions around him in the "great Black City," he confines himself to the rich neighborhoods and suburbs.[65]

Chicago of the 1880s and 1890s had a powerful reality peculiar to itself, which Chicago's writers wished to capture but felt alienated from. Even William Dean Howells, the foremost exponent of the new realism, who was lured to Chicago after the Haymarket Riot, contented himself with writing a fable, *A Traveler from Altruria* (1894). Alienated himself, the architect in fiction was closest to the novelist's own sensibility. Despite his efforts to identify with the conditions of a fundamentally new American urbanism, he fails. The architect, whether successful or not, is always ill at ease. When not instructing the rich or drowning in his own ambition, he is embattled, struggling against and never identifying with the infidel native population. "Like the Christians at Ephesus, he, too, had 'fought with wild beasts'—with time, with the elements, with Labor, with National niggardliness, with a hundred-headed management; and he had expanded and ripened in the struggle."[66] Part of a fundamental modern story, the Chicago architect is involved through his own actions, not as an inert commentator on the passing scene. He is no longer detached, but is implicated in the city from which Henry James felt dispossessed, thrown into the middle of a struggle he cannot dominate.

In the end, these novels are just variations on the Chicago business novel. The introduction of the architect as a character provides a way to enter and gain some purchase on a hostile environment. It is impossible to make a large claim for these works individually. But in the aggregate they do reveal a shift towards an interest in the lives of the new urbanite. They prepare the ground for later writers who were able to get further inside their subject, like Upton Sinclair in *The Jungle* (1906), which moves to the center of factory life in the city's industrial neighborhoods. Crucial to *The Jungle* is Sinclair's understanding that the story must also be told from the point of view of a person who lives the life. Jurgis Rudkus is one of the young immigrants building the city; he is not seen as a beast or alien, but as Chicago's natural inhabitant.

Upton Sinclair assumed the authority to write about the city as it was. Initially in *Sister Carrie* (1900) and then in *The Titan* (1914), which was the first of a trilogy based on the life of Chicago streetcar baron Charles Tyson Yerkes, Theodore Dreiser broke the Jamesian code and wrote entirely from the experience of a Chicagoan after the fire. *The Titan* is set in the last quarter of the nineteenth century. Frank Cowperwood is an artist of the practical, a builder, deal maker who relies only on his own wits and ruthlessness to make his way. His architect, Taylor Lord, is little more than a dandy whom he orders around. Without a pedigree, Cowperwood had gone west after serving time at Philadelphia's Eastern District Penitentiary. He is a conscious parody of the artist arriving from Philadelphia, Boston, or New York, a type who uses himself as subject, able to make himself over every day. To Cowperwood Chicago is perfect. "What a city! Presently a branch of the filthy, arrogant, self-sufficient little Chicago River came into view, with its mass of sputtering tugs, its black, oily water, its tall red, brown, and green elevators, its immense black coal pockets and yellowish-brown lumberyards. Here was life; he saw it at a flash." [67]

Born poor to German immigrants, Dreiser did not require a translator. He felt at home. In Chicago "the world was young . . . Life was doing something new." [68] Dreiser found the city hospitable because it favored a protean identity; its newness mitigated against the formation of static elites. Cowperwood's criminal record is forgotten in a place where an individual is known by only his last act. Dreiser's plot is free of the melodramas that confined Fuller, Payne, and Herrick's characters. Cowperwood openly has a mistress and openly plays the city power game. His defeats and victories are not measured against his character but are observed neutrally. The action's rise and fall follows logic and not predetermined rules. Dreiser detonated Victorian convention as surely as Wright did when he pushed his piano through the wall of his proper home. He did not attempt to redeem Chicago, to make it appear like a New England city, but took it on its own. "By its shimmering lake it lay, a king of shreds and patches, a maundering yokel with an epic in its mouth, a tramp, a hobo among cities. . . . Here hungry men, raw from the shops and fields, idylls and romances in their minds, builded them an empire, crying glory in the mud." [69]

The story of Chicago high and low was presented to the world during the years of the World's Columbian Exposition. The problem of imagining Chicago became an international event as millions visited the city and walked through the exposition grounds. The city's modern period, which had begun with a great unifying event, was celebrated by a second. The fair was to show off the city as it wished to be known. But the contradictions and nagging facts remained that had fueled a vital literature of observation and a stripped new architecture. Like the Great Fire, for over twenty years remembered and legendized, the fair became a symbolic center around which the real life of the city swirled. There would never be one Chicago. Cowperwood observes, "Along with a sense of the new green life everywhere came a breath of the stockyards."[70] Chicago continued to prosper but, contrary to the boosters' prophecies, remained fundamentally in contradiction. Imagining the new Chicago would have to include many inharmonious aspects, like its pretensions to respectability, its armies of poor and its wealthy elites, its constant flirtation with the new and dangerous. From the rejection of Jenney's fire memorial and to the acceptance of Burnham's White City, modern Chicago had difficulty unapologetically representing itself. These failed novels, Jenney's tower of debris, Wright's piano, the shanty, and the skyscraper all remain as fragments, cartoons for an unrealized epic.

While the businessman was the usual protagonist of Chicago literature, the architect was its new emanation, a character inseparable from the city's awkward cosmopolitanism. A figure like Baudelaire's Parisian boulevardier or flaneur, Dostoevsky's or Gogol's St. Petersburgian bureaucrat or double, Dickens's London urchin, he embodied the city's twin obsessions with power and cultural respectability. He appeared as a convenient and safely gentrified representative of the city's burned-out shells and crumbling Loop of the panic years, but invariably optimistic, selling the future with a reassuring New England accent and dressed in the latest European fashions. He was a slightly outside, vulnerable insider who conveyed the city's mixture of pride and acute embarrassment over itself. Like Constantin Guys in Baudelaire's "The Painter of Modern Life," he was a vehicle for a larger narrative, a way to understand the city.

The fire's violence provided a rare modern opportunity for architecture to reassume, for a time, its ancient primacy. Frank Lloyd Wright was particularly obsessed with this notion. He thought of the city in ruins as blasted back to a pre-Gutenbergian world, a place where the printed word was subordinated to the architect's elemental manipulations of form and space. He found support for this fantasy in Victor Hugo's *Notre-Dame de Paris*, in which "architecture was the chief writing of the human race."[71] Wright appropriated the novelist's discussion of architecture in his autobiography. In this way Chicago's literary backwardness became its greatest attribute. Chicago in ruin ushered in Wright's nostalgic Golden Age, when poetry, painting, and sculpture were all subordinated to architecture. "If a man was born a poet he turned to architect."[72]

Wright's medieval master was only one personification of the architect, joining Hunt as Cimabue and Burnham as Roman emperor. While architects had to wait for Ayn Rand to receive the complete heroic treatment, Chicago's early urban literature responded to these figures and scaled them down to help register the changes at home. Frederick Jackson Turner, in an address delivered in Chicago during the fair, understood the West's newness in terms of the loss of the frontier, although in the end, it proved much easier to describe what was lost than the conditions that replaced it. Chicagoans attempted to describe this sense of loss through a direct rendering of the world they inhabited. The architect in fiction is a bridge between the outer or primary "business" narrative, a version of the conventional Victorian or melodramatic tale of success and its excesses, and an inner one that holds the seeds of a realistic, and relatively unmoralized, view of the new city.

At their best, these primary urban novels remain interesting in their strongly rendered detail, which recall eyewitness accounts of the fire—a realistic technique successfully transformed and made vivid by Norris and Dreiser and later perfected by Bellow. They reflect a city in conflict with itself. The architect is essential to the inner or shadow narrative of the city. The persistent, often shapeless, drama, of the city manages to percolate up, subverting momentarily the smug surface, to create genuine moments. The novelist's discovery of the architect as a convenient subject inevitably led his imagination back to the ruins and forward to a world that "was no longer simple and could not express itself simply."[73]

Chicago was difficult to size up.[74] The attempt of writers between the time of the fire and the fair to think and write about the city was an experiment. Lacking transforming imaginations like Hawthorne's, James's, or Melville's, Chicago writers created only a city of fragments, as raw in fiction as in fact. The ruin, the shanty, the mansion, the skyscraper were all pieces of a fractured whole. When the city competed for and won the right to host the World's Columbian Exposition in 1893, it was provided with a chance to reimagine itself for the world.

Chicago Black and White

The Court, the University, the Midway, and the Street

Chicago was America's most dynamic city between 1871 and 1894. A period that began with a disaster ended with a celebration of triumph. Having demonstrated its ability to transform apocalypse into profit, Chicago exploited the opportunity of hosting the world's fair to seize worldwide attention. But this time it did so in a selective way. Visitors were not encouraged to see the Loop, but were lured to an invention further south on the lakefront. A city celebrated in ruin invited people back to view its success, not in its remarkable actuality, but in an organized form that allegorized the reality. An imperial Chicago was temporarily erected to distract from the city's real life. The real Chicago was avoided as if it had again been burned away. Images of unity conjured by the fire—visions of the "one Chicago"—were built in plaster for the Court of Honor organized by Daniel H. Burnham. No less a visitor than Henry Adams accepted the illusion as fact and declared that "Chicago was the first expression of American thought as a unity; one must start there."[1]

An artificial order reigned during the fair's six-month run that helped make the fair a popular and financial success. In that brief time it grossed nearly fourteen million dollars.[2] Burnham's staged neoclassicism was an awkward admission that Chicago's success was still embarrassing, even when presented in the form of the new steel-frame architecture that he, prominently among others, had made commercially viable. He deferred to Charles F. McKim, one of the five principal architects invited to participate in the master plan. Burnham's desire for order and a unifying style neatly fit the argument made by McKim and the other East Coast architects for a return to the classics, despite the fact that "the choice of the classical motive, however, was absolutely new to Chicago, no architect having used it up to the time of the Fair."[3] Why

195

retreat to a grammar that he and his contemporaries had already brilliantly transformed? At the time of the fair, Chicago architects inspired by H. H. Richardson's Marshall Field Wholesale Warehouse (1885–87) were involved in abstracting and not replicating classical language for new ends.[4] Using Richardson's example as a guide for the massing of the Chicago office tower, they employed ancient rules governing base, shaft, capital, and entablature to provide complex structures with unified elevations, resolving a problem endemic to early skyscraper design. So in Chicago of all places, Burnham's literal use of antiquity was a serious step back. To the fair's organizers, the idea of Chicago as the youngest international city was more compelling in idea than in fact. It was as if to them there was something shameful about the city as it stood.

It is clear now that the real city was never Burnham's object. He knew instinctively that Americans were uneasy with the pace of urbanism and the modern city's distinctly foreign and lower-class accent. Chicago's fantasy of built-to-order Roman architecture was meant to soften the accumulated effect of the modern that Burnham and the other refiners of a high-density commercial style had built in the Loop. Under Burnham's direction, one might for the moment imagine that no other Chicago existed. Old after twenty years, the new Chicago was already darkened with soot and compromised by time. In emulation of Baron von Haussmann, and using a monumental architecture that culminated in his Chicago Plan (1909), Burnham sought to divert attention from Chicago's "black" architecture and its dynamic streets to a theatrical substitute on the lake shore. The desired effect was easily appreciated. Will Payne described a couple visiting the Court: "The great white palaces of the Fair rose around them in the mellow sunset light. All was colossal and harmonious, and, coming abruptly from the cluttered ugliness of the city itself, it was like a dream. . . . All bore the air of something ancient, august, haunting the mind with an idea of power."[5] The Court of Honor cheated time. There history became irrelevant and a "timeless" architecture linked "the beautiful with the sublime, the present with the past, the finite with the infinite."[6] A generalized history of humanity's progress, framed by the classical architectural orders, was substituted for a contemporary sense of place. Burnham retreated from the vagaries of his day to a safe "imitation of an admired model" that created a nostalgia for a world that never existed.[7] A popular English writer, Walter Besant, at the time wrote: "Never before, in any age, in any country, has there been so wonderful an arrangement of the lovely buildings as at Chicago in the present year of grace." He loses himself in praise for Burnham's efforts: Chicago's "wealth is boundless, but it has been able to conceive somehow, and has carried into execution somehow, the greatest and most poetical dream that we have ever seen. Call it no more the White City on the Lake. It is Dreamland."[8]

The desire to substitute something sublime and harmlessly abstract, like the image of the phoenix, to distract from the city's conflicts remained into the 1890s. Seen as an era of common purpose, stripped of tragedy, the fire (confused with the rebuilding) was popularized as a positive agent of change. The losses and displacements were conveniently forgotten. In the 1890s nothing was obliterated. The fair was neither replaced nor rebuilt. The fairground existed in an awkward kinship with the city it sought to obscure. The illusion often worked. Charles Eliot Norton joined his fellow Bostonian Henry Adams in praising the city's reform. Norton had recently been troubled by the attempts at urban realism of his friend Henry B. Fuller, and warned him in a letter written on October 30, 1893: "It is the man of imagination, the poet, who alone sees things as they really are; it is the writer who has a natural genius for style who can present with equal worth the charm of Italy, or the *repulsiveness of that aspect of Chicago which you depict.*" Having seen the fair, he pointed to another Chicago that redeems Fuller's "repulsive" one: "My recent visit there showed me another and a better aspect of it. I do not wonder that you detest the Chicago that you have drawn, but I think you should have sympathetic admiration, nay, even affection, for the *ideal Chicago* which exists not only in the brain, but in the heart of some of her citizens. I have never seen Americans from whom one could draw happier auguries for the future of America, than some of the men whom I saw at Chicago. The Fair, in spite of its amazing incongruities, and its immense *'border' of vulgarities*, was on the whole a great promise, even a great pledge. It, at least, forbids despair."[9] Mr. Norton need not have bothered writing. His friend had already recognized the virtues of American "classicism." Before the public dedication, in a newspaper article of September 14, 1892, Fuller described his first impressions: "An architectural style is not the product of one man, however inventive, nor of one day, however rapid. It is the product of a race, of an epoch—the slow result of evolution and selection. There is one historical style which is safe, stable, serviceable and universally adaptable. This is the style of the Romans."[10] Chicago proper was instantly relegated to the edge,

73. Chicago stockyards at the time of the fair: A machine for moving animals that served as a model for the design of sports stadiums.

the "vulgar border," as the fair became the new center. The fire's radical reorganization was, for the moment at least, accomplished by decree and did not have to await another dangerous act of God.

Four separate environments, each with a distinctive architectural form, existed simultaneously in this new Chicago of the nineties. The neoclassical Court of Honor and the vernacular Midway were temporary creations; the new Gothic university and the clutter of streets were permanent. These ecologies affected each other and shaped modern Chicago, not as an imagined unity but as four fragments of an historically divided whole. Instead of establishing a convincing statement of communal action, the fair, compared with its surrounding neighborhood, merely vivified old divisions, making them more visible because of the fair's profound contrast with life as it was lived. When the fair was over, the street remained. Visiting the city in 1899, Wallace Stevens notes in his journal that there he found no relief from "modernity . . . so plain, so unmeditative."[11]

The implied dialectic that Chicago had lived with since the fire, between an old-world downtown worthy of destruction and a new order dedicated to progress, which was waiting to replace it, was expressed again in Jackson Park. Between May 1 and October 28, 1893, when the assassination of Mayor Car-

ter H. Harrison ended the World's Columbian Exposition two days earlier than planned, there were two Chicagos separated by only seven miles. For the locals, the fair proved to be a relief from the Loop, where the increasingly militant labor unions agitated for reform as the unemployed roamed the streets, finding shelter where they could at night. "In the City Hall, all through December, the stone corridors were filled at night with sleepers. The impromptu dormitory was so overcrowded that the men were forced to sleep with their heads against a wall, a narrow path being left between the rows of outstretched feet."[12] The city to the south had a "miracle of beauty in this lower world . . . a realization of the possibilities of the Celestial City."[13] To hundreds of thousands of visitors, the fair was the true Chicago. Arriving by train from the Loop on a shuttle run by the Illinois Central, they exited the main terminal and directly entered the Court of Honor. There grand, columned buildings arranged around a closed court, following strict Beaux Arts plans, provided an impression of stability. At a uniform cornice height and color, these central buildings housed fabulous inventions of new industrial and military power, among them, the Bethlehem steam hammer, Krupp guns, and Nicola Tesla's "high-tension" electricity. Throughout the Court the architecture contained the force of the displays and projected a sense of calm. From tractors to

74. Illinois Central Van Buren Street viaduct, the station for trains from the Loop to the Columbian Exposition.

75. Crowds arriving at the railway station on Chicago Day. World's Columbian Exposition.

76. View west from the roof of the Liberal Arts Building. World's Columbian Exposition.

77. Chicago Day. World's Columbian Exposition.

78. "World's Columbian Exposition, Chicago 1893," from the Roosevelt Family Album.

massive electric dynamos, the White City was a great stage.

But outside the gates the aura of calm was shattered. Along the lake, on hundreds of acres of what had been sandy scrub only a little more than a year before, the fair reenacted in microcosm Chicago's process of settlement, from first sighting through catastrophic fire. When he arrived in the city in October 1893, Paul Bourget described the impression of change. As he approached the lake, where the pastoral was wed to ugly images of development, he provided a snapshot of progress's underside. "Vague lots, inclosed by wooden fences smeared with posters, with cows inside munching the scanty grass; then more hovels, more building; here a concrete sidewalk, carefully tended, there a battered one of wood; one moment a paved street, the next a sea of mud where the gripcar tracks glistened with a metallic luster. Never has the unfinished state of that enormous city impressed me more. A hundred years ago it did not exist. Twenty years ago it ceased to exist. It began again. It grows still." [14] Bourget's observations help us recover the planners' real motives. Building again on a wasteland, Chicagoans, in little over a year, had made a new city, ostensibly to commemorate the four-hundredth anniversary of Columbus's discovery of America. The fair served the permanent impulse toward self-dramatization, a drama that featured a discarded central city and a new one made to order. The White City was *intentional*,[15] a willful replaying of the pioneer days by a group of businessmen and community nabobs with a fifteen-million-dollar stake raised by large investments and the public sale of stock. The transformation of a wilderness was accelerated. A group of entrepreneurs, not so different from the originals Ogden and Wright, executed grandiose plans knowing their city had succeeded once. Reviving old passions, the fair was teleological. The happy outcome was thought safely known in advance.

A new city was provided where none was required. The white buildings on the lake and the old new city of the Loop existed not in a linear sequence, with one replacing the other as they might have had there been another catastrophic fire, but locked together, one informing the other. Grotesquely, Chicago for a time had to live with two versions of itself. The Court and the streets of the Loop were contrasts that teased the imagination. A city cracked apart offered two realities, as vividly as during the first days after the fire, when the electric impressions of the street conflicted with the steadying rhetoric of recovery. Rather than a single, purified Chicago, two, in sharp contrast, existed side by side.

The White City dream of a pure rebirth was accompanied

by a nightmare of decay on the "vulgar border." Chicago, which had once provided the nation with a palpable sense of the modern, expressed as a sudden meteoric transformation, again presented a way to imagine the present, not as a single kitsch image of neoclassical unity but as a double in a collision with reality at the edge. The fair ironically intensified rather than obliterated the failures of contemporary life reported in Jane Addams's *Twenty Years at Hull House* and William T. Stead's *If Christ Came to Chicago*. The city of fact and the urban fantasy were interdependent. A promise of violent release was frustrated by a steady diet of class violence with no resolution, a fact brought to public awareness by the Haymarket Riot, the McCormick Works and Pullman strikes, and a summer of economic panic. Even the opening-day ceremonies on May 1, 1893, were shadowed by impending disaster. Despite attempts by the fair's organizers to satisfy creditors, the Chemical National Bank failed within a week of the opening, after it was learned that the directors had used deposits of foreign exhibitors for their own purposes. In reality, the city which began as a few lines on the Howard Projection (1830) was in a chronic state of overdevelopment.

But Chicago would not be permitted to get old. Following the fire by a generation, the fair was planned to do what the flames had done unintentionally. Frederick Law Olmsted came to town this time not as a reporter of disasters but in his primary role as a landscape designer. After the rejection of his suggestion for a more congenial site on the North Side, he bulldozed and graded Jackson Park into a fairground. Daniel Burnham invited America's most celebrated architects, including Richard M. Hunt and George B. Post from the East. Reporters, artists, and writers joined the hundreds of thousands who daily visited the fair. Their articles, paintings, and novels about the "newest" American city soon followed.

Illuminated by electricity and ringed by the best transportation, the fair exploited the same technology that it celebrated in its large exhibition spaces. The largest, George Post's Manufactures Building, was advertised as having almost twice the area of the Great Pyramid. The interior was a giant free space of hinged-arch framing which created a span of three-hundred eighty-six feet. Burnham's conceit was to outdo the other Chicago. The Loop already boasted two of the nation's tallest buildings, the Auditorium and D. H. Burnham and Company's massive Masonic Temple. Set against the

79. View from the Illinois Central tracks, showing the Administration Building under construction. World's Columbian Exposition.

fair, the Loop's pragmatic architecture and obedience to function seemed out of an alien civilization. Montgomery Schuyler commented on the subtle negative effect of the fair's gigantism: "The Great Pyramid appeals to the imagination by its antiquity and its mystery as well as to the senses by its magnitude, but it would be impossible to erect anything whatever of the size of the Manufactures building or even of the Great Pyramid that would not forbid apathy in its presence."[16]

Hunt's Administration Building, the centerpiece of a new high-minded civic religion, had a larger dome than the capitol in Washington. Far from needing to encourage the New York architect, Burnham found that he had to tone down some of his extravagant effects. A version of Hunt's building would later reappear as the focus of Burnham and Bennett's plan of 1909. A comparison between the later plan, prepared for the city's Commercial Club, and the architecture of the fair reveals Burnham's intention from the beginning to build a real metropolis out of the "models" in Jackson Park. A real city based on an imperial baroque plan, with Haussmannic axial boulevards and clean streets, would envelop and dwarf the old city—a new St. Petersburg looking east to New York, Boston, and Europe for civilization, as Peter the Great's invention pointed west for cultural reassurance.

Burnham's fair was another intentional move to assure Chicago's turnaround from a disordered western metropolis to one with a single identity, finally secure in the orbit of the great cities of the East. According to his first biographer, Charles Moore, Burnham considered the Columbian Exposition the "third great American event, comparable to 1776 and 1861."[17] Burnham added later, "Chicago, in common with other great cities, realizes that the time has come to *bring order out of chaos* incident to rapid growth, and especially to the influx of many nationalities without common traditions or habits of life. Among the various instrumentalities designed to accomplish this result, a plan for a well-ordered and convenient city is seen to be indispensable."[18]

The Court of Honor and the infrastructure that supported it were not only metaphors for a new Chicago but a blueprint for the transformations to come. Burnham revived the fire-era

80. Grand Basin, looking west to the Administration Building. World's Columbian Exposition.

81. Burnham and Bennett, *Plan of Chicago* (1909), plate 131: Elevation showing the proposed civic center.

82. Burnham and Bennett, *Plan of Chicago* (1909), plate 122: Railway station scheme west of the river, showing the relationship to the civic center.

"spirit of Chicago" for his planned reordering and reorientation of the city from west to east: "The origin of the plan of Chicago can be traced to the World's Columbian Exposition. The World's Fair of 1893 was the beginning, in our day and in this country, of the orderly arrangement of extensive public grounds and buildings." [19] Jules Guerin's bird's-eye axial and oblique projections, in melting water colors, made the actual postfire city seem to vaporize. Burnham's Court and his white metropolis replayed a poetic of nostalgia, a retreat to a presumed innocent original; he and his cohorts distrusted the present and the human disorder of the street.

Burnham, the fair's director of works was not simply after world records in size, though he knew enough to use them as a spectacular lure to the new city. "White Chicago" was a powerful idea that gave a convenient shape to the negative associations that since the fire had attached themselves to downtown. Hunt's Administration Building was a mock capitol that closed the formal Court the way Jefferson's Rotunda terminated the main axis of the original, freer plan of the University of Virginia. Seen from the lake or close up as one entered from the Central Railway Terminal, the meaning of the illusion was unmistakable. The World's Columbian Exposition was not a grand-scale trade and agricultural show or a celebration of new machines, but a capital, the gateway to a western empire, marked by Hunt's dome (meant to be larger than the dome of St. Peter's), which respectfully looked back across the great inland lake to an older America. A city without a resident population, it was daily composed of the crowds that paid fifty cents to get past the turnstiles. Dwarfed by the new buildings and giant statuary, visitors

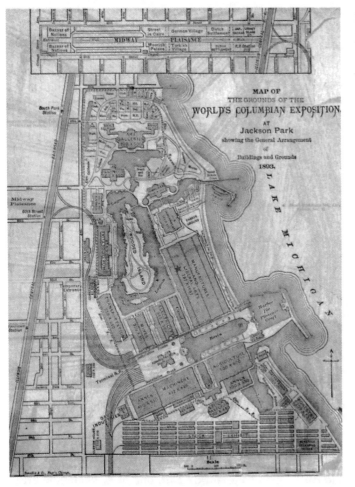

83. World's Columbian Exposition: Map of the grounds.

were symbolically renationalized into a pristine state suggested by the architecture that the city's elite, led by the Commercial Club, hoped would eventually be extended to the city as a whole. As early as the day of public dedication, October 12, 1892, the metaphor of renaturalization was firmly established when the crowds were encouraged to recite the Pledge of Allegiance, which had been composed in the same year by *Youth's Companion* editor Francis J. Bellamy. Over a hundred thousand people attended the patriotic opening ceremonies, which included the spectacle of schoolgirls dressed in red, white, and blue forming a "living flag."[20] Burnham's Court demanded single allegiance; it was a place where the disorder of many nationalities without common traditions could be reformed through design into a homogeneous whole. Even the modern "street" was given attention and tamed to some degree; national differences and cultural peculiarities were given their own architectural treatment on the Midway Plaisance, extending a mile west off the fair's main axis.

Fairgoers could come and go without ever having to enter the real city. Daniel Burnham understood his public. Henry James asserted in the preface to *Daisy Miller* that the kind of city that interested him was "uptown," as opposed to the "downtown" that fascinated the urban realists like Crane, Norris, and Dreiser. Even William Dean Howells, who several times tried to write a "downtown" novel, descended on the fair with relief. Howells was not prepared to write about what he saw in the city proper. He retreated to writing utopian tales of an "Altrurian" traveler set against a background of what Dreiser called the fair's "snowy" architecture. All this planning and building never completely obliterated the real Chicago; in a crazy way it perversely heightened the impression it made.

A novelist of limited merit, Clara Louise Burnham, used the Fair as background in *Sweet Clover: A Romance of the White City*.[21] For her the city was a character—not only the built-up Loop but also the inchoate metropolis to the south. She begins by recording the changes in the areas neighboring the fair site and boasts that her upstart city beat out its more urbane competitors for the honor of "hosting the world." She accepts the steam dredges and excavating equipment as a liberating army that "improves" her old Hyde Park neighborhood and invades the bordering "wilderness." She adds that there were many in New York and Boston holding their "sides with merriment over the exquisite humor of the idea that upstart, pork-packing Chicago should undertake to conceive and carry out a true World's Fair, one fit to follow the great similar achievements of the Old World nations, and to be an adequate embodiment of the high ideas which gave birth to the enterprise."[22] So Chicago again found itself in mudwrestling. The architecture critic M. G. Van Rensselaer pointed to the city's struggle with the environment as its characteristic route to the sublime. "I believe that no place of its extent in the modern world has been so impressive, so magnificent, so imperial in its beauty. . . . Man had here to conquer Nature in one of her more recalcitrant moods. But having conquered her, the result is more admirable as well as more individual than could have been any result won by a less desperate struggle."[23]

Mrs. Burnham was instinctively drawn to what George Santayana would in a lecture at Berkeley in 1911 call the "genteel tradition." Santayana viewed attacks on the vernacular culture as the desire to replace a new culture with an edited version of the old. The vitality of the street is seen as "unhappy," as desire builds for a "purer medium" to take its place. "Music and landscape make up the spiritual resources of those who cannot or dare not express their unfulfilled ideals in words. Serious poetry, profound religion (Calvinism for instance) are the joys of an unhappiness that confesses itself; but when a genteel tradition forbids people to confess that they are unhappy, serious poetry and profound religion are closed to them by that; and since human life, in its depths, cannot then express itself openly, imagination is driven for comfort into abstract arts, where human circumstances are lost sight of, and human problems dissolve in a purer medium."[24] Santayana further illuminates the Chicago condition: "This division may be found symbolized in American architecture: a neat reproduction of the colonial mansion—with some modern comforts introduced surreptitiously—stands beside the skyscraper. The American Will inhabits the sky-scraper; the American Intellect inhabits the colonial mansion. . . . The one is all aggressive enterprise, the other is all genteel tradition."[25]

The "genteel tradition" was daily taking form through "desperate struggle" in Jackson Park. Mrs. Burnham had little to invent. For a Chicagoan, Santayana's formulation was the city's contemporary reality. After all the talk about Chicago's "bravery" and its heroic ascendancy, Mrs. Burnham remained unsettled by the city's rawness. In Chicago of the 1890s, the downtown vernacular was opposed by the gentrified model city. The "genteel" fair was temporary compensation for something thought lost in the streets to the north and west. For Mrs. Burnham's transplanted New Englanders, the Court of Honor was "the realization of the possibilities of the Celestial City"[26] that allowed them to avoid contemporary vulgarity. Even within the fairground she could see expressed the modern conflict between idea and act. Set against the nostalgic abstractions of "whiteness," even a visitor could instantly articulate the local drama: "That Midway is just a representation of matter, and this great White City is an emblem of mind."[27]

Sweet Clover is more than a literary oddity. Relying upon the sentimental dime-novel style, it is in the tradition of early naturalist fiction in trying to heighten the experience of the moment. *Sweet Clover* haltingly manages to exploit Chicago's formative events. Specifically, Mrs. Burnham insightfully yokes the apocalyptic imagery of the Great Fire to the fair.

The city's Gotterdammerung and its scenes of horror are recalled only so they may later be aestheticized against the White City backdrop. The fair domesticates modern Chicago's defining moment, rescuing it from the haunting of individual memory, and provides it with a soothing genteel form.

But inadvertently Chicago neoclassicism, beyond its "stupendously beautiful architectural panorama," also carried unsettling negative associations.[28] All memories of a time and place that did not fit the contemporary idea of heroic dominance could not be completely suppressed. Mrs. Burnham does manage to divorce the fire's destructive force from its pleasing promethean effect. She treats it as pure show. The crown of the Administration Building dome, "*shone out in immobile fire,* while torches of flame, yellow, golden, glorious, flamed across its facades."[29] Electric lights, illuminating the fountains and buildings, glorified the white "city of preternatural loveliness," as people glided through the dark to find a spot to view the fireworks.[30] On October 9, 1893, the anniversary of the fire, the official attendance was 716,881. Fireworks "made the heavens as luminous as on that night, twenty-two years ago, when she was made the victim instead of the instigator of her pyrotechnics."[31] Fire made "immobile" is a "gorgeous spectacle."

Mrs. Burnham's aboriginal Chicagoans and new-wave New Englanders achieve a state of ecstasy in the presence of Chicago's technological display, made spiritual through controlled conflagration. "The shore was black. . . . Volcanoes and serpents of flame, bouquets of a hundred rockets at once, filled the night with brightness, paling the stars, and illuminating the surging water; and when a succession of fiery white cascades slowly unrolled their graceful curves and stood poised in air, showering a light of day upon the scene."[32] The effect does "everything possible toward annihilating space."[33] Enjoying this choreographed apocalypse, a visitor feels "enchanted," out of time. Clover, Mrs. Burnham's female protagonist, has the "usual curious experience in World's Fair minutes. In a city of enchantment, how could it be expected that sixty seconds should be of the conventional length?"[34] For the moment, all is well as the city belongs again to her and her friends.

Mrs. Burnham's sentimental novel provides a comfortable narrative for the history being told and legendized daily in the local newspapers and national press, an instant documentation that had its origins in the eyewitness literature of the fire. Books were quickly published to satisfy the huge tourist trade. Julian Ralph's *Chicago and the World's Fair* (1893),

The Chicago Record's History of the World's Fair, Joseph and Caroline Kirkland's *The Story of Chicago* (1894), and Hubert Howe Bancroft's *The Book of the Fair* (1894) are the best of the comprehensive guides. They built on a tradition begun in 1866 with the publication of *Chicago: A Stranger's Guide,* in which the authors combined fact and myth to celebrate the new town. The Kirklands borrowed from this tradition in their chapter "The Tramp of Coming Millions," on the building of the fair. A mix of naturalism and hyperbole native to the city mark a description which would not have been out of place in Mrs. Kinzie's descriptions of Fort Dearborn: "Horses sank up to their bellies in the spongy surface, and temporary plank-ways had to be made to carry the vehicles engaged in preparing permanent roads, foundations for majestic structures, water-ways for floating pleasure craft, and standing room for countless feet. Even soil for the sustenance of vegetation had to be brought from afar. Progress was inch by inch, foot by foot and yard by yard. It is well that the human mind could not grasp, in advance, the greatness of the task; it would have staggered if not recoiled at the conception."[35]

Mrs. Burnham's romance takes form against this background of "fact." Clover views the fairground and declares "a deserted, unpromising, monotonously level bit of country, surely to be chosen as a cynosure for the eyes of all nations; to be destined to become 'the dazzling focus of a world's ac-

84. Work crews on the Midway, Winter 1891–92. World's Columbian Exposition.

85. Application of plaster facade to the Art Building. World's Columbian Exposition.

tivity'."[36] To her the fair rises "like a perfect superb lily from its defiling mud."[37] The fair was a pageant that recalled the three previous rituals of founding—from Fort Dearborn, through incorporation, to rebuilding after the fire. Together they refined the city's myth of origin. For the fourth time in less than a hundred years, Chicago seemed brand new.

Four new Chicagos in less than a century did not allow space for what the boosters considered a gentrified culture to compete with the "Prairie hedonism" that drove the city in the early 1890s.[38] Somewhere between the myth of the White City and the reality of the buildings being assembled in Jackson Park were clues to Chicago's split identity. Even this completely synthetic place, isolated seven miles from the Loop, was infected. Its reversion to classical architecture indulged the popular nineteenth-century legend of the Veiled Lady.[39] Behind the sheer plaster, molded to look like marble, were impressive modern structures. Before the veil was applied to provide an illusion of permanence, when the great exhibition spaces were being framed in steel in the winter of 1891–92, the expectations of an observer on the site might reasonably have been for an ordered arrangement of functional contemporary buildings. The unclad walls were transparent. Viewing these temporary structures in their uncompleted state undermined their intended effect. With the veil not in place, visitors to the site were forced to see architecturally.

In this form, the hulking skeletons appeared as a series of European train sheds of the sort refined by Labrouste, Baltard, and Lefeul and Dutert.[40] For example, George B. Post's Manufactures Building, the most imposing of the structures, revealed a utilitarian free space extended to its last available inch by the thin-walled envelope. In form and void, the steel-ribbed roof, open-loft interiors, and massive footings were familiar objects particularly appropriate to Chicago, whose office buildings, train stations, and bridges routinely exploited the same technology. Before they were clad, these imposing steel frames memorialized Chicago as it was. But like Jenney's first fire monument scheme, they were thought to be insufficiently dignified. In section, these buildings were not out of a dead or remote culture but were familiar to all. These monumental train sheds—proper symbols of what made Chicago—were more appropriate to house a pioneering technology of energy and movement than the buildings were in final form, complete with trompe l'oeil facades.[41]

86. Wooded Island, looking east. World's Columbian Exposition.

87. Transportation Building under construction. World's Columbian Exposition.

88. View of construction from Illinois Central tracks. World's Columbian Exposition.

89. Interior of the Manufactures Building, under construction. World's Columbian Exposition.

90. Central Station at Park Row, Illinois Central Railroad (1894).

While strong in symbolism, Chicago neoclassicism was thin, an expedient solution to the problems raised by any central planning scheme that seeks out an accepted style to establish its authority. Ironically, Sullivan's fulminations against the "white cloud" that settled over American architecture after the fair did more to institutionalize the symbol than had it been left to fade in memory. He complained that "the damage wrought by the World's Fair will last for half a century from its date, if not longer. It has penetrated deep into the constitution of the American mind, effecting these lesions significant of dementia."[42] For Sullivan, the myth of a "lost cause" was useful to explain his own fall from favor but more importantly to obscure the fact that his own rationalized medievalism, based on Richardson's manipulations of the Romanesque, had reached a dead end.[43] He held fast to the superficial argument, current at the fair's earliest planning sessions, which maintained that if Root had not died prematurely, but had continued in his prominent role as consulting architect, the architecture would have been more eclectic. Root's surviving sketches of what appear to be the Administration Building and some general exposition structures in fact might have caused Sullivan as much alarm. They indicate a rather sentimental approach inspired by the Brighton Pavilion's emphasis on picturesque stylistics.

Sullivan missed the opportunity to clarify the contemporary state of architecture rather than involving himself in a

peripheral debate about style.[44] In a revealing way he was as dependent on the fair, to define what he was not (rather than what he was), as were the detractors of downtown who used the White City to make their antiurban case. Both sides adhered to a habit of mind, born of the experiences of the fire and the rebuilding, in which a continued longing for cataclysmic resolutions to static problems replaced a will to reform. The White City/Black City binary was useful to flatten the refractory reality of Chicago aspiring to genteel stability within a turbulent vernacular culture. Seduced by the experience of dramatic and conclusive change, neither saw any middle ground. In the absence of one, Sullivan's vague formulations of a "democratic architecture" can be seen as his attempt to connect a rhetoric of change with building types already assigned to the dominant commercialism of his time. Through language and idiosyncratic romantic ornamentation, he tried to reinscribe utilitarian structures with a pastoral allegory of work that no longer existed. Daniel Burnham simply changed the inscription. To a contemporary critic, the fair's classical mantle was a default, in the absence of any formal attempts at synthesis between uptown and downtown. Style was substituted for form. "The only safe pilot between the Scylla of servile imitation on the one hand and the Charybdis of an eccentric originality on the other is a thoroughly disciplined and cultured taste."[45] As Santayana later saw it, taste replaced belief in a higher power as the final authority in America of the late nineteenth century.

Schuyler was close to the mark when he wrote about the fair's "decorative envelope" of plaster bonded with hemp, called "staff."[46] He went beyond the question of style and declared the conflict to be between skin and structure. In its architecture, including John Root's aborted plans, Louis Sullivan's Transportation Building, and Henry Ives Cobb's Fisheries, Chicago revealed its need to cover with a gentrified or flashy skin its utilitarian soul. In skeleton, before the skin was fitted and while the classical elevations were still suppressed, the Court of Honor was a collection of contemporary forms massed together to exhibit a technology with which Chicago was already acquainted. This assemblage of buildings was for a short time the accurate manifestation of a country and city in perpetual transition. It was, for a short time only, the "thing itself."

As he toured the building site, Schuyler was struck by the incongruity between the powerful forms he observed in construction and the conservative aspirations the planners had for them. The distance between aspiration and the undressed

91. Agriculture Building at early stage of construction. World's Columbian Exposition.

actuality produced for Schuyler an incongruity that shad-owed the fair through its entire run. He offered an example: "A four-foot column, apparently of marble, may have aroused such a sentiment (of incongruity) during the process of con-struction, when it might have been seen without a base and supported upon little sticks, with its apparent weight thus emphatically denied." The spectacle of a floating architecture was evocative for the fire survivors who had witnessed the same sort of surreal spectacle as they first moved through the ruins. Schuyler continues: "Such a sentiment may have been aroused again in the closing days of the Fair, when it was no longer thought necessary to repair defects as fast as they showed themselves, and where the apparent masonry dis-closed in places the lath-backing. But when the buildings were ready for the public no such incongruity was forced upon the observer, as it would have been forced upon him if the forms that were used had been such as are still associated with the structure that gave rise to them." [47] But particularly for those who had seen the site under construction, the in-congruity, although not "forced upon the observer," was never completely suppressed and was threatening always to crack the surface.

Art had been stretched to the limit. With its essentially modern structure closeted behind a thin skin, the architecture was the weakest link in a chain of illusions. More fundamen-tal to the desired effect was Olmsted's brilliant engineering of Burnham's "city beautiful" plan on a site that was little more than a flood plain when he found it. [48] He made the project work. He saw the highly allegorical architecture of the Court as only one element of the fair. Particularly successful was his juxtaposition of the Court's orthogonal basin to the assymet-

92. World's Columbian Exposition: Early stage of construction, view northwest from the tower of the Fire Engine House.

rical lagoon that organized the extended fairground to the north. The imagery of the formal grid placed beside a picturesque landscape recalled the western city's trials with the land. A system of pool, lagoon, and canals domesticated the flooding waters of Lake Michigan in a way that memorialized the act of founding, when repeated interventions of the machine on the landscape had made settlement possible.[49] But still the White City illusion did not go very deep.

Paul Bourget, who in *Outre-Mer* embraced Chicago's dynamic contrariness as a refreshing counterpart to the dulling seriousness of European cities, saw beyond the Court: "By a singular contrast, the White City I left, constructed only for a season and finished to the minutest detail, must disappear forever, while the black city, which will endure forever is only at its commencement. Strange contrast. I felt it was unique. I saw it presented the exceptional feature of this exposition, distinguishing it from all others."[50] Bourget, who adopted the established White City/Black City distinction as naturally as a native, viewed Schuyler's "sentiment of incongruity" not as a defect but as the impermanent Fair's strongest feature. Even with complete control over the intentional city in Jackson Park, Chicago could not admit failure or build a middle ground between what it was and what it aspired to be. Olmsted aestheticized this indecision in the moderated site planning between basin and lagoon.[51] An urban hydra, Chicago proliferated desired versions of itself. But also like a hydra, all these new heads were on the same old body. The contrasts remained incongruous and resistant to decisive reform.[52] Whereas in Europe an exposition was a "supreme result" of cities that were already finished, Chicago was just beginning. Bourget continued, "The White City of Jackson Park, with its palatial monuments of human achievement lacking only in stability, standing at the gates of a city still incomplete, is not an apotheosis, it is a hope."[53]

Chicago's incongruity was its defining spirit, an imp of the perverse that always found a way to cheat respectability.[54] What would reclaim the city to the north when the fair was gone? Asked by the *Atlantic* to make the case for the city, Henry Blake Fuller encountered the difficulty of life in Chicago without the White City illusion. A powerful sense of unity and common action was short-lived. What remained was the familiar double: white Chicago perversely amplifying rather than annihilating the black. "The date of the Fair was the period at once of the city's greatest glory and of her deepest abasement." Fuller recognizes that addiction to cataclysmic change and faith in healing metaphors was the booster's inside game. At a time when the natives thought themselves to be "associated in a worthy effort under the unifying and vivifying impetus of a noble ideal," foreign critics viewed their city as "the Cloaca Maxima of modern civilization."[55] With the veil removed again, Chicago required a way to institutionalize the "passion for a superior civilization."[56] Required was a permanent preserve of high culture.

One was under construction, bordered snugly on the south by the Midway and on the east by the already moldering Court. Symbolically placed in the intersection of the Black and White Cities, the new University of Chicago filled the breach between the high-culture aspirations of the fair and the ragged democracy of the central city. Neo-Gothic rather than Roman, the University was a permanent Court to continue the "city's intellectual and social annexation to the world at large"[57] and to tame "this vast, ingenuous commonwealth, fed unceasingly by heterogeneous elements which it must assimilate; this vast civilization, with its contrasts of extreme refinement and primitive cruelty unmistakably symbolized by its central city."[58]

Many people received their first impressions of the university from atop the Ferris Wheel at the Midway. A few stone buildings lumbered at the borders of the naked quadrangles, the only disturbances on a barren plot of land that had been offered on generous terms by Marshall Field. Made to last, the new University of Chicago campus would supplant the Court long after the fair was little more than a memory. The University's alma mater memorializes the conceit:

The City White hath fled the earth,
But where the azure waters lie
A nobler city hath its birth,
The City Gray that ne'er shall die.

Hugging the lake front, the newly reorganized university, along with the new Art Institute of Chicago on a prominent site off the Loop, created a relocated cultural axis, a center for the new international Chicago, built at the eastern edge of the old city.[59] A mixture of white and black, university gray was as close to a middle ground as Chicago could produce.

There was a University of Chicago as early as 1857.[60] The following year, Illinois's popular senator, Stephen A. Douglas, deeded ten acres north of its current site, where a building in an eclectic Gothic style was immediately begun. The institution grew quickly under Baptist auspices. After the fire, it continued an imprudent expansion, until it accumulated a fatal debt and was foreclosed on in 1886. At the same time that planning intensified for the fair, the cause of a new university was taken up by leading citizens, most prominently Thomas Wakefield Goodspeed, secretary of the local Morgan Park Seminary. He did much of the work to persuade the nation's wealthiest Baptist, John D. Rockefeller, to endow a reborn University of Chicago rather than to complete his original plans to fund a national university. Given the scale of Rockefeller's resources, the city was again in the now-comfortable role of wooing national attention. Through a combination of salesmanship and appeals to Baptist piety, Goodspeed convinced the New York financier to give six-hundred-thousand dollars if four-hundred-thousand dollars were provided by the local Baptist churches. After the initial goal was met, Rockefeller, without solicitation, provided an additional one million dollars before the university opened. Identifying itself intimately with the romantic fate of the city, and with the phoenix at the center of its heraldic seal, the new school with international ambitions opened on October 1, 1892.

William Rainey Harper, a Yale professor of Hebraic studies, was appointed first president. Although famous for innovative programs with a populist appeal in adult education and home study, Harper also understood the city's passion for credentials. This would be no parochial Bible college. From its inception, the new institution was modeled on the universities of the East, with a special modern concentration on the sciences. Harper thought religion was "something in itself and for itself, fulfilling a separate role, and not in any way to

be confounded with art, or philosophy, or even with morality." [61] To help accomplish the goal of a modern, secular institution, he searched the country for his first faculty of one
hundred twenty. Offering in some cases three times as much
as the going rate of pay, Harper assembled an excellent staff
that included nine former college presidents. He planned to
house the university in heavy gray stone buildings north of
the Midway. Henry Ives Cobb, a celebrated local architect at
the fringe of the modern movement, was retained to design
Gothic spires at the best possible price. When all the quadrangles were completed and the buildings were occupied, the
campus might look as if it had always been there. Cobb's use
of a stone that appeared dirty when new reinforced the general impression of instant academic tradition in a city where
almost nothing built was more than twenty years old. He
helped the University concentrate the city's intellectual ambitions in one architecturally coherent place.

Along with the relocated Art Institute and Theodore Thomas's Chicago Symphony Orchestra, the university bound
the city's intellectual life to a definite space on the city grid. It
was hoped that these institutions, encouraged by the fair and
allegorized so successfully by the White City, assured the
city's consolidation of high culture. Up to this time, what
Fuller called Chicago's "upward movement" was by nature

93. View of the Univer-
sity of Chicago campus
from the Ferris Wheel.
World's Columbian Ex-
position.

94. The University of Chicago campus, viewed from Stagg Field.

"discordant in character."[62] The examples of gentrification were diffuse and difficult to locate. William Morton Payne had earlier observed that the city was in such an early stage of its "higher" development that the "'inarticulate poet,' of the 'maker' (architect) of substantial realities rather than of insubstantial phrases" would determine Chicago's future.[63] At the same time, an editorial in *The Dial* entitled "Chicago's Higher Evolution" cited the university as evidence that the city was "passing to a higher and maturer stage" and that it would "set standards that shall mitigate and transform the grossness of our hitherto material life."[64] Chicago's considerable accomplishments in this vein were lost to the general impression of a city of railroad lines, stockyards, and industrial works. They required an architecture to concentrate the impression of high culture. Fuller regretted that the city's clubs, libraries, churches, and museums, spread over town, were nearly invisible. He might have gone further. In addition to their built work, architects, through their writing and public lectures, provided a characteristic Chicago cultural imprint that blended high and low. The mix of the practical and theoretical in the form of architectural discourse made it a natural outlet for the city's indigenous culture, which was rooted stubbornly in the "grossness . . . of material life."

While *The Dial* (founded 1880), based on a New England model and a forerunner of Harriet Monroe's influential *Poetry* (founded 1912), is justifiably regarded as Chicago's leading journal of the period, a more original and representative publication was *The Inland Architect* (1883–1908). Editor Robert Craik McLean conceived his journal as an instrument in the struggle to organize the profession and did not want it confused with Boston's *American Architect and Building News*, which reflected the views of the national AIA. *The Inland Architect* grew to have a wide readership and remains a critical source for the history of the period. It was a unique institution with roots in a time before architecture in the city successfully accomplished gentrification. With a blend of high-blown oratory from the likes of Jenney, Burnham, Root, and Sullivan, interspersed with practical information concerning what was grandly called the "building arts," the journal was a defining Chicago publication. Editorials extolled the elevated status of architects, encouraged suspicion of trade unions, and cautioned against strikes. In a typical issue (March 1887), articles on ornamental ironwork and architectural history were printed next to a note about a "well-known mason" contractor's trip to California and a thoughtful speech by John Root delivered at the Illinois State Association. In *The Inland Architect*, along with the less complex *Building Budget* (1885–87), we can trace the city's struggle with its hybrid soul.[65] A professional journal filled with advertisements for locks and plumbing features became a forum for the city's ratty intellectual life before it was successfully rooted in a genteel sense of place. The art museum, the symphony, and the university were attempts to create a pedigree breed from a mongrel line.

Robert Herrick was witness to the latest of the city's makeovers. A member of the first group lured west by Harper's charm and cash, Herrick provided a vivid sense of the university's first improbable days in *Myself* (1898), an unpublished memoir. As a young instructor at MIT, he had no special interest in Chicago, although the city seemed at least to offer relief from his "nightmare vision of the stiff, dried up pedagogue" in Boston.[66] For Herrick, the death of Longfellow a decade earlier had marked the end of two hundred fifty years of New England intellectual dominance. He followed the architects in a second-generation brain-drain, drawn to Chicago as the place that offered the "glittering prospect of immediate results."[67]

When a critical part of the city was again under construction, Chicago's primal rawness nourished the imagination. The city in ruin, or in the process of reasserting a new identity, fractured seemingly fixed relationships. Herrick attempted to explain why he made the city the center of his fiction: "I never thought and never intended to give the impression in my stories that I thought Chicago was baser or more corrupt than any other American city in its greedy race for physical satisfactions. But I saw the race there near at hand, and it was staged so to speak in an environment that did not relieve it of any of the sordid and mean aspects of the predatory individual game. Everybody knew more or less what everybody was after, and there was little of the beauty and old social customs that soften the harsher aspects of a people whose energies are centered upon 'Success'." [68] His vision of unadorned ambition could be asserted but still not fully dramatized. The raw "thing itself," in an environment unrelieved by New England social ballast, seemed to him too dark to imagine without reverting to the sentimental deus ex machina of redemptive love, the literary equivalent of the White City. It was easy while observing Chicago to fall into that dulled habit of mind. The imagery was all around in a city that seemed superior to any available novelist. It is revealing how quickly Herrick abandoned his intention to write outside of his "traditional puritan point of view" and withdrew to a conventionally moralized narrative. [69] He was a privileged eyewitness to change occurring at a pace that he could not quite assimilate.

The condition Herrick discovered upon his arrival lacked any softening romance. Harper's language had created a place in advance of its reality. Absent is the casual irony of the transplanted Ivy League professor who earlier had referred to President Harper's dream as "Elevator University," after the grain towers that were seen everywhere on the landscape. He reported, "I shall never forget my sensation as I stood stranded at the northside of the muddy stream of Fifty Seventh street, gazing at the unfinished gray stone buildings scattered loosely over the immense campus which was nothing more than a quagmire with a frog pond at the south end near the administration building, and beyond the irregular roofs along the famous Midway." [70] As Herrick muddied his polished shoes trying to get around the campus, he got a clearer idea of the life he had chosen for himself. "The whole thing was the strangest travesty of a university that I had ever dreamed, something between a boiler house, the celebrated grain elevator, and an intelligence office." [71] The Midway School, as it was commonly called, in its present reality made it difficult for the young New Englander to believe Harper's claims. Only its neighbor, the fair, got Herrick through the tough early days. Like Juliette and John Kinzie or William Ogden and John Wright among the aboriginal generation, he learned to look beyond the present fact to a saving idea. He looked not to the "sprawling overbuilt city along the lake" but to the "great Fair." He displaced a threatening environment with its opposite. "The Fair in a way was Chicago, its dream, its ideal, its noblest self incarnated in magnificent building, in splendor of size and pomp and beauty. . . . It was the fete day of our new world, the big backbone of America, when it proclaimed to everybody that in spite of all the haste and ugliness and makeshift character of its civilization it had preserved its love of the ideal, of beauty and could accomplish it too—could achieve anything." [72]

In town for less than a month, Herrick could not locate a middle-ground between the taunting actuality of the mud and the city's teasing promise of transformation. Desperate for some grounding, he found even the fair's obviously self-serving classicism to offer some relief against material Chicago, where the crass making of money or the absolute lack of it were oddly equated. Herrick associated material success and failure (the daily involvement with money as an object) with the streets beyond the cloistered Court and university, be they LaSalle Street or Conley's Patch. The young professor was not alone in worrying about Chicago on its own, without a large idea to sustain its myth. Will Payne observed that even the city's modern architecture, closely observed, betrayed its roots. He described the Loop at the time of the fair in *The Money Captain:* "He faced west in which direction the buildings grew taller. The mismated halves of the Great Northern towered fourteen and sixteen stories at his right hand, and to the left loomed the *dismal and vast facade of the Monadnock, like the gigantic projection of a mud fence.*" [73]

Henry B. Fuller also failed to locate a "higher life" in the city that will outlive the fair. In *With the Procession,* the people who built the city, represented by the dying patriarch David Marshall, have already been replaced by arrivistes like Mrs. Granger Bates, who originate nothing and only conspicuously consume. Her belief in Chicago as a "big town" has paid off. She lives well and boasts that she reserves one bed for only her visitors' coats. In contrast, David Marshall has the old values. He still believes that work and not money measure a man's worth, but he's a dinosaur in the new city. His daughters live in the suburbs, and his son Truesdale has been off in Europe pursuing an education that he feels he could not get at home. The old man is in danger of being buried alive in his own backyard by cinders falling from the local factories and passing suburban trains. When Truesdale returns home, he is disconcerted by the absence of a diverting urbanism. He sounds very much the dandy when he declares, "No journals, no demi-tasse, no clientele, no leisure. No, nor any excursions; nor any general market; nor any militia or even any morgue. And five francs for a cab. *Quelle Ville.*"[74]

Chicago offers little reassurance. Fuller's all-purpose radical character, Theodore Brower, lecturing under a bust of Emerson at the Consolation Club, complains: "This town of ours labors under one peculiar disadvantage: it is the only great city in the world to which all its citizens have come for one common, avowed object of making money. There you have its genesis, its growth, its end and object; and there are but few of us who are not attending to that object very strictly. In this Garden City of ours every man cultivates his own little bed and his neighbor his; but who looks after the paths between?"[75] Brower wants to found an institution that fits in between the White and the Black. Truesdale reacts quickly: "I should *want* to put an architectural monument in such a ghastly town as this; I should as soon think of ramming an angel into a coal-hole."[76]

Along with others of the young faculty, Herrick recalled feeling homesick for the "pleasant East from which we came." But something kept him there, "faithful to the hope of the West."[77] Caught between the lake and sprawling south-side Chicago, he found himself on the margin of the grid as he "dreamed" his new stories on the "lonely walks beside the sandy lake shore with the cavernous hum of the great city behind."[78] Part of Harper's "huge venture beside the desolate Midway," he was also psychologically in between east and west.[79] The streets that so fascinated him and separated him in his own mind from the "dried up pedagogues" back home still remained foreign and remote. His new job put him at the juncture of two worlds. For all he knew of Chicago, he could have been a young recruit transferred to Fort Dearborn during the Indian campaigns. Harvard had not prepared him for the indeterminacy of a school in embryo and a rugged young city that would not yet yield to his "hope."

In this western city in which he had chosen to live and work, he was forced to confront his "puritan misapprehension of modern life."[80] While the university immediately claimed a kinship with the Court, in advance of any real evidence, in its raw and barren state it resembled the abandoned strip of land connecting the exposition to the vast city in the western flats. By its name, the Midway suggested something mediatory. Herrick felt that it reinforced the impression of the city's incomplete passage from the "state of a 'live town' to the self-consciousness of metropolis, with its own university, the greatest ever, its own symphony orchestra, the first in America, etc. and it could not tolerate any suggestion that it was not the Paris and Berlin of the United States combined with certain purely American advantages over anything that ever had been before."[81]

Until it was absorbed into the city proper, unlike most of the fair, which deteriorated quickly and was reclaimed by nature or sold as scrap, the Midway Plaisance existed as a concession to the realities of an urban exposition, to satisfy the need for recreation. It accommodated and contained all that did not fit into the highly rationalized scheme in Jackson Park. Available on the Midway was all the fun that fairgoers desired at night after the exhaustion of a day's education in the great white buildings. As J. Seymour Currey, a contemporary historian, attempted to explain: "The Midway offered an admirable location for picturesque displays characteristic of the customs of foreign and remote nations, aboriginal and half-civilized tribes; and for various forms of amusement, refreshment, comfort and rest. It gave an opportunity for isolating special features which would not harmonize well with the more dignified buildings and exhibits in the main part of the Exposition grounds." Currey was quick to add that the Midway's forty-one separate shows were also "educational and instructive" but conceded that the "object is simply to amuse."[82]

The Midway Plaisance, a six-hundred-foot wide, one-mile-long avenue, ran west to east from the ragged border streets to one of the fair's most gentrified attractions. An open allée, unlike the closed Court, the Midway functioned as a planned double-size street, retaining its direction and force within the larger city. Originating at Cottage Grove Avenue, the Midway, divided by a covered walk, terminated after passing under the Illinois Central tracks at Stony Island Avenue in front of the classical Women's Building. Set between 59th Street on the north and 61st Street on the south, the Midway Plaisance both engaged the Chicago grid and seemed independent from it because of its width and parklike qualities.

Sandwiched between Jackson and Washington parks, the Midway bridged the two cities. At the Cottage Grove entrance, as one moved toward the Court, the intended imagery of the axis was first revealed. Considered a practical introduction to modern ethnography—so even simple amusement would be elevated to the higher status of education—various exhibitions were arranged in what was thought to be the order of their cultural, and not biological or Darwinian, evolution. The African and Asian exhibits were placed furthest out, nearest to the city proper. A fairgoer moving toward the lake passed from black to white. At one of the most popular sites, sixty-nine Dahomeyans, from what was known as the Slave Coast of West Africa, whooped and whirled in a stockade-like structure reminiscent of the old western cavalry forts. A mass-circulation magazine reported, "In these wild people we easily detect many characteristics of the American negro."[83]

The pretense to pure science continued to erode as one proceeded down the Midway. One passed the Arab villages, where the popular dancer Little Egypt performed. Her gyrations were protested by citizen groups, but the act was never banned. Thought no more than half-civilized, she performed in the shadow of the Ferris Wheel, near the symbolic midpoint of the Plaisance.

The Midway predated the fair; this was not the first time it had served as a divide. For almost twenty years before the Midway was built as part of the planning of the South Parks system, the Washington Park neighborhood to the west had been predominantly working class Irish and Germans who made their livings from truck farming and laboring in the Rock Island Line yards. The railroad tracks that gave the neighborhood its irregular shape effectively separated poor from rich. Those more well off kept close to the lake. When the Midway was laid out along with Jackson and Washington parks, the prime beneficiaries were the established suburbs of neighboring Hyde Park and Kenwood.[84] Even Prairie Avenue, nearer the Loop, profited from these landscape changes to the south. In 1884, the Washington Park Club for breeding and racing horses was established. The steady gentrification of the neighborhood, aided in the 1890s by the new university, was tied at an earlier date to the diminishing effect of the railroad on the grid and to the development of parks and broad avenues.[85] From the earliest settlements, the pattern of development had been established on a relatively narrow north-south corridor. The west side was neglected.

During the fair days the Midway was reborn. Here one metaphorically passed from black to white, past to future, from barbarism to civilization, reinforced by the west-to-east plan of the street. Not far from "Little Egypt" were "Turkish dancing girls" who were just exotic enough to permit good people to ogle, but not too wild or black, like the Africans, to be considered completely beyond the limits of respectability.

Islam served as a convenient point of transition on the street, between paganism and the marshmallow spirituality of the Christian fair and its White City. The colored dancer was thought to be, as Ishmael describes Queequeg, "a creature in the transition state—neither caterpillar nor butterfly. He was just enough civilized to show off his outlandishness in the strangest possible manner. His education was not yet completed."[86] An entry in one of the official guidebooks captured the same dominant tone of restrained license, a droit-du-seigneur fantasy on the democratic street with the aristocratic name.[87] "Turkish dancing girls and the veiled maidens who sell flowers at the entrance to the temple of Luxor wear slippers which are as dainty as any made in Paris. They are of red and blue silk with flowers and filigree designs of gold or silver thread. The heels are rather low. Some are fastened above with fancy buckles or else bows of gay ribbon."[88] In the interest of complete reporting, an anonymous writer from *The Religious Herald* permitted himself a very long look at the tabooed attractions but still managed to pull back in time and keep the faith. His *Guide to the World's Fair* gave the Midway scant attention, referring to the heathen section adjacent to the Ferris Wheel under the category "Novel, Quaint and Curious Things." He mentioned "A Street in Cairo" but neglected to locate it. Some of his discomfort was inadvertently revealed by a printer's error in the published text. The normally flat, descriptive language was suggestively mangled to read "strange things from foreign lards."[89]

Having survived these temptations of the Midway, one continued a pilgrim's progress past a model of St. Peter's and the German Village. Before passing under the Illinois Central tracks and exiting, one found an exhibit of Irish industries. The straight-back, stiff-step dancing provided a reassuring contrast to the wild howling and dervishing on the west, city end of the Midway.

The Midway terminated at the entrance to the Women's Building, clad confidently in snow-white Italianate plaster, which completed the progression from darkness to light. Its architecture fit nicely the nineteenth-century European colonial model of the white building on the hill. But here the land's flatness required the architecture to work harder to assert its intrinsic cultural superiority. Care was taken not to assert too strongly. Everything was done in moderation; no Moorish hip-swaying here, no gentlemen drinking gin and ordering servants around. The building that looked down the length of the Midway was a monument to progressive American womanhood, a mile on axis away from the Dahomeyans and by extension, away from the streets on the far west side of the turnstiles. This controlled turnstile urbanism was

95. Midway Plaisance, looking west toward the Ferris Wheel. World's Columbian Exposition.

96. On the Midway. World's Columbian Exposition.

97. Midway scene. World's Columbian Exposition.

98. Yucatan ruins on the Midway—Chicago's approved, fake ruins. World's Columbian Exposition.

symbolically presided over by women—definitely not dressed provocatively to gain the attention of men. Here modern women could be observed at work in the domestic arts and in the formerly exclusively male professions. In fact, to underscore this new reality the building itself was designed by Sophia G. Hayden, an MIT graduate, who had won the commission after a competition limited to women architects. An eighty-thousand-square-foot structure provided room for women's sculpture, paintings, crafts, and industries. Set on the lagoon and next to the Horticulture Building (with a glass dome modeled after the 1862 World's Fair in London), its relaxed classicism offered relief from the hectic environment of the Midway and the strictness of the Court. The building's upper porch, employing a modified Corinthian order and using caryatids as pilasters, provided a relaxed setting from which to view the surrounding activities. Hayden minimized the structure's monumental effect by setting relatively small windows between the columns to indicate the comparatively modest domestic scale of the rooms inside. It was an implicit criticism of the gigantism of the great shed interiors of the Machinery and Manufactures buildings. In practice her building provided an immediate reacculturation for fairgoers who had ventured out to the Midway, welcoming home those who had tentatively left the safe precincts of Jackson Park. The busts of Susan B. Anthony and Elizabeth Cady Stanton and a relief of Sappho brought one back into the realm of strong female authority. At its core, the building had its own Court of Honor with a tunnel-vaulted, skylit roof, where a relatively empty central space, surrounded on both the long and narrow sides by double-height loggias, offered a rare respite from both education and serious amusement.

During the day everything was fixed in its proper place, just as the planners and their academic consultants intended. The passage from Cottage Grove Avenue to the safe precincts of Jackson Park along the Midway had been coordinated by Frederick Ward Putnam, Director of Harvard's Peabody Museum, and Sol Bloom, a young Californian responsible for the various Midway concessions. Bloom emulated the sideshow scheme that had made profitable the recent Paris Exposition. Some of the ethnological exhibits were housed in the Women's Building, but the majority were exhibited in mock-natural surroundings on the Midway. Dominated by Hayden's work at its terminus and tamed by Professor Putnam, chief of the exposition's Archaeological and Ethnological Department, the Midway succeeded in the day as a controlled street, a "living museum" or an "ethno-zoo," depending on

99. View from intra-
mural powerhouse.
World's Columbian Ex-
position.

100. View from the
Ferris Wheel, looking
east along the Midway.
World's Columbian Ex-
position.

101. Behind the Midway: 60th Street, looking east. World's Columbian Exposition.

your point of view.[90] In this mixture of carnival and science the city street was given an architectural hierarchy, progressing from vernacular native villages to classical architecture on the lake shore. This easy-to-read hierarchical order was reassuring to those disquieted by the city's new European immigrants and its constant class conflict. A contemporary observer reported that on the Midway each race "has its place." "Undoubtedly, the best way of looking at these races is to behold them in the ascending scale, in the progressive movement; thus we can march forward with them starting with the lowest specimens of humanity, and reaching continually upward to the highest stage." But the Plaisance ran in two directions. One could walk west to east as the cultural evolutionist suggested, or in reverse to trace "humanity in its highest phases down almost to its animalistic origins."[91]

But this clarity was dependent on daylight, when all that was foreign was nicely ordered and controlled. At night the same street that seemed securely to belong to the fair was reclaimed by the city. "Every clime has the night-bird. Its present home is the Midway Plaisance. If one walks there at 10 o'clock p.m. one begins to catch a flavor of the international bohemian strip. But if one waits until the last express train has gone . . . one will really begin to find out. It is the 'sur-

vival of the fittest'."[92] The street was a vector with force in two directions. The reporter continued: "As midnight comes nearer the transformation is complete. The international business mart of the day has become the playground of the revelers. The rolling-chairs, the catalognes [*sic*], the prim old ladies, the children, the family caravans, the dignified men with spats, the timid young men have gone and the nightbirds have begun to flap their wings. The tom-toms are silenced, but other sounds have taken their place."[93] In the light the "Anglo-Saxon is officiating," looking in at the people behind the bars in the ethno-zoo. However, in the dark, "the night air has an alcoholic whiff to it, but you can't put your finger upon any one who is actually reeling ripe. As for the dissipation, it is what you might call riotous but not particularly wicked. It is an outdoor orgy without the element of sin."[94]

At night the Midway's chief exhibit became a version of the Chicago street, modified enough to accommodate an Anglo-Saxon orgyist who dissipated discreetly, still distancing himself from activities in which he never completely participated. The architecture and planning allowed him to leave unchanged, essentially unaffected—a funky Disney street with the balance between order and disorder tilted just to the safe

102. Interior of the Women's Building. World's Columbian Exposition.

side of experience. Compare it to Theodore Dreiser's account of the real street he visited in 1890: "To me Chicago at this time seethed with a peculiarly human or realistic atmosphere. . . . It sang, I thought, and in spite of what I deemed my various troubles—small enough as I now see them—I was singing with it. These seemingly drear neighborhoods through which I walked each day, doing collecting for an easy-payment furniture company, these ponderous regions of large homes where new-wealthy packers and manufacturers dwelt, these curiously foreign neighborhoods of almost all nationalities; and lastly, that great downtown area, surrounded on two sides by the river, on the east by the lake, and on the south by railroad yards and stations, the whole set with these new tall buildings, the wonder of the western world fascinated me."[95] Dreiser had no need for an ethnographic exhibit. It was all already there to see if one desired: "Always the miseries of the poor, the scandals, corruptions and physical deteriorations which trail folly, weakness, uncontrolled passion."[96]

Dreiser's interest in street life was part of his growing fascination with the world beyond the towers of the Loop and the Court. However, unlike the novelist, most others did not wish to get close to the outlands. The Midway provided the curious a safe way to view the city, complete with the thrill of motion. Chicago, which often lacked refinement, had a genius for self-satire. Although it chose to present itself dressed virginally in white, a more accurate manifestation of the city of the nineties was placed almost dead center on the Midway's street-fair axis. The two-hundred-sixty-five-foot-tall Ferris wheel was the perch from which one could see Chicago whole. A writer at the time noted: "It seemed as if the earth were sinking away out of sight slowly and quietly. Going up, the passengers had the whole of Chicago and the prairies for miles beyond laid before them unobscured."[97] George Ferris, a Pittsburgh engineer, had invented this gigantic spinning wheel years earlier; the Exposition Corporation provided him the opportunity to build it in steel and run it as an amusement. Over a year in construction and seven weeks late in opening, the wheel, more than the Court or Olmsted's pastoral lagoon, was the city's monument. Boldly modern in construction, it employed the architectural technology of downtown and Machinery Hall for pleasure. Shaped like the forks of a bicycle, two unclad one-hundred-forty-foot steel towers held the two-hundred-fifty-foot circumference wheel fifteen feet off the ground. Thirty-six passenger cars, allowed to pivot and swing in sympathetic motion, could hold a total of

103. Ferris Wheel, from the University of Chicago campus. World's Columbian Exposition.

104. Ferris Wheel base and cabs. World's Columbian Exposition.

105. Ferris Wheel. World's Columbian Exposition.

close to fifteen hundred riders. Kept in motion by two thousand-horsepower engines and stopped by air brakes, the entire structure weighed twelve-hundred tons.[98] Chicago had done Paris one better by building a revolving Eiffel Tower. Eiffel's thousand-foot structure was a freak in a city where the tallest buildings were little more than a twentieth its height. In Chicago, the Ferris Wheel was in scale with the great towers of the Loop. The wheel's three-hundred-fifty-square-foot, nine-foot-high wood and glass rooms resembled business offices suspended like cradles above the ground. The parodic allusion to the Loop was apparent to those entering the cars. A rider recalled the business tower transformed into a carnival attraction: "This doorway opens into a sunshiny room with two rows of chairs at either side. There are windows all about and these are barred with wide iron grating. So much of a view as can be gathered through the side window shows other cars poised silently in the air above. They are so close to one another that they seem like upper stories of buildings near at hand, except that they are cris-crossed by the shade from a network of slim girders." He continued, "It combines the gliding motion of the railroad train with the upward jerk of the passenger elevator."[99] With its combination of modern engineering and honky-tonk, steel-framed and bare, the wheel was a skyscraper that moved, and moved predictably, with the clockwork of an induction motor, from the basement to the penthouse and back again. To add to the delight of the promoters, this building could be rented not by the month but by the minute. There was public interest in retaining it as a permanent attraction, and after the fair it was moved further to the interior, to North Clark near Diversey, where it would not compete with the university's Gothic spires. This proved only a temporary reprieve. In 1904 the wheel was transported to St. Louis for the Louisiana Purchase Exposition and soon after it was demolished and sold for scrap.[100]

*W*hen the Midway attractions were demolished and the Court lay in ruin, the streets of the neighborhoods remained. A sociologist called this sprawl in the "looming shadow of the skyscraper" a "tidelands of city life."[101] "As the Loop expands it literally submerges the areas about it with the traffic of its commerce. Business and industry encroach upon residential neighborhoods. As the roar of traffic swells, and the smoke of industry begrimes buildings, land values rise. The old population moves slowly out, to be replaced by a mobile, shifting, anonymous population bringing with it transitional forms of social life."[102] Frank Norris, looking out over the web of tracks bisecting the city, thought of the combination of man and machine that developed Chicago: "Great strength, prodigal of its wealth, infinite in its desires. In its capacity boundless, in its courage indomitable; subduing the wilderness in a single generation, defying calamity, and through the flame and the debris of a commonwealth in ashes, rising suddenly renewed, formidable, and Titanic."[103] Dreiser, a reporter for the *St. Louis Republic*, stared back toward the west from the top of the Administration Building. It was night as he observed "one vast blaze of lurid fire." In the glow of the new electric searchlight "the whole distant prospect is lighted up and distant many blocks one may see people walking, distinguish the finer outlines on buildings and see small objects."[104]

Norris's and Dreiser's works were some of the latest additions to a literature interested in the life of the street that began developing in Chicago as early as the fire.[105] Agnes Leonard Scanland's *Heights and Depths* (1871) was one of the earliest titles. It is a conventional narrative, which follows a girl's rise from poverty to respectable servitude. Little of Chicago as a specific locale enters the book. Shang Andrews's *Chicago After Dark* (1882) and the anonymous *Suppressed Sensations; Or, Leaves from the Note Book of a Chicago Reporter* (1883) are more sensationalistic attempts at dealing with life in the tidelands. Anticipating the opening of the fair, a local publisher printed an illustrated edition of *Chicago By Day and Night: The Pleasure Seeker's Guide* (1892). The streets of Chicago beyond the Loop had become as foreign and exotic as the streets of Cairo. The alienation of the city from itself can be traced back to the Great Fire's first hours, when Chicago's lakeside elite saw the eruption of the masses fleeing the flames. A progression of labor demonstrations stigmatized as dangerous the areas where working people lived, although a prurient interest remained in the uninhibited life that was thought to go on there. These streets beyond the pale of mainstream Chicago's day life proved perversely alluring at night. Frank B. Wilkie's *The Gambler: A Story of Chicago Life* (1888) and Lilian E. Sommers's *For Her Daily Bread* (1887) gave a look over the line from Prairie and Michigan avenues. In these books city streets on the edge of gentrified Chicago were viewed as a permanent Midway. This violent fiction was an echo of the violent facts.

The first mob action after the fire took place during the winter of 1872. Responding to rumors of embezzlement at the Relief and Aid Society, a group of the unemployed rioted outside its offices. After the panic the following year, groups of homeless were a frequent sight and many took shelter in public buildings, including the first floor of the new five-hundred-million-dollar City Hall. There were frequent street fights that gave a pervasive sense of general disorder. In the summer of 1877, a national railroad strike spread to Chicago. In response to an increased police presence, workers organized their own defense teams with names like the Irish Labor Guards, Bohemian Sharpshooters and Lehr-und Wehr-Verein. The foreign language press, representing the interests of immigrant workers, used the situation to call for a general strike. On July 21, an outdoor rally of nearly a thousand laborers was held at Halsted and Twelfth streets. Other peaceful meetings followed where crowds of working men were addressed by political activists like John Schilling and Albert Parsons. These legitimate protests organized by socialist and anarchist factions were joined by apolitical gangs of the unemployed as well as by thieves and petty criminals. Mayor Monroe Heath, convinced that he had another Paris Commune on his hands, mobilized the city, swearing in new policemen and encouraging the citizenry to defend itself against the Reds. Violent confrontations between the authorities and demonstrators followed, culminating in full-scale riots at Halsted and Sixteenth streets on July 26. At least thirteen were reported dead and many more wounded. Two companies of federal troops fresh from the Indian wars were called in to calm things down. In the next decade relations between the city's business interests and its immigrant labor force deteriorated. In the public imagination, the streets became the scene of violent engagement. The International Working People's Association (IWPA) organized its National Information Bureau in Chicago. The city quickly became the most active center of the IWPA with seventeen affiliated groups by 1885.

Public awareness of the labor movement was accelerated in the middle eighties. A series of large public demonstrations began with the 1884 Thanksgiving Day protest meeting, continued with a march on the new Board of Trade Building on April 28, 1885, and culminated at the Haymarket, May 4, 1886. In addition, there were weekly Sunday labor meetings by the lake with as many as a thousand attending. Other demonstrations staged at busy intersections signaled a chronic social malaise; particularly for a city schooled in cataclysmic change, they seemed to indicate that the city's next transformation would begin violently from below. Chicago had survived the fire's test to its status quo, but such manmade disorder was not as easy to unify or mythologize into a blessing.[106] Also this form of disorder had its own voice. There was no way for the boosters easily to incorporate the language of August Spies, editor of the *Arbeiter-Zeitung*, or George Engel, editor of *Anarchist*. Failing this, the daily press resorted to cartooning and editorializing against the foreign-born worker and his native sympathizers.

The most significant of these radical publications was Albert Parson's English language *Alarm*, which permitted the population to read its nightmares. For example, on April 4, 1885, *Alarm* published an article, "A Practical Lesson in Popular Chemistry—The Manufacture of Dynamite Made Easy." In addition, for years the German language *Freiheit* and *Arbeiter-Zeitung* contained information on explosives and weaponry. To Chicagoans barely secure on a middle rung of the social ladder, such material gave evidence that the very technological tools that had secured success and the city's progress were now inverted toward destruction. A journal reported, "The latest scare about the Terrorist Socialist is in Chicago, where the police have discovered that they are trying to destroy the city by infernal machines, dynamite bombs and electricity."[107] The bomb in the hands of a dark-complexioned, wild-eyed, unshaven man was a widely circulated portrait. It became the image of a technology perverted for demonic ends. What had begun as agitation for an eight-hour work day in a peaceful May Day rally outside the McCormick Works became caricatured, after the Haymarket Riot three days later, as anti-American anarchy. Seven radicals were sentenced to death, four men were hanged—some on trial were not even at the Haymarket that day—in retribution for the deaths of eight policemen.[108]

Serious labor disputes continued into the next decade. At the time of the fair, the connection between labor (particularly foreign and radical) and violence was tied to bombs pictured as sinister black cannonballs with tail-like fuses. A strike that began at the Pullman Works on May 11, 1894, became a general railroad walkout at the end of June. Labor unrest was given as one of the causes for the series of arson fires that plagued the deserted White City. The Chicago street, inland from the lake, was where the bomb and the frustrated agents of order collided.[109]

An Englishman, William T. Stead, wrote the most widely read account of the other Chicago. Seventy thousand copies of his book, *If Christ Came to Chicago*, were ordered before the initial Chicago press run (1894). He observed, "The first impression which a stranger receives on arriving in Chicago is that of the dirt, the danger and the inconvenience of the street."[110] The provocative title was illustrated by a frontispiece in the first English edition that pictures Christ chasing the money changers from a temple opposite the Administration Building. The book unmasked the circumstances of urban poverty in the tradition of Jane Addams, Lincoln Steffens, and Jacob Riis. Stead's account relied on the work of a local writer, George Wharton James, who edited a report by a "corps of specially appointed commissioners"; *Chicago's Dark Places* (1891) established the language and argument that Stead employed in his account.[111] Like Stead's, the earlier book's goal was to argue for moral over material progress, although James reluctantly admitted, "It must be acknowledged that it is the too great temptation of ordinary Chicago humanity to look only on the side of the prosperity, progress, magnificence and splendor of their city, and in the feelings of honest pride that spring up with such contemplation to forget, or wilfully overlook, the other side."[112]

In November 1893, Stead presided over a conference at the Central Music Hall. Returning the following year for a three-month stay, he found the city in a more critical condition than he had on his first visit. A year of economic depression, the trial of Prendergast (Mayor Harrison's assassin), and the Pullman strike were factors that made Stead sensitive to the city's dark side. "If a stranger's first impression of Chicago is that of the barbarous gridironed streets, his second is that of the multitude of mutilated people whom he meets on crutches. Excepting immediately after a great war, I have never seen so many mutilated fragments of humanity as one finds in Chicago."[113] Like other writers, Stead was drawn to violence. But his imagination ranged beyond polarities of cops and Reds to a permanent Chicago condition. His interest was not in the bomb, but in the daily explosions of urban life. Chicago was structurally violent because of its class conflicts,[114] which he saw demonstrated in the frequent accidental deaths occurring at the intersections of its "barbarous" transportation grids. Stead portrayed the scenes as massacres, suggesting the connection between the anonymous traffic victims and the original Fort Dearborn martyrs. The railroads are the Indians who are outside Christian values because of their "plutocratic despotism." They are modern pagans. He proclaimed: "I do not think that it is too much to say that in the last five years we have had fewer soldiers killed in our wars all round the world than have been slaughtered in the streets of Chicago at the grade crossing. The figures are: in 1889, 257; 1890, 294; 1891, 323; 1892, 394; 1893, 431. . . . In the city of Chicago there are under 2500 miles of roadway, but there are 1375 miles of railroad track within the same area. The railroads traverse the streets at grade in 2000 places."[115]

At the Harrison Street Police Station he found an elemental architecture, functional to the point of despair, a counterarchitecture to the White City. "There is something dreary and repelling about a police station even in the least criminal districts. But Harrison Street Station stands in the midst of darkest Chicago." Here the "most desolate ruffians of both sexes" are penned "behind the iron bars of its underground cages."[116] Some who are not incarcerated have to improvise their shelter. These "homeless out-of-works" sleep in empty trucks, in basements of saloons and in outhouses. Up to two thousand a night camp out at City Hall, and another five to six hundred at the Pacific Garden Mission at Van Buren and Clark streets. The Harrison Street Police Station, not the Court of Honor, was Chicago's center. At the heart of the cosmopolitan nineteenth precinct of the first ward, it was the city with its ceremonial toga off, free of universal architecture or a redemptive narrative.[117] Stead feels that he is observing human behavior unmodified: "The novelist who had at his command the life story of those who, in a single week, enter this prim brick building surrounded by iron palings, would never need to draw on his imagination for incident, character, plot, romance, crime—every ingredient he could desire is there ready to hand, in the terrible realism of life." [118]

Unemployment and homelessness characterize life in the tidelands. The tramp is the failed double of the entrepreneur who founded and rebuilt Chicago, and in the year of the fair celebrated himself. A throwback to an earlier stage of evolution, he is an urban hunter and gatherer. A judge told Stead, "You can always tell the bum by his smell. There is an ancient stink about him which you can detect in a moment." [119] Only seven miles north of the spot where fairgoers celebrated unfettered progress was the chronic, unprogressive norm. Stead found compensation for his time on the street. "Even in this nethermost depth," he believed he was on the "bed-rock of actual fact, face to face with the stern realities of things as they are." [120]

Stead was only one in a long line of visitors to the city searching for the "bed-rock of actual fact." The search yielded a mixture of fact and myth. But the experience of the city was something quite different. Finally, Chicago could not be understood as a unity. There was no bedrock. At best, the fire and the fair were simply two poles between which the city might be known, mixtures of facts and legends that revealed the city in advance of its real history. Chicago was always floating itself a loan to be paid off at some indefinite time in the future. It could not seem to wait for history to establish it in its own ideal image. Little more than two decades separated the city's near-annihilation from an international celebration in praise of its dominance. The distance in time between the two events was thought to symbolize the triumph of will over the vagaries of fate. A cataclysmic fire was God's will, the fair was man's. The two were thought to be in separate realms. But inevitably, they came together, on Independence Day 1894.

An arson fire, conveniently attributed to radical workers then on strike against the Pullman Company, made efficient work of the abandoned White City. The pasteboard facades melted in a parody of the 1871 catastrophe, when iron and stone liquified in the fifteen-hundred-degree firestorm. The White City in flames linked Chicago again to the source of its myth. Chicago was not another American city of seemingly undeterred progress, but the perpetual creature of fire and ash, truly a phoenix. Other cities developed, prospered, and kept on developing, with periodic reversals that they soon overcame. However, more like a Biblical city, Chicago's fate was more tragic; it would be repeatedly tested, and tested severely. Chicago's newness and incongruity as an international metropolis made the apocalyptic model attractive. Chicago was important not because of venerable history, but like Job it was great because of the depth of its adversity. An intentional city like St. Petersburg, it had sprung complete out of the mind of its creators, a completely manmade place in a hostile environment. Slave labor made the northern Russian capital; a shared vision of greatness and heroic labor raised Chicago out of the mud. It took a century for a poet to legendize St. Petersburg in language complex enough to carry the contradictions of its founding. Alexander Pushkin's *The Bronze Horseman* expressed the city as a conflict between the power of a unified idea—European Russia—and the reality of the land. Peter ruled with a ruler as he laid out the plans for an imperial city in the swamps. He built it only to have it periodically reclaimed by floods. The pure idea was locked forever with the tragic inevitability of nature; architecture only seemed to triumph over the former chaos of the unruled land. The "luminous Admiralty spire," Chicago's skyscrapers and White City domes, reassured a newly urbanized population with a precarious hold on existence.

Pushkin's poem is a hymn to development and the primordial urge to build:

> A hundred years have passed, and the young city,
> The grace and wonder of the northern lands,
> Out of the gloom of forests and the mud
> Of marshes splendidly has risen; where once
> The Finnish fisherman, the sad stepson
> Of nature, standing alone on the low banks,
> Cast into unknown waters his worn net,
> Now huge harmonious palaces and towers
> Crowd on the bustling banks; ships in their throngs
> Speed from all ends of the earth to the rich quays;
> The Neva is clad in granite; bridges hang
> Poised over her waters; her islands are covered
> With dark-green gardens, and before the younger
> Capital, ancient Moscow has grown pale,
> Like a widow in purple before a new empress.[121]

In the poem, upstart St. Petersburg has displaced Moscow as the new capital, but its fate is never secure. The danger of its site insures the precariousness of its condition. Pushkin understood that the fate of modern Russia could be found at the intersection of St. Petersburg's heroic architecture and the land's intractable condition. The Neva is "clad in granite" but not contained. The great poem, subtitled *A Tale of St. Petersburg*, begins with a celebration of an extraordinary city and ends with a description of a killing flood. A peasant couple is separated forever when one of the lovers drowns. But the bronze equestrian statue of Peter endures forever. Cities like Rome, Paris, and Moscow are eternal, rich in history. The St. Petersburgs and Chicagos are perpetually new, churning a mix of fact and myth to justify their grand sense of themselves. The dialectic of development and tragedy creates an odd sense of reassurance. Urban Jobs, Noahs, and Jonahs, these cities survive apocalyptic tests severe enough to annihilate more venerable and storied places. The severity of the tests might be seen to confirm that the gods are involved with the city. In this way even failure is transformed into another myth of success. Disaster helps further claims to primacy.

Chicago had no Pushkin to legendize its claim. But the impulse was there. It helps explain the overindulgences of Wright and Sullivan, the imperial posturings of Daniel Burnham. In a rare moment of self-criticism, Louis Sullivan admitted the problem of being both the builder Peter and the poet Pushkin. At his career's end he confided: "Words are most malignant, the most treacherous possession of mankind. They are saturated with the sorrows of all time. They hold in most unstable equilibrium the vast heritage of man's folly, his despair, his wrestling with the angel whose name is Fate; his vanity, pride before a fall, his ever-resurrecting hope—arising as a winged spirit from the grave of disaster, to flit in the sunshine for a while, to return to the dust, and arise again as his civilizations, so laboriously built up, have crumbled one by one." [122] Architecture was less complicated. It was easier to literalize a vision with the Admiralty, Winter Palace, or Court of Honor. Language proved to be less under control.

An understandably forgotten pseudonymous poet, H. H. Van Meter, was compelled to write his own *Bronze Horseman*, which he entitled *The Vanishing Fair*. He recognized that architecture was a proper occasion for literature; language began where the buildings left off. A poor man's Pushkin, he is oddly appropriate to a democratic city with an imperial flair. The Russian epic holds the tension between the heroic aspirations of city builders to control nature and nature's inevitable periods of rebellion, but Van Meter's, of course, cannot.

Like the Great Fire, the burning of the fair is referred forward to a time when all will be better:

> When the world beheld with pity
> As the fiery cyclone's flame,
> Swept across our smitten city
> Then began its greater fame.

In Van Meter's kitsch epic, Chicago is defined not by Pushkin's dialectic, a tension between ideal and actual, but by alternate prosperity and suffering. Long periods of unity suddenly give way to cataclysmic moments of disorder, only to be followed by another era of supposed unity and common purpose. St. Petersburg would be allowed to get old, Chicago not. In perpetual transit between founding and destruction, Chicago's realities are made to conform to its myths:

> As we stand above the ashes
> Of the fairest scenes of time
> May each fiery flame that flashes
> Light to visions more sublime.[123]

A more accomplished writer, Robert Herrick, tried to deal in his memoir precisely with what he was feeling as he contemplated the failure of the fair. The longed-for displacement

106. Frontispiece from H. H. Van Meter, *The Vanishing Fair* (1894). From top: "Vacant site"; "White city"; "After the flames." Compare the progression of the scenes to that of Thomas Cole's series of paintings, *The Course of Empire*.

107. The White City on fire and in ruins, photographs from H. H. Van Meter. *The Vanishing Fair* (1894).

of the Black City by the White had never occurred except in metaphor or in the memories of visitors who came and quickly left after their tour of the remade South Side was over. Herrick wrote from the point of view of a marooned traveler. Lured to stay by President Harper, he was forced to see Chicago in between its apocalyptic moments of transformation. During the first winter following the fair, Herrick saw the city in the shadow of its flamboyant times of change. The city was authentic again in ruin. He relived in slow motion the instantaneous eruptions of buildings in 1871. He walked through Jackson Park and recalled: "During these culminating weeks of the Fair the university was naturally even less real than it became as soon as the savage December winds began to howl through the empty Court of Honor, and the dream city began to crumble into staff. Then the university became a very real and somewhat dreary fact. That part of the city about the university and the fair grounds had been badly overbuilt in anticipation of the Fair, and now these flimsy, tawdry, ill built structures were empty, deserted by all save rats." Herrick tried to capture the city's essence the way the *Bronze Horseman* expressed the aspirations of St. Petersburg (or the Ringstrasse, those of Vienna, or the Rue de La Paix, those of Paris). He was struck by the discontinuity of Chicago, how it had to stop and start over and over. For him, it was as much a city of ruin and wasteland as it was the overdeveloped Loop or pristine White City: "It was a dreary picture of a new city deserted, a city of huge brick booths built for a holiday left to moulder into unsightly ruin. And how unsightly that southern stretch of the city was for years after the closing of the World's Fair, only those who lived in it and went to and fro daily through its deserted, squalid streets can know." Any history of Chicago, much less an epic poem, would have to contain these contradictions, somehow embody the simultaneous urge to create and the compulsion for destruction. Herrick could not reimagine it into an epic, but only remark on the phenomenon. "I believe Chicago was never so forlorn as immediately after its great celebration, and it took years for it to regain its buoyant energy, to flow into the empty corners once more with a flood tide."[124]

Herrick could feel that there was something powerfully American in Chicago's reassertion of the Puritan apocalyptic condition. But he was too much the liberal Christian to live with the contradiction of a place seemingly so much at war with itself, without attempting to redeem it. When it came time to heighten what he had discovered into fiction, he never could improve on his original raw observations. He used the fire at the fair as a means of authenticating the fiction, but he could not leave it alone. The scenes from his memoir were revised to become scenes in *The Web of Life* and *Waste*. On July 4, 1894, he "turned into the desolate Midway, where the unsightly wheel hung an inert, abortive mass in the violet dusk."[125] He cannot resist elaborating, and he transposes the real fire into an act of the gods. The turgid writing follows: "Flames finally licked up the fantasy of the great Fair, a fit apotheosis . . . [he watched] the fire eat into the huge Transportation Building, throwing torches of smoky light out to the prancing horsemen of the Colonnade, into the surrounding lagoons. As though wearied by men's neglect of their toy, those gods invoked by the builders of the play city swept down out of the northwest on the wings of fire and reduced to ashes and twisted steel, to the amorphous and inchoate, the dream of beauty made of plaster upon the flat, unfinished prairie. . . . That was America, eager, hurried, unfinished."[126]

Will Payne also understood the significance of the burning of the White City. For his generation, it was the reenactment of the Ur-Chicago event, the Great Fire, which itself had replayed the earlier spectacles of settlement and resettlement it helped legendize.[127] "He had watched them build the Fair, and had seen it in its glory, when it had seemed serenely to affirm the immortality of the system which produced it. But this sight was the greatest of all . . . exceeded by this triumph of mere destruction. This fire was the end of the old order." [128] At least in a fragmentary way, Chicago was trying to understand itself. The key to the city would not be the permanence of its architecture, but its vulnerability. Displacements of white for black, gentry for poor, native-born for immigrant would continue to create new social forms reflected in architecture but never solidified into self-satisfied Ringstrasses or imperial boulevards. Chicago newly rebuilt would always be on the verge of calamity, be it from Indians, fire, anarchy, or Al Capone. The architecture of the eighties and nineties seemed to acknowledge this. It became less ornamented, planar, and more pragmatic. Stacks of empty shells, as neutral as the frames that supported them, rose higher off the ground than any inhabited buildings had ever risen before. Modern architecture developed in Chicago as a silent acknowledgment that the iconography of the era was not yet known and could no longer be confidently imposed.

When Robert Herrick wrote *Waste* toward the end of his career, he was looking back on this critical period when Chicago was building its deepest aspirations for itself. Like a dream told in the light of day, it made the teller vulnerable. "The city itself was left to recover from its aspiration for beauty. It was singularly empty. With the end of the great Fair somehow the city had crumpled exhausted. Those specters of threatening disaster, unemployment and panic, that had haunted the imagination of its leaders during the summer of 1893 had arrived to take possession. Thousands of idle, starving people prowled the ice-cold streets and slept in the filthy alleys. Violence broke forth. Once more Chicago became the frontier village, unkempt and unsafe." [129] But it is the city's eternal return to something primitive, its constant doubling back on itself, that finally defines Chicago, the American city that most expressively embodies the conflicting representations of modern life. The prosaic urban grid became the medium that appeared to organize these contradictions. Like Easter Islanders, Chicagoans exposed their psyches in the odd assortment of things they built. There was "no steady unretracing progress" in the nineteenth century. [130] The Court, university, Midway, and street were all authentic representations of the modern. In the year of the fair, Chicago incongruously contained them all.

Notes

Introduction

1. Separated by two oceans from the rest of the world, America has not suffered the repeated threat of invasion. War fought on our own soil has been the exception, not the rule. So the status of a natural disaster, an event fought at home and affecting a large population, is raised to a greater level of interest. The fact that the Chicago fire followed the end of the Civil War by only six years added to the interest. The war had stimulated the appetite for spectacle. During its first battles, bleachers were erected so that spectators might observe the drama at a safe distance. Later, the San Francisco Earthquake was a similar sort of event. But the audience had already been prepared by the reporting and legendizing of Chicago; the 1906 eyewitness reports and earliest narratives exploited the analogy between the two cities.

2. Elias Canetti, *Crowds and Power* (New York, 1963), p. 76.

3. In 1865, both the North Chicago Rolling Mill, responsible for the first steel rails, and the Union Stock Yards were built. In the year of the fire, the yards received 2,400,000 hogs and 500,000 cattle. In 1867, Armour and Company opened its first packing plant, with a capacity to butcher 30,000 hogs annually.

4. Theodore Dreiser, *Sister Carrie* (New York, 1927; first published 1900), p. 9.

5. Nathaniel Hawthorne, "Earth's Holocaust" (1844), in *Mosses from an Old Manse* (Columbus, Ohio, 1974), p. 401.

6. Ibid.

7. Patrick F. Quinn, ed., *Edgar Allan Poe: Poetry and Tales* (New York, 1984), p. 666.

8. Ibid.

9. The compression of time and narrative provides a period of some duration with a dramatic unity. In the 1988 fiftieth-anniversary commemoration of Kristallnacht (November 10–11, 1938), the Nazi attacks on Jewish property and persons were seen as the beginning of the Holocaust; a twenty-four-hour holocaust stood as metaphor for the larger crime.

10. Saul Bellow, *Herzog* (New York, 1967), p. 316.

11. Walt Whitman, "The Wound Dresser" (1865), in Richard Maurices Bucke et al., eds., *The Complete Writings of Walt Whitman*, vol. 2 (New York, 1902), pp. 75–76.

12. Jack London, who experimented with new forms of realism, discussed the problems of reporting on conditions of the modern city, in a letter written from London at the time he was researching *People of the Abyss* (1902). He too was interested in seeing twice: "I've read of misery, and seen a bit; but this beats anything I could even have imagined. Actually, I have seen things, & looked the second time in order to convince myself that it was really so." Letter to George and Caroline Sterling, August 22, 1902, in Earle Labor, Robert C. Leitz III, and I. Milo Shepard, eds., *The Letters of Jack London*, vol. 1, *1896–1905* (Stanford, 1988), p. 306. His ambition was to write "merely a narrative of things as they are" (p. 318).

13. Hawthorne, "Earth's Holocaust," p. 398.

14. In the same year as the fire, the imperial sense of classical order imposed by Baron Haussmann's executed plan of Paris (1850–70) was shattered by Communards occupying and then torching the Hotel de Ville.

15. Quoted in Simone de Beauvoir, *America Day By Day* (London, 1952), p. 81.

16. Ibid., p. 85.

Chapter One

1. Frederick Law Olmsted, *Nation* (November 9, 1871): 303.

2. Ibid.

3. Frank Luzerne, *The Lost City: Chicago As It Was and As It Is and Its Glorious Future* (New York, 1872), p. 19.

4. See John Higham, *Strangers in the Land: Patterns of American Nativism, 1860–1925* (New Brunswick, 1963), for the effect of nineteenth-century immigration.

5. Interestingly, this was more a feeling than a fact, since 80 percent of Chicago's infrastructure was left intact.

6. Compare Dostoevsky's St. Petersburg and the Goncourts' Paris.

7. There are three suggestive recent works on modernity's effects: Marshall Berman's *All That Is Solid Melts into Air* (New York, 1982); T. J. Jackson Lears, *No Place of Grace* (New York, 1981); and Alan Trachtenberg, *The Incorporation of America* (New York, 1982).

8. Charles Butler, Autograph Letters, 1881 (based on 1833 diaries and letters), Chicago Historical Society, vol. 31.

9. William Bross, *History of Chicago* (Chicago, 1876), p. 64.

10. Edward L. Peckham, in Pierce, ed., *As Others See Chicago*, p. 167.

11. William Howard Russell, in Pierce, ed., *As Others See Chicago*, p. 173.

12. J. W. Sheahan, *Scribner's Monthly* 10, no. 5 (September 1875):529.

13. Ibid.

14. Bessie L. Pierce, *A History of Chicago*, vol. 3 (Chicago, 1957), 3–5.

15. *Report of the Chicago Relief and Aid Society of Disbursements of Contributions for the Sufferers of the Chicago Fire* (Cambridge, 1874), pp. 9–10.

16. Elias Colbert and Everett Chamberlin, *Chicago and the Great Conflagration* (Chicago, 1871), p. 276.

17. H. A. Musham, quoted in *The Great Chicago Fire of 1871* (Ashland Ore., 1969), p. 10.

18. "Chicago in Ashes," *Harper's Weekly* (October 28, 1871) in *The Great Chicago Fire of 1871*, p. 22.

19. Ibid., p. 17.

20. Joseph Kirkland, "The Chicago Fire," *New England Magazine* 6, no. 4 (June 1892):726.

21. Ibid., p. 727.

22. Quoted in ibid., p. 737.

23. David Swing, "Historic Moments: A Memory of the Chicago Fire," *Scribners* 11 (January–June 1892):693.

24. Ibid., p. 696.

25. The urban idyll derives from a modern translation of Virgilian and Hebraic ideas of the pastoral, transformed into a largely sentimentalized sense of harmony.

26. "Chicago in Ashes," p. 25.

27. Ibid., p. 27.

28. *The Great Chicago Fire of 1871*, p. 11.

29. Colbert and Chamberlin, *Chicago and the Great Conflagration*, p. 451.

30. Eyewitness account in the *World*, quoted in *The Great Chicago Fire of 1871*, p. 15.

31. John R. Chapin, *Harper's Weekly* (November 4, 1871), reprinted in Angle, ed., *The Great Chicago Fire of 1871*, p. 40.

32. Pierce, *History of Chicago* 3:9.

33. Ibid., p. 17.

34. Emmett Dedmon, *Fabulous Chicago* (New York, 1953), p. 124.

35. Pierce, *History of Chicago* 3:10.

36. Ibid., p. 19.

37. Colbert and Chamberlin, *Chicago and the Great Conflagration*, p. 445.

38. The idea of a "fortunate fall" or *felix culpa* had its most popular expression in Nathaniel Hawthorne's *The Marble Faun* (1860). See particularly pp. 183, 311, and 329 of the Signet edition (1961). In this formulation one sins or fails only to succeed later.

39. Kirkland, "The Chicago Fire," p. 726.

40. Swing, "Historic Moments," p. 691.

41. Colbert and Chamberlin, *Chicago and the Great Conflagration*, p. 462.

42. Ibid., p. 450.

43. Ibid., p. 446.

44. Jonathan Edwards, "Sinners in the Hands of an Angry God"

(July 8, 1741), in Ola Elizabeth Winslow, ed., *Jonathan Edwards: Basic Writings* (New York, 1966), p. 158.

45. Colbert and Chamberlin, *Chicago and the Great Conflagration*, p. 446.

46. Pierce, *History of Chicago* 3:12. Colbert and Chamberlin, *Chicago and the Great Conflagration*, p. 448.

47. Colbert and Chamberlin, *Chicago and the Great Conflagration*, p. 455.

48. "Chicago in Ruins," in Angle, ed., *The Great Chicago Fire*, p. 55.

49. Robert Cromie, *The Great Chicago Fire* (New York, 1958), p. 110.

50. Later there developed a romance about entry into the city: modern Chicago confers status on all those who arrive. See Carl S. Smith's excellent discussion of this phenomenon in *Chicago and the American Literary Imagination, 1880–1920* (Chicago, 1984), pp. 107–20.

51. Cromie, *The Great Chicago Fire*, p. 1.

52. Sheahan, *Scribner's Monthly*, p. 531.

53. Swing, "Historic Moments," p. 694.

54. Kirkland, "The Chicago Fire," p. 741.

55. Pierce, *History of Chicago* 3:4.

56. William Bross, *History of Chicago* (Chicago, 1876), p. 100.

57. As the fire burned down the Tribune Building, an editorial was being prepared for the next day: "Chicago Shall Rise Again." Reported by James W. Sheahan and George P. Upton, *Chicago: Its Past, Present and Future* (Chicago, 1871), Appendix.

58. Bross, *History of Chicago*, p. 101.

59. Ibid., p. 36.

60. There were three other novels explicitly about the fire: Martha J. Lamb's *Spicy* (New York, 1873); John McGovern's *Daniel Trentworthy: A Tale of the Great Fire of Chicago* (Chicago, 1889); and Janet Ayer Fairbanks's *The Smiths* (1925).

61. Edward P. Roe, *Barriers Burned Away* (New York, 1886; first published 1872), p. 469.

62. Ibid., p. 471.

63. Roe, *Barriers Burned Away*, p. 389.

64. John R. Chapin, in Angle, ed., *The Great Chicago Fire*, p. 40.

65. Roe, *Barriers Burned Away*, p. 21.

66. Ibid., p. 3.

67. Ibid., p. 9.

68. Ibid., p. 23.

69. Ibid., pp. 21–22.

70. Ibid.

71. Ibid., p. 181.

72. Ibid., p. 231.

73. Roe's was the first novel to feature the conflict between the artist and Chicago's practical culture of commerce. Robert Herrick, Henry B. Fuller, and Theodore Dreiser, among others, later explored the same subject.

74. Henry B. Fuller, *With the Procession* (Chicago, 1965; first published 1895), p. 65.

75. Roe *Barriers Burned Away*, p. 44.

76. No modern hero could immediately compete with the myths of the first generation so cleverly exploited by Juliette Kinzie in *Wau-Bun* (New York, 1856) and *Mark Logan, The Bourgeois* (New York, 1870).

77. Roe, *Barriers Burned Away*, p. 90.

78. Ibid., pp. 74–75.

79. Ibid., p. 132.

80. Ibid., p. 225.

81. Ibid., p. 370.

82. Colbert and Chamberlin, *Chicago and the Great Conflagration*, p. 450.

83. Roe, *Barriers Burned Away*, p. 407. Note a similar description of class mingling in Sheahan and Upton's factual report, *Chicago: Its Past, Present and Future*: "Along the beach were judges, merchants, doctors, workingmen, women and children" (p. 113).

84. Roe, *Barriers Burned Away*, p. 463.

85. Ibid.

86. Ibid., p. 39.

87. Ibid., p. 397.

88. Ibid., p. 470.

Chapter Two

1. Kirkland, "The Chicago Fire" (1892), p. 733.

2. Frank J. Loesch, *Personal Experiences during the Chicago Fire, 1871* (Chicago, 1925), p. 10.

3. Thomas Knudtson, *Chicago, The Rising City* (Chicago, 1975), p. 2.

4. Ibid., p. 3.

5. Herbert Butterfield, *The Whig Interpretation of History* (New York, 1951). The Whig fantasy of uninterrupted progress was a dominant idea in the nineteenth century. Mark Twain was particularly susceptible to it. Roger Salomon, *Twain and the Image of History* (New Haven, 1957), pp. 9–10.

6. Kinzie, *Wau-Bun* (1856), p. 95.

7. Kinzie, *Mark Logan, The Bourgeois* (1870), p. 90.

8. Mabel McIlvaine, *Reminiscences of Chicago During the Great Fire* (Chicago, 1915), p. 119.

9. Ibid., pp. 121–22.

10. Ibid., p. 36.

11. Ibid., p. xxx.

12. Unsigned report in *Chicago Post*, October 16, 1871, quoted in Kirkland, "The Chicago Fire," p. 737.

13. McIlvaine, *Reminiscences of Chicago*, p. 39.

14. Ibid., p. 63.

15. Ibid., p. 32.

16. Lennox B. Grey, *Chicago and "The Great American Novel"* (Ph.D. diss., University of Chicago, 1935) is still the best source on the city's frontier writers.

17. Letter of Jonas Hutchinson to his mother, midnight October 10, 1871, in Paul M. Angle, *The Great Chicago Fire* (Chicago, 1946), p. 22.

18. Letter of Mrs. Aurelia King to friends, October 21, 1871, in Angle, *The Great Chicago Fire*, pp. 141, 143.

19. Ibid., p. 43.

20. McIlvaine, *Reminiscences of Chicago*, p. 48.

21. Close, first-hand reports of labor disturbances and life in the ungentrified quarters of the city were elementary exercises in realism. These fragmentary reports of Chicago reality look forward to later, more fully-realized works of Robert Herrick and Henry B. Fuller in the 1890s. Such budding naturalism was mostly discouraged in the frantic rebuilding that followed the fire.

22. E. J. Goodspeed, *History of the Great Fires in Chicago and the West* (New York, 1871), p. 110.

23. Ibid., p. 11.

24. Goodspeed is the natural source of all the fire's evangelical interpretations, including those of Roe, Kirkland, and Swing (all cited above).

25. Goodspeed, *History of the Great Fires in Chicago and the West*, p. 111.

26. Ibid., p. 35.

27. Ibid., p. 517.

28. Lamb, *Spicy* (1873), p. 120.

29. Ibid., p. 159.

30. Ibid., p. 133.

31. Ibid., p. 134.

32. Joseph Kirkland's later novels (*Zury*, 1887, *The McVeys*, 1888, and *The Captain of Company K*, 1890) successfully revived some of the frontier romance. They indicate a continuing interest in a controlled presentation of the past.

33. Lamb, *Spicy*, p. 148.

34. Ibid., p. 149.

35. Ibid.

36. Ibid., p. 151.

37. Ibid., p. 158.

38. Ibid., p. 160.

39. Letter from Horace White to Murat Halstead, October 1871, in McIlvaine, *Reminiscences of Chicago*, p. 69.

40. Swing, "Historic Moments," p. 694.

41. Ibid.

42. Lamb, *Spicy*, p. 133.

43. Such negative events were substantially supported by the public record. See especially Pierce, *History of Chicago*, vol. 1.

44. Lamb, *Spicy*, pp. 174–75.

45. Images of Chicago as a risen Christ augmented those of the phoenix as the city's emblem. See George Alfred Townsend's poem

"The Smitten City," written October 13, 1871, for extensive use of
Christian imagery: "With all my thorns, I wear my civic crown."

257

Notes to Pages 58–73

46. Lamb, *Spicy*, p. 175.

47. McGovern, *Daniel Trentworthy* (1889), p. 5.

48. A. A. Hayes, "The Metropolis of the Prairies," *Harper's* 61(1880):718.

49. Luzerne, *The Lost City* (1872), p. 131.

50. Ibid.

Chapter Three

1. Joseph Kirkland, *The Story of Chicago* (Chicago, 1892), pp. 354–55.

2. Ibid., p. 355.

3. "The Loop" conveniently describes Chicago's downtown business district, even though the encircling elevated rail tracks were not built until 1897.

4. See especially Colbert and Chamberlin, *Chicago and the Great Conflagration* (1871), and Sheahan and Upton, *Chicago: Its Past, Present and Future* (1871), for discussions of the city's lack of fire and disaster planning. Alfred L. Sewall's *The Great Calamity: Scenes, Lessons and Incidents of the Great Fire* (Chicago, 1871), the first book published on the fire, makes a specific issue (p. 74) of drunkenness in the fire department.

5. Charles H. Mackintosh, *The Doomed City: Chicago During an Appalling Ordeal* (Detroit, 1871), p. 31.

6. Subsequent "antifire" legislation disproportionately penalized the working poor who owned their own wooden homes. Eventually they were allowed to rebuild in wood only outside the city's enlarged commercial district, but the stigma of their responsibility for the fire remained.

7. Mackintosh, *The Doomed City*, p. 22.

8. Sewall, *The Great Calamity*, p. 27.

9. Thomas Eddy Tallmadge, *Architecture in Old Chicago* (Chicago, 1941), p. 74.

10. Mackintosh, *The Doomed City*, pp. 11, 32.

11. John G. Shortall in Kirkland, *The Story of Chicago*, p. 315.

12. Mackintosh, *The Doomed City*, p. 16.

13. Ibid., pp. 16–17.

14. Sewall, *The Great Calamity*, p. 31.

15. Mackintosh, *The Doomed City*, p. 30.

16. F. B. Wilkie, "Among the Ruins," *The Lakeside Monthly* 7 (January 1872):51.

17. H. R. Hobart, "The Flight for Life," *The Lakeside Monthly* 7 (January 1872):42.

18. Sewall, *The Great Calamity*, p. 18.

19. Thomas Carlyle, "Letter to Varnhagen," quoted in Will Payne, "Literary Chicago," *The New England Magazine* (February 1893):683.

20. Payne, "Literary Chicago," p. 18.

21. Sigfried Giedion, *Space, Time and Architecture*, 5th ed. (Cambridge, 1974; first published, 1941), pp. 346–54. Paul Sprague, "The Origin of Balloon Framing," *Journal of the Society of Architectural Historians* 40 (1981):311–14. Tallmadge, *Architecture in Old Chicago*, pp. 38–39.

22. Reconceptualized in terms of the extraordinary tensile qualities of Bessemer steel, the balloon frame became the mainstay of urban design and permanently associated with Chicago architecture's contribution to the skyscraper.

23. J. B. Runnion, "Our Aesthetical Development," *The Lakeside Monthly* 7 (January 1872):18–19.

24. Mackintosh, *The Doomed City*, p. 8.

25. Newspaper accounts of such urban homesteading are documented in Christine Meisner Rosen's *The Limits of Power: Great Fires and the Process of City Growth in America* (New York, 1986), pp. 101, 354, an excellent study of the public policy issues raised by the fire. See especially: *Chicago Tribune*, January 15, 1872; *Chicago Times*, January 13, 15, 1872; and Anton Hesing's letters in *Chicago Evening Post*, January 17, 1872, and *Chicago Tribune*, January 18, 1872.

26. *The Lakeside Monthly* 7 (January 1872):261.

27. For prefire demographic, political, and economic surveys, see Elias Colbert, *Chicago: Historical and Statistical Sketch of the Garden City,* (Chicago 1868).

28. McGovern, *Daniel Trentworthy* (1889), p. 72.

29. Rosen, *The Limits of Power*, pp. 162–63, 174.

30. This and all quotes above refer in order to McGovern, *Daniel Trentworthy*, pp. 190, 8–9, 17, 215, 111, 279, 190.

31. Sewall, *The Great Calamity*, p. 78.

32. Ibid., p. 77.

33. Wilkie, "Among the Ruins," p. 53.

34. Ibid.

35. A. T. Andreas, *History of Chicago* (New York, 1975; first published 1884–86) 3:64.

36. "The Melting Pot Explodes," in Dedmon, *Fabulous Chicago* (1953), pp. 148–62, provides a good summary of labor and political agitation in the period from the fire to the world's fair. The use of the term "Chicago School" was popularized and given international academic authority by Sigfried Giedion in *Space, Time and Architecture*.

37. A notable exception is Tallmadge, *Architecture in Old Chicago*. Carl W. Condit's invaluable study, *The Chicago School of Architecture* (Chicago, 1964), is subtitled *A History of Commercial and Public Building in the Chicago Area, 1875–1925*, indicating that he felt the period 1871–74 to be of little architectural interest.

38. The invention of the electric elevator, experiments with poured-concrete construction, and pioneering work in effective fireproofing all took place during the seventies.

39. Root's letter to his sister, April 29, 1875, in Harriet Monroe, *John Wellborn Root* (Park Forest, Ill., 1966; first published, 1896), p. 28.

40. Ibid., pp. 30–31.

41. Root's letter home to his family, January 1876, in Monroe, *John Wellborn Root*, pp. 34–35.

42. Kirkland, *The Story of Chicago*, pp. 331–32.

43. Rosen, *The Limits of Power*, p. 107.

44. Kirkland, *The Story of Chicago*, p. 356.

45. H. W. Thomas in Andreas, *History of Chicago* 3:55.

46. Ibid., p. 54.

47. This and all quotes above refer in order to ibid., pp. 60, 64, 63.

48. Tallmadge, *Architecture in Old Chicago*, p. 76.

49. *Industrial Chicago*, p. 57.

50. Ibid., p. 56.

51. Jenney's successful transformation or abstraction of the Gothic—referred to at the time as Ruskinized—is the counterpart to the modernizing, a decade later, of Richardsonian Romanesque by Root and Sullivan. Jenney appears to have turned away from his early experiments with "transforming" or stripping down medieval styles. The following year, his Lakeside Building (1873) employed a more literal use of Gothic elements.

52. *Industrial Chicago*, p. 62.

53. Condit, *The Chicago School of Architecture*, p. 23.

54. Louis H. Sullivan, *The Autobiography of an Idea*, (New York, 1954; originally published by AIA Press, 1924), p. 201.

55. For photographs of the fire see *Chicago History: The Magazine of the Chicago Historical Society* 1, no. 4 (Fall 1971); David Lowe, *Lost Chicago* (Boston, 1975); and David Lowe, ed., *The Great Chicago Fire*, (New York, 1979).

56. Sullivan, *The Autobiography of an Idea*, p. 201.

57. Marshall Berman, "Goethe's Faust: The Tragedy of Development," in *All That Is Solid Melts into Air* (1982), pp. 37–86.

58. Sullivan, *The Autobiography of an Idea*, p. 199.

59. Louis Sullivan, *Kindergarten Chats and other Writings* (New York, 1947; first published 1901, 1918), p. 22.

Chapter Four

1. Wilkie, "Among the Ruins" (1872), p. 51.

2. Whenever possible I will refer to the principal designer rather than to the firm when crediting architects.

3. Sullivan discovered in H. H. Richardson's use of the Romanesque an efficient way to rationalize and unify large building design without resorting to more vernacular neoclassical sources. Romanesque was still at that time exclusively associated with professional architects. For further discussion of this matter see Tallmadge, *Architecture in Old Chicago* (1941), pp. 157, 158, 171, and Hugh Morrison, *Louis Sullivan: Prophet of Modern Architecture* (New York, 1962), p. 87.

4. Monroe, *John Wellborn Root*, (1896), p. 141.

5. Mrs. Glessner's journals, kept over a fifty-year period between the 1870s and the 1920s, are in the Chicago Historical Society.

6. Jenney's Home Insurance Building's designation as the first steel- or iron-frame building is based more on myth than fact. Carl Condit, among others, has demonstrated that there were antecedents. Particularly see Gerald R. Larson, "The Iron Skeleton Frame: Interactions between Europe and the United States," in John Zukowsky, ed., *Chicago Architecture: 1872–1922* (Munich and Chicago, 1987), pp. 38–55.

7. Morrison, *Louis Sullivan*, p. 90. Root earlier had employed steel-frame construction in all the Rookery (1885–86) except its main elevations. See also Condit, *The Chicago School of Architecture*, p. 63, and Donald Hoffmann, *The Architecture of John Wellborn Root* (Baltimore, 1973), pp. 69–70, for excellent technical discussions of the Rookery's structure.

8. Sullivan, *The Autobiography of an Idea* (1924), p. 292.

9. Within a week of the fire politicians and builders were planning new uses for the burned land, including a comprehensive central railroad passenger terminal on the lakefront. See Rosen, *The Limits of Power*, p. 94.

10. Sullivan, *The Autobiography of an Idea*, p. 187.

11. G. W. Steevens, *The Land of the Dollar*, (New York, 1897), pp. 149–50.

12. See Condit, *The Chicago School of Architecture*, pp. 9–11, for a brief discussion of those like Ralph Waldo Emerson, Horatio Greenough, and James Jarves with earlier claims to the idea. Its many authors testify to the fact that the idea was firmly grounded in the American experience.

13. Dolores Hayden, *Seven American Utopias: The Architecture of Communitarian Socialism, 1790–1975* (Cambridge, 1976). See Gwendolyn Wright, *Moralism and the Model Home: Domestic Architecture and Cultural Conflict in Chicago, 1873–1913* (Chicago, 1980), and *Palliser's Model Homes, 1878* (Bridgeport, Conn., 1878) for the sentimental tradition in nineteenth-century American architecture that complemented the high functional art of the utopian settlements.

14. Sullivan, *Kindergarten Chats* (1901, 1918), p. 138.

15. Wright's early dislike of tall buildings probably had more to do with the lack of a suitable client than ideology. As early as 1912 he prepared a slab design for San Francisco, in the 1920's St. Mark's in the Bowery and National Life Towers, and the aborted Lake Front and Mile High towers of the 1950s. As with Sullivan, his rhetoric was not always consistent with his buildings.

16. Sullivan, "The Tall Office Building Artistically Considered," first published in *Lippincott's* (March 1896), in *Kindergarten Chats*, p. 202.

17. Ibid., pp. 202, 206, 213.

18. Henry B. Fuller, *The Cliff-Dwellers* (New York, 1893), pp. 240–41.

19. See the *Chicago Tribune* of December 8, 10, 12, 1889.

20. Montgomery Schuyler, "Architecture in Chicago," in William H. Jordy and Ralph Coe, eds.. *American Architecture and Other Writings* (Cambridge, 1961), p. 378.

21. Paul Bourget, *Outre-Mer,* quoted in Schuyler, "Architecture in Chicago," p. 382.

22. Frank Norris, *The Pit* (New York, 1956; first published 1902), pp. 5–6.

23. Ibid., p. 65. See also David Goodwin, *The Dearborns* (Chicago, 1884), for a contemporary sense of the dynastic meaning of the name.

24. Norris, *The Pit,* p. 23.

25. Ibid., p. 63.

26. Sullivan, *The Autobiography of an Idea,* p. 63. In addition to writing books and lectures, Sullivan was an important contributor to *The Inland Architect* (1885–1908), which began as a trade journal like *Building Budget* (1885–87) but later took on the character of a journal of opinion. All of Chicago's principal architects contributed to it.

27. Henry B. Fuller, *With the Procession* (Chicago, 1965; first published 1895), p. 155; *Industrial Chicago,* p. 63. The primary influence of the time was East Coast neoclassicism, championed by the great modern architectural firm of McKim, Mead, and White.

28. John Root, "A Great Architectural Problem," in Donald Hoffmann, ed., *The Meaning of Architecture* (New York, 1967), p. 133.

29. The Boston developer Peter Brooks originally wished to build a hotel in anticipation of the world's fair for Darius Ogden Mills. See Hoffmann, *The Architecture of John Wellborn Root,* p. 206. Owing to the developer's delays, Root was only able to design the first four stories of the Reliance Building before his death. Credit for the completed skyscraper goes to Charles Atwood, Root's successor at the firm.

30. Montgomery Schuyler, "D. H. Burnham & Co.," in Jordy and Coe, eds., *American Architecture and Other Writings,* pp. 407–8.

31. This is not in any way to diminish Burnham's considerable architectural abilities, seen most dramatically in New York's Flatiron Building (1903). For the fullest treatment of Burnham's own career, see Charles Moore, *Daniel H. Burnham Architect, Planner of Cities,* 2 vols. (Boston, 1921), and Thomas Hines's excellent modern biography, *Burnham of Chicago* (New York, 1974).

32. Hoffmann, *The Architecture of John Wellborn Root,* p. 182.

33. Henry Van Brunt, "Architecture in the West," *Atlantic Monthly* 64 (December 1889):777.

34. Frank Lloyd Wright, Sullivan's protégé, never built a commercial building in Chicago. His Unity Temple in Oak Park was a self-conscious throwback to the early synagogues of Adler and Sullivan, who would design a religious structure with the same care as a modern office tower.

35. See Robert Prestiano's *The Inland Architect: Chicago's Major Architectural Journal, 1883–1908* (Ann Arbor, 1985), for a study of the magazine's wider cultural importance.

36. Root, "A Great Architectural Problem," p. 132.

37. See the culmination of their approach in Burnham's contribution to the Chicago Plan of 1909. Hines's *Burnham of Chicago,* pp. 312–45, is a particularly good critical source.

38. Root, "A Great Architectural Problem," p. 141.

39. Ibid.

40. Ibid.

41. Schuyler, "D. H. Burnham & Co.," p. 410.

42. Fuller, *The Cliff-Dwellers*, p. 5.

43. Drawings to this effect are in the collection of the Canadian Centre for Architecture in Montreal.

44. Hoffmann, *The Architecture of John Wellborn Root*, pp. 180–81.

45. *Economist* (August 17, 1889) 2:717.

46. Hoffmann, *The Architecture of John Wellborn Root*, p. 156, and Donald Hoffmann, "John Root's Monadnock Building," *Journal of the Society of Architectural Historians* 26 (December 1967).

47. For the full effect of Sullivan's remarks, think of New York's Sixth Avenue of the 1960s and 1970s.

48. Donald Hoffmann, in *The Architecture of John Wellborn Root*, suggests that P. B. Wight's "On the Present Condition of Architectural Arts in the Western States," *American Art Review* 1 (1880), influenced developers and architects against conspicuous ornamentation.

49. John Root, "Fire Insurance and Architecture," *American Architect and Building News* 20, no. 561 (September 25, 1886).

50. Fuller, *The Cliff-Dwellers*, p. 1.

51. Root, "A Great Architectural Problem," p. 141.

52. Saul Bellow, *Humboldt's Gift* (New York, 1975), p. 101.

53. The modernism of the Loop contrasted with the white neoclassicism of the World's Columbian Exposition. In the years immediately after the fair, Chicago architects began to indulge in more blatantly historicist design. The Tribune Tower competition in 1922 furthered the influence of the East Coast style of building in Chicago. Raymond Hood's neo-Gothic design won out against an expressionist entry, like a Hugh Ferris drawing, by Eliel Saarinen and an international-style submission by Walter Gropius. Chicago's return to derivative architecture at this time has not yet been adequately examined.

54. Such an explosive period of invention has been repeated in our own time in California's "Silicon Valley," where production of extraordinary quality has kept pace with invention.

55. Wilkie, "Among the Ruins," p. 51.

56. Rosen, *The Limits of Power* (1986), pp. 119–20.

57. Hobart, "The Flight for Life" (1872), p. 42.

58. Sigmund Freud, "Mourning and Melancholia," in Philip Rieff, ed., *General Psychological Theory* (New York, 1963), p. 164 (first published 1917).

Chapter Five

1. For further discussion of this critical component in the development of the tall commercial structures see Frank A. Randall, *History of the Development of Building Construction in Chicago* (Urbana, 1949), pp. 14, 65, and *Chicago History* (Summer 1987), pp. 64–72.

2. Montgomery Schuyler, "Modern Architecture," in Jordy and Coe, eds., *American Architecture and Other Writings*, pp. 113–14.

3. Henry-Russel Hitchcock, *Architecture: Nineteenth and Twentieth Centuries* (Pelican History of Art, 1971), pp. 337, 341.

4. William H. Jordy, *American Buildings and their Architects: Progressive and Academic Ideals at the turn of the Twentieth Century* (Garden City, 1972), p. 26.

5. James Jackson Jarves, *The Art-Idea* (Cambridge, 1960; first published 1864), p. 227

6. Rufus Blanchard, *Discovery and Conquests of the Northwest with the History of Chicago* (Chicago, 1881), p. 697.

7. F. H. Stead, "The Civic Life of Chicago," *Review of Reviews* (August 1893):179.

8. Ibid.

9. Fuller, *With the Procession* (1895), p. 77.

10. See Andrew Saint, *The Image of the Architect* (New Haven, 1983), and Spiro Kostof, ed., *The Architect: Chapters in the History of the Profession* (New York, 1977), for two excellent discussions of the architect's professional role.

11. Paul Bourget, *Outre-Mer* (New York, 1895), p. 117.

12. Ibid., p. 115.

13. Ibid., p. 116.

14. Ibid.

15. Anthony Trollope, *North America* (Philadelphia, 1863), 1:176.

16. Steevens, *The Land of the Dollar* (1897), p. 186.

17. Ibid., p. 189.

18. Ibid., pp. 192–93.

19. Ibid., p. 193.

20. In the plans for the first memorial scheme, Jenney tried to invent a new response to disaster. This was unprecedented, breaking radically with Christopher Wren's celebrated and imitated monument to the Fire of London. Jenney experimented with a form of populist or primitive art that culminated in Simon Rodia's Watts Tower (1921–54) in Los Angeles, in which the architecture is composed of waste materials—soda bottles, china, shards of tile.

21. Theodore Jurak, *William Le Baron Jenney: A Pioneer of Modern Architecture* (Ann Arbor, 1986), p. 91.

22. "The Report of the West Chicago Park Commissioners for 1873," p. 49.

23. Ibid.

24. John C. Van Horne, ed., *The Correspondence and Miscellaneous Papers of Benjamin Henry Latrobe*, vol. 3, 1811–1820 (New Haven, 1988), p. 916.

25. See Howard C. Rice, Jr., *Thomas Jefferson's Paris* (Princeton, 1976), and Rich Bornemann, "Some Ledoux-Inspired Buildings in America," *Journal of the Society of Architectural Historians* 13, no. 1 (March 1954).

26. See Anthony Vidler, *The Writing of the Walls* (Princeton, 1987), for an excellent discussion of French postrevolutionary architecture.

27. William Henry Furness, Closing Address, November 9, 1870, *Proceedings of the Fourth Annual Convention of the American Institute of Architects* (New York, 1871), in Don Gifford, ed., *The Literature of Architecture: The Evolution of Architectural Theory and Practice in Nineteenth Century America* (New York, 1966), p. 391.

28. Horatio Greenough, "American Architecture" (1853), in Harold A. Small, ed., *Form and Function* (Berkeley, 1947), p. 53.

29. Calvert Vaux, *Villas and Cottages* (New York, 1970; first published 1857), p. 25.

30. Furness, Closing Address, in Gifford, ed., *The Literature of Architecture*, pp. 393–94.

31. Jarves, *The Art-Idea*, p. 227.

32. Richard Guy Wilson and William B. Rhoads have written extensively on this subject. J. Meredith Neil's *Toward a National Taste* (1975) is another good source. I am indebted to John Zukowsky, Curator of Architecture, the Art Institute of Chicago, for his comments on this subject.

33. Bourget, *Outre-Mer*, p. 117.

34. Jarves, *The Art-Idea*, pp. 236–37.

35. See David Van Zanten's "The Nineteenth Century: The Projecting of Chicago as a Commercial City and the Rationalization of Design and Construction," in *Chicago and New York: Architectural Interactions* (Art Institute of Chicago Exhibition Catalog, 1984), pp. 30–49.

36. A contemporary of Burnham, quoted in Saint, *Image of the Architect*, p. 87.

37. Sullivan, *The Autobiography of an Idea* (1924), p. 76.

38. Paul Starrett, *Changing the Skyline* (New York, 1938), p. 110.

39. Ibid., p. 29.

40. "High brow populism" is my term, an attempt to characterize Sullivan's and Wright's attempt to find a mass audience. But like Hawthorne, Whitman, and Twain before them, they were also concerned about educating or leading any mass audience that they might ultimately find.

41. Upon Richardson's premature death shortly after this photograph was taken, his Boston firm was renamed Sheply, Rutan, and Coolidge. In the 1890s, Coolidge established offices in St. Louis and Chicago. Based on a classic tripartite organization, the firm fast became one of Chicago's sturdiest, if uninspired, architectural businesses.

42. The photograph can be found reprinted in *Western Architect* (January 1925).

43. Letter from Daniel Burnham to his mother, May 11, 1868. In manuscript collection of the Burnham Library, Art Institute of Chicago.

44. Frank Lloyd Wright, *Genius and the Mobocracy* (New York, 1971; first published 1949), p. 94.

45. Letter from Wright to Dr. Hendrick Petrus Berlage, November 30, 1922, in Bruce Brooks Pfeiffer, ed., *Letters to Architects* (Fresno, 1984), p. 54.

47. Ibid.

48. Sullivan, *Kindergarten Chats* (1901, 1918), p. 31.

Chapter Six

1. Charles Moore, *Daniel H. Burnham: Architect Planner of Cities* (New York, 1968; first published 1921), pp. 16–17.

2. Ibid., p. 17.

3. As quoted by Sarah Bradford Landau, *P. B. Wight: Architect, Contractor and Critic, 1838–1925* (Chicago, 1981), p. 54.

4. Meredith L. Clausen, "Paris of the 1880's and the Rookery," in Zukowsky, ed., *Chicago Architecture: 1872–1922* (1987), pp. 157–71.

5. Frank Lloyd Wright, *An Autobiography*, (New York, 1977; first published 1932), p. 151. There is no absolute documentation for this offer, but it has been generally accepted as fact. See Giorgio Ciucci, Francesco Dal Co, et al., *The American City: From the Civil War to the New Deal* (Cambridge, 1979), p. 42, and Wright's most recent biographer, Brendan Gill, in *Many Masks: A Life of Frank Lloyd Wright* (New York, 1987), p. 117.

6. Louis Sullivan,"Revulsion," in *Kindergarten Chats* (1901, 1918), p. 94.

7. Sullivan, *Kindergarten Chats*, p. 202.

8. Fuller, *The Cliff-Dwellers*, (1893), p. 94.

9. W. D. Howells, "Certain of the Chicago School of Fiction," *North American Review* 176 (1903):740.

10. Fuller, *The Cliff-Dwellers*, p. 5.

11. Henry B. Fuller, "Art in America," *Bookman* 10 (September 1899–February 1900):223.

12. Fuller, *The Cliff-Dwellers*, pp. 4–5.

13. Ibid., pp. 3–4.

14. Robert Herrick, *The Common Lot*, (New York, 1904), p. 319.

15. Robert Herrick, *The Web of Life*, (New York, 1900), p. 167.

16. Will Payne, *Mr. Salt* (Boston, 1904), pp. 138–39.

17. H. H. Van Meter, *The Vanishing Fair* (Chicago, 1894).

18. Will Payne, *The Money Captain* (Chicago, 1895), p. 1.

19. Ibid., p. 5.

20. Ibid.

21. Ibid., pp. 103, 5.

22. Robert Herrick, "The Background of the American Novel," *Yale Review* 3 (January 1914):222.

23. Ibid., p. 215.

24. Henry B. Fuller, "The Downfall of Abner Joyce," in *Under the Skylights* (New York, 1901), pp. 16–17.

25. Ibid., p. 27.

26. Ibid., p. 31.

27. Ibid., p. 139.

28. Henry B. Fuller, "Little O'Grady vs. the Grindstone," in *Under the Skylights*, p. 148.

29. Ibid., p. 149.

30. Ibid., p. 208.

31. Ibid., p. 197.

32. Ibid.

33. Ibid.

34. Ibid., p. 272.

35. Ibid., p. 289.

36. Ibid., p. 322.

37. Henry James, *The American Scene* (Bloomington, 1968; first published 1907), p. 86.

38. Herrick, *The Common Lot*, p. 22.

39. Robert Herrick, *Literary Love Letters*, (New York, 1897), p. 21.

40. Herrick, *The Common Lot*, p. 187.

41. Will Payne, *Jerry the Dreamer* (New York, 1896), pp. 53–54.

42. Ibid., p. 118.

43. Ibid., p. 117.

44. Ibid., p. 118.

45. Fuller, *With the Procession*, pp. 72–73.

46. Payne, *Jerry the Dreamer*, p. 56.

47. Herrick, *The Common Lot*, p. 28.

48. Ibid., p. 55.

49. Ibid., p. 10.

50. Ibid., p. 21.

51. Ibid., p. 6.

52. Ibid., p. 24.

53. Ibid., p. 63.

54. Ibid., p. 336.

55. Ibid., pp. 381–82.

56. Ibid., p. 313.

57. Ibid., p. 315.

58. Ibid., p. 320.

59. Ibid., p. 322.

60. Fuller, *The Cliff-Dwellers*, p. 50.

61. Ibid., p. 57.

62. Ibid., pp. 95–96.

63. Ibid., p. 97.

64. Ibid., p. 217.

65. Fuller, *With the Procession*, p. 10.

66. Ibid., pp. 132–33.

67. Theodore Dreiser, *The Titan*, (New York, 1965; first published 1914), p. 11.

68. Ibid., p. 12.

69. Ibid., p. 13.

70. Ibid., p. 84.

71. Victor Hugo, *Notre-Dame de Paris* (London, 1979; first published 1831), p. 168.

72. Ibid., p. 169.

73. Henry Adams, *The Education of Henry Adams* (Boston, 1961; first published 1918), p. 317.

74. Leo Marx, "The Puzzle of Anti-Urbanism in American Literature," in *The Pilot and the Passenger: Essays on Literature, Technology, and*

Culture in the United States (New York, 1988). Marx wisely cautions against a sort of literary argument that proposes a direct relation between the "urbanizing America out there in reality and the imagined world we encounter in literature." (p. 211) He adds that an enduring naturalistic fiction must have what Dostoevsky called a higher realism. Marx is right in arguing that classic American writers like Hawthorne, Melville, and James remained "nonrealistic in the sense that they represent place not chiefly for what it is, but for what it means." (p. 220) The writers I have been considering were more bogged down in detail and fact. They were never completely successful in reimagining what they observed.

Chapter Seven

1. Adams, *The Education of Henry Adams* (1918), p. 343.

2. *The Chicago Record's History of the World's Fair* (Chicago, 1893), p. 253.

3. Moore, *Daniel H. Burnham* (1921), p. 42; see also Hines, *Burnham of Chicago* (1974), pp. 86–87. The move back to neoclassicism also broke with the fair's most recent precedent, the Paris Exposition (1889), where the Eiffel Tower—a denuded version of Chicago architecture—lured fairgoers to the city. Burnham consciously turned away from using the novelty of the skyscraper as a gateway to the city.

4. Louis Sullivan found Richardson's example so compelling that his Walker Warehouse (1888–89) was strictly modeled on the Boston architect's earlier work. The Auditorium Building also owes an immediate debt to Richardson.

5. Payne, *Mr. Salt* (1904), pp. 56–57.

6. Lyman Gage, *The World's Columbian Exposition: First Annual Report of the President* (Chicago, 1891).

7. Greenough, "American Architecture" (1853), p. 57.

8. Quoted in J. Seymour Currey, *Chicago: Its History and Its Builders: A Century of Growth* (Chicago, 1912), p. 82.

9. Sara Norton and M. A. DeWolfe Howe, eds., *Letters of Charles Eliot Norton* (Boston, 1913) 2:216. (Emphasis mine.)

10. Henry B. Fuller, *Wednesday Morning News Record*, September 14, 1892.

11. Quoted in Eric Homberger, "Chicago and New York: Two Versions of American Modernism," in Malcolm Bradbury and James McFarlane, eds., *Modernism* (New York, 1976), p. 152.

12. Lloyd Lewis and Henry Justin Smith, *Chicago: The History of its Reputation* (New York, 1929), p. 217.

13. Clara Louise Burnham, *Sweet Clover: A Romance of the White City* (Boston, 1894), p. 181.

14. Paul Bourget, "A Farewell to the White City," *Cosmopolitan* 16 (December 1893):134–35.

15. Fyodor Dostoevsky in *Notes from the Underground* (1864; Jessie Coulson, trans., 1972) declared St. Petersburg to be different from its European models. "For ordinary human life it would be more than

sufficient to possess ordinary human intellectual activity, that is to say, half or quarter as much as falls to the lot of an educated man in our unhappy nineteenth century, and especially one having the misfortune to live in St. Petersburg, the most abstract and intentional city in the whole round world." Joseph Brodsky further explores the modern phenomenon of willed cities in "A Guide to a Renamed City," in *Less than One* (New York, 1986).

16. Montgomery Schuyler, "Last Words about The World's Fair," in Jordy and Coe, eds., *American Architecture and Other Writings*, p. 569.

17. Moore, *Daniel H. Burnham*, p. 43.

18. Daniel H. Burnham and Edward H. Bennett, *Plan of Chicago* (Chicago, 1909), p. 1. (Emphasis mine.)

19. Ibid., p. 4.

20. Robert W. Rydell, *All the World's a Fair* (Chicago, 1984), p. 46.

21. Robert Herrick's *The Web of Life* and *Waste*, Will Payne's *Mr. Salt*, and Frances Hodgson Burnett's *Two Little Pilgrims' Progress* are other novels by Chicago authors that make substantial use of the fair as background.

22. C. L. Burnham, *Sweet Clover*, p. 125.

23. M. G. Van Rensselaer, "The Artistic Triumph of the Fair-Builders," *Forum* 14 (December 1892):528.

24. George Santayana, "The Genteel Tradition in American Philosophy," in Douglas L. Wilson, ed., *The Genteel Tradition: Nine Essays by George Santayana* (Cambridge, Mass 1967), p. 51.

25. Ibid., p. 40.

26. C. L. Burnham, *Sweet Clover*, p. 181.

27. Ibid., p. 200.

28. Van Rensselaer, "The Artistic Triumph of the Fair-Builders," p. 531.

29. C. L. Burnham, *Sweet Clover*, p. 182. (Emphasis mine.)

30. Ibid., pp. 178–79.

31. Ibid., p. 397. Will Payne, in *Mr. Salt*, pp. 58–59, exploited the same analogy between the uncontrolled great fire and the controlled light of the fair: "The entire Fair stood forth in light. It was like a spectacle of creation."

32. C. L. Burnham, *Sweet Clover*, p. 191.

33. Ibid., p. 206.

34. Ibid., pp. 214–15.

35. Joseph Kirkland and Caroline Kirkland, *The Story of Chicago*, vol. 2 (Chicago, 1894), p. 19.

36. C. L. Burnham, *Sweet Clover*, p. 34.

37. Ibid., p. 152.

38. Theodore Dreiser used this phrase to describe Carrie Meeber in *Sister Carrie* (1900). She is a midwestern counterpart to Henry James's "new woman." In Chicago, she is a materialist, motivated by things. Frank Norris in *The Pit* (1903) described a similar phenomenon: in Chicago "everywhere the eye was arrested by the luxury of stuffs."

Most prominently among nineteenth-century writers, Nathaniel Hawthorne used the story of the Veiled Lady as the focus of
The Blithedale Romance (1852).

40. Dimitri Tselos, "The Chicago Fair and the Myth of the 'Lost
Cause'," *Journal of the Society of Architectural Historians* 26, no. 4 (December 1967):265.

41. Hugh Morrison, in *Louis Sullivan: Prophet of Modern Architecture*(1962), looked beyond the walls of the Transportation Building.
He concluded that the golden doorway had to be considered as only
an isolated fragment, inflating the impression of what was simply "a
great shed." Carl Condit's recent work does much to focus interest
on the railroad as Chicago's principal resource. In this regard, the
train shed had great iconographic power.

42. Sullivan, *Autobiography of an Idea*, (1924), p. 325.

43. Tselos, "The Chicago Fair and the Myth of the 'Lost Cause',"
p. 259.

44. See David H. Crook, "Louis Sullivan and the Golden Doorway," *Journal of the Society of Architectural Historians* 26, no. 4 (December 1967).

45. A. D. F. Hamlin, "The Battle of the Styles," *Architectural Record* 1, no. 3:274.

46. Schuyler, "Last Words about the World's Fair," p. 562.

47. Schuyler, "Last Words about the World's Fair," p. 562.

48. See Joan E. Draper's recent discussion, "Paris by the Lake:
Sources of Burnham's Plan of Chicago," in Zukowsky, ed., *Chicago
Architecture 1872–1922* (1987).

49. The best source for this subject remains Leo Marx's *The Machine in the Garden* (New York, 1964) and his recent collection of essays, *The Pilot and the Passenger* (1988). In addition, Norman T. Newton's *Design on the Land: The Development of Landscape Architecture*
(Cambridge, 1971) and John Brinckerhoff Jackson's *American Space*
(New York, 1972) are critical studies of the history of American land
planning.

50. Bourget, "A Farewell to the White City," p. 135.

51. Chicago legend has it that the city beat out New York for the
honor of hosting the fair. But as early as 1889, when plans were first
being discussed, there was considerable agitation to take New York
out of the running. The influential *Garden and Forest* ran an editorial
by Professor C. S. Sargent, Director of Harvard's Arnold Arboretum,
arguing that the exposition would violate the idea of Central Park as
an urban preserve. He wrote that he felt such a commercial use
would violate "pleasure grounds absolutely indispensable to the
well-being of those who are subjected to the complex conditions of
modern city life." *Garden and Forest*, (September 25, 1889):457. J. Seymour Currey in *Chicago: Its History and Its Builders*, 3:90, quotes the
Chicago Record's History of the World's Fair to this effect: "Most of the
visitors to the Fair grounds must have been impressed by the great
contrast between their southern and northern sections. In the first
the effect aimed at is that of the formal, the academic, the ceremo-

nial. In the second, art makes some concession to nature and the balance and symmetry required by the classic style give way to an adjustment that permits a free expression of the informal and the picturesque."

52. Mayor Daley's postwar redevelopment kept to a narrow alley on a north-south axis near the lake, at the expense of the inland neighborhoods.

53. Bourget, "A Farewell to the White City," p. 135.

54. Edgar Allan Poe, "The Imp of the Perverse" (1845). The story concerns a man who commits a perfect crime only to perversely admit his guilt.

55. Henry B. Fuller, "The Upward Movement in Chicago," *Atlantic Monthly* 80, no. 480 (October 1897):534.

56. Bourget, "A Farewell to the White City," p. 136.

57. Fuller, "The Upward Movement in Chicago," p. 534.

58. Bourget, "A Farewell to the White City," p. 135.

59. After two earlier buildings, the Art Institute was housed in Shepley, Rutan, and Coolidge's Renaissance palazzo. Despite the new quarters, it could not escape the old incongruities. Built on landfill from the fire and straddling the rails near the Loop, the Art Institute was still in the Chicago condition.

60. I am indebted to Richard J. Storr's comprehensive history of the university's early years, *Harper's University: The Beginnings* (Chicago, 1966), and to W. M. Murphy and D. J. R. Bruckner, eds., *The Idea of the University of Chicago* (Chicago, 1976).

61. Quoted in Storr, *Harper's University*, p. 183.

62. Fuller, "The Upward Movement in Chicago," p. 534.

63. William Morton Payne, "Literary Chicago," *The New England Magazine*, n.s., 7, no. 6 (February 1893):683.

64. *Dial*, 13, no. 151 (October 1, 1892):206.

65. We can see how remarkable *The Inland Architect* was when we directly compare it to *Building Budget*. Also conceived and published in Chicago, it remained a sectarian trade journal and never became a forum for ideas outside narrow professional concerns.

66. Robert Herrick, *Myself*, unpublished typed manuscript, 1898, University of Chicago Library, p. 39.

67. Ibid., p. 50.

68. Ibid., p. 78.

69. Ibid., p. 76.

70. Ibid., pp. 46–47.

71. Ibid., p. 47.

72. Ibid., p. 48.

73. Payne, *The Money Captain* (1898), pp. 4–5. (Emphasis mine.)

74. Fuller *With the Procession*, p. 117.

75. Ibid., p. 203.

76. Ibid., p. 204.

77. Herrick, *Myself*, p. 52.

78. Ibid.

79. Ibid., p. 51.

80. Ibid., p. 64.

81. Ibid., p. 61.

82. Currey, *Chicago: Its History and Its Builders*, p. 82.

83. *Frank Leslie's Popular Monthly* 36 (October 1893):415.

84. A fine mapping and history of the Loop and South Side neighborhoods can be found in Glen E. Holt and Dominic A. Pacyga's *Chicago: A Historical Guide to the Neighborhoods* (Chicago, 1979). Particularly useful is their discussion of the development of Paul Cornell's Hyde Park and Dr. John A. Kennicott's Kenwood communities in the 1850s.

85. We can observe a similar positive effect on contiguous land values after the building of Central Park. See my "Building Urban Parks," in Neil Larry Shumsky and Timothy J. Crimmins, eds., *American Life, American People*, vol. 1 (San Diego, 1987).

86. Herman Melville, *Moby-Dick* (Evanston, 1988; first published 1851), p. 27.

87. Gentrification extended to the designation of the Midway as a plaisance, a variation of pleasance; a pleasure ground or garden attached to an estate or mansion.

88. "On Midway Plaisance," in *The Chicago Record's History of the World's Fair*, p. 247.

89. *Picturesque Chicago and Guide to the World's Fair* (Hartford, 1893), p. 286.

90. Rydell, "'And Was Jerusalem Builded Here'," in *All The World's A Fair* is particularly strong in demythologizing the Midway's cultural implications and exploring its ethnic hierarchies.

91. Denton J. Snider in *The Chicago Tribune*, as quoted in ibid., p. 65.

92. "On Midway Plaisance," p. 249.

93. Ibid.

94. Ibid.

95. Theodore Dreiser, *Newspaper Days* (New York, 1922), p. 1.

96. Ibid., p. 65.

97. Currey, *Chicago: Its History and Its Builders*, p. 85.

98. David F. Burg, *Chicago's White City of 1893* (Lexington, 1976), p. 224.

99. "On Midway Plaisance," p. 237.

100. Currey, *Chicago: Its History and Its Builders*, p. 85.

101. Harvey W. Zorbaugh, *The Gold Coast and the Slum* (Chicago, 1929), p. 3.

102. Ibid., pp. 2–3.

103. Norris, *The Pit* (1903), p. 98.

104. T. D. Nostwich, ed., *Theodore Dreiser Journalism: Newspaper Writings, 1892–1895* (Philadelphia, 1988), pp. 126–27.

105. This earliest urban literature differs from the main-line Chicago literature of Fuller, Herrick, and Payne in the absence of a mediating high-culture character (architect or artist).

106. Carl Smith, "Cataclysm and Cultural Consciousness: Chicago and the Haymarket Trial," *Chicago History* 15, no. 2, (Summer 1986):49–50. Smith makes a strong point about the way radical politics quickly became the subject of potboilers and melodramas, i.e.,

the New York Detective Library's *The Red Flag; or, The Anarchists of Chicago* (1886) and Frank Harris's *The Bomb* (1908). In both cases the anarchists were quickly transformed into a commodity with their politics caricatured.

107. *John Swinton's Paper,* January 24, 1886, as quoted in Henry David, *The History of the Haymarket Affair* (New York, 1936), pp. 125–26.

108. Paul Avrich's *The Haymarket Tragedy* (Princeton, 1984), and William J. Adelman's *Haymarket Revisited* (Chicago, 1976) and *Pilsen and the West Side* (Chicago, 1979) provide excellent background for the Haymarket in particular and labor history in general. In addition, Dave Roediger and Franklin Rosemont's *Haymarket Scrapbook* (1986) is a fine collection of primary sources.

109. It is interesting in this regard to note that Burnham and Root designed the fortresslike First Regiment Armory (1889–91) in response to the Red scare.

110. Stead, *If Christ Came to Chicago,* p. 174.

111. Stead acknowledged his debt to *Chicago's Dark Places* but several times provided a misleading citation.

112. George Wharton James, *Chicago's Dark Places* (Chicago, 1891), p. 14.

113. Stead, *If Christ Came to Chicago,* pp. 174–75.

114. Ibid., p. 210. Stead documents the unprogressive table of assessments for the rich and poor. Not only did this add to the divisions between rich and poor, it also divided the poor from the poorest.

115. Ibid.

116. Ibid., p. 2.

117. Ibid., p. 112.

118. Ibid., p. 3.

119. Ibid., p. 9.

120. Ibid., p. 54.

121. Alexander Pushkin, *The Bronze Horseman,* trans. D. M. Thomas (New York, 1982; first published 1833).

122. Sullivan, *The Autobiography of an Idea,* pp. 198–99.

123. Van Meter, *The Vanishing Fair* (1894).

124. Herrick, *Myself,* p. 49.

125. Herrick, *The Web of Life,* (1900), p. 171.

126. Robert Herrick, *Waste,* (New York, 1924), p. 117.

127. Evidence of continued interest in the city's rituals of founding was the publication in 1884 of Daniel Goodwin's *The Dearborns* for the Chicago Historical Society.

128. Payne, *Mr. Salt,* p. 139.

129. Herrick, *Waste,* p. 117.

130. Melville, *Moby-Dick,* p. 492.

Photo Acknowledgments

1. Claes Oldenburg, Proposal for a Skyscraper for Michigan Avenue, Chicago, in the form of Loredo Taft's Sculpture "Death" (1968). Collage, ink, pencil on postcard on paper, 11¾" × 9¾". Photo by Dorothy Zeidman.

2. A collaboration between Red Grooms and Mimi Gross with "Ruckus Construction Company," *City of Chicago* (1967). Mixed media. Courtesy of the Art Institute of Chicago.

3. Prefire Chicago: Grain elevators on the Chicago River. Collection of David R. Phillips.

4. Chicago: Prefire Chicago: Illinois Central yards. Collection of David R. Phillips.

5. Prefire Chicago: Shipping on the Chicago River. Collection of David R. Phillips.

6. Prefire Chicago: Buildings along the Chicago River. Collection of David R. Phillips.

7. Magazine Illustration: "Scene on the Chicago River. Grain Elevators on Fire" (1871). Collection of David R. Phillips.

8. Title page of *Through the Flames and Beyond,* a book published immediately after the fire. Collection of David R. Phillips.

9. Title page of *The Lakeside Memorial of the Burning of Chicago* (1872). Courtesy of the J. Paul Getty Museum.

10. W. D. Kerfoot's Real Estate Office (1871), the first building constructed after the fire. Collection of David R. Phillips.

11. State Street in the 1890s, showing the Masonic Temple under construction. Collection of David R. Phillips.

12. Ruins of Chicago: Tribune Building, corner of Dearborn and Madison Streets. Albumen print by George N. Barnard reproduced from *The Lakeside Memorial of the Burning of Chicago* (1872). Courtesy of the J. Paul Getty Museum.

13. J. M. Van Osdel, Court House (1853, 1858). Engraving reproduced from *The Lakeside Memorial of the Burning of Chicago* (1872). Courtesy of the J. Paul Getty Museum.

14. Home Insurance Building demolition. Courtesy of the Art Institute of Chicago.

15. W. W. Boyington, Board of Trade Building (1882–85). Photo by J. W. Taylor. Courtesy of the Art Institute of Chicago.

16. J. M. Van Osdel, Reaper Block (1873). Courtesy of the Art Institute of Chicago.

17. William Le Baron Jenny, Portland Block, Dearborn at Washington (1872; photo c. 1878). Courtesy of the Chicago Historical Society.

18. W. W. Boyington, Inter-State Industrial Exposition Building (1872–73). Photo of Litho, 1873. Rider and Barnard Photo. IChi-20354. Courtesy of the Chicago Historical Society.

19. Ruins in Columbia, S.C. (1875). Albumen print by George N. Barnard. Courtesy of the J. Paul Getty Museum.

20. Columbia, S.C., from the capital (1865). Albumen print by George N. Barnard. Courtesy of the J. Paul Getty Museum.

21. Grand Facade, Hôtel de Ville, Paris (1871). Albumen print by A. Liebert. Courtesy of the J. Paul Getty Museum.

22. Interior of the Ballroom, Hôtel de Ville, Paris (1871). Albumen print by A. Liebert. Courtesy of the J. Paul Getty Museum.

23. "Successful Intermediate Excision of the Head and three inches of the Shaft of Right Humerus for Gunshot Fracture" (1874). Albumen print by William Bell. Courtesy of the J. Paul Getty Museum.

24. "Case of Corporal Bemis, thrice severely wounded in Three Battles" (1864). Albumen print by William Bell. Courtesy of the J. Paul Getty Museum.

25. Ruins of Chicago: Entrance to Insurance Exchange, LaSalle Street. Albumen print by George N. Barnard, reproduced from *The Lakeside Memorial of the Burning of Chicago* (1872). Courtesy of the J. Paul Getty Museum.

26. Ruins of Chicago: Field, Leiter & Co.'s Store, corner of State and Washington Streets. Albumen print by George N. Barnard, reproduced from *The Lakeside Memorial of the Burning of Chicago* (1872). Courtesy of the J. Paul Getty Museum.

27. Ruins of Chicago: Chamber of Commerce, corner of LaSalle and Washington Streets. Albumen print by George N. Barnard, reproduced from *The Lakeside Memorial of the Burning of Chicago* (1872). Courtesy of the J. Paul Getty Museum.

28. Ruins of Chicago: Court House, from corner of Clark and Washington Streets. Albumen print by George N. Barnard, reproduced from *The Lakeside Memorial of the Burning of Chicago* (1872). Courtesy of the J. Paul Getty Museum.

29. Ruins of Chicago: Clark Street, looking south from Court House. Albumen print by George N. Barnard, reproduced from *The Lakeside Memorial of the Burning of Chicago* (1872). Courtesy of the J. Paul Getty Museum.

30. Ruins of Chicago: LaSalle Street, looking north from Monroe Street. Albumen print by George N. Barnard, reproduced from *The Lakeside Memorial of the Burning of Chicago* (1982). Courtesy of the J. Paul Getty Museum.

31. Ruins of Chicago: Clark Street, looking north from Court

House. Albumen print by George N. Barnard, reproduced from *The Lakeside Memorial of the Burning of Chicago* (1872). Courtesy of the J. Paul Getty Museum.

32. "Among the Ruins in Chicago. No. 25, Post Office, Interior View, North End" (1871–72). Albumen prints by George N. Barnard. Courtesy of the J. Paul Getty Museum.

33. "Among the Ruins in Chicago. No. 29. Tribune Building, corner of Madison and Dearborn Streets" (1871–72). Albumen prints by George N. Barnard. Courtesy of the J. Paul Getty Museum.

34. H. H. Richardson, Marshall Field Wholesale Warehouse (1885–87). Collection of David R. Phillips.

35. Louis Sullivan, Walker Warehouse (1888). Courtesy of the Art Institute of Chicago.

36. H. H. Richardson, Glessner House, c. 1888. All rights reserved, Chicago Architecture Foundation. Reprinted with permission.

37. H. H. Richardson, Glessner House Courtyard, c. 1888, showing servant petting the Glessner's dog, Hero. All rights reserved, Chicago Architecture Foundation. Reprinted with permission.

38. John W. Root, First Regiment Armory, Chicago (1889–91). Courtesy of the Art Institute of Chicago.

39. Adler and Sullivan, Auditorium Building (1889). Chicago Architectural Photo Co. Collection of David R. Phillips.

40. Louis Sullivan, Chicago Stock Exchange Building (1893–94). Collection of David R. Phillips.

41. Notice sent out by Adler and Sullivan at completion of the Auditorium Building. Chicago Architectural Photo Co. Collection of David R. Phillips.

42. Louis Sullivan, Auditorium Theater stage, Auditorium Building (1889). IChi-14707. Courtesy of the Chicago Historical Society.

43. Louis Sullivan, Carson, Pirie, Scott Building (1899). Chicago Architectural Photo Co. Collection of David R. Phillips.

44. John W. Root, Reliance Building, 32 N. State Street. Chicago Architectural Photo Co. Collection of David R. Phillips.

45. John W. Root, Montauk Block, Chicago (1881–82). The Goodspeed Publishing Co. Courtesy of the Art Institute of Chicago.

46. John W. Root, Monadnock Building (1889–91). Chicago Architectural Photo Co. Collection of David R. Phillips.

47. John W. Root, Rookery Building (1884–86). Courtesy of the Art Institute of Chicago.

48. John W. Root, Rookery Building, interior court. Courtesy of the Art Institute of Chicago.

49. Frank Lloyd Wright, Larkin Building (1904), Light Court. Courtesy of the Buffalo and Erie County Historical Society.

50. Frank Lloyd Wright, Larkin Building, view across Light Court, fifth-floor level. Courtesy of the Buffalo and Erie County Historical Society.

51. Frank Lloyd Wright, Larkin Building, Seneca Street elevation. Courtesy of the Buffalo and Erie County Historical Society.

52. Frank Lloyd Wright, Larkin Building, intaglio relief and foun-

tain on Seneca Street facade of annex (Bock and Wright). Courtesy of the Buffalo and Erie County Historical Society.

53. Glass slide, Chicago Fire—Rebuilding: view from Court House looking southeast, c. 1872–73. IChi-02833. Courtesy of the Chicago Historical Society.

54. Detail of photo, Chicago Fire—Rebuilding: view from Water Tower, south, 1872–77. Stereo by Copelin & Son, 244 W. Washington. IChi-16678-D. Courtesy of the Chicago Historical Society.

55. Photo, Chicago Fire—Rebuilding: view from Water Tower, southwest, 1872–77. Stereo by Copelin & Son, 244 West Washington. IChi-16677. Courtesy of the Chicago Historical Society.

56. Photo, Chicago Fire—Rebuilding: view from Water Tower, west, 1872–77. Stereo by Copelin & Son, 244 W. Washington. IChi-16675. Courtesy of the Chicago Historical Society.

57. William Le Baron Jenney, Fire Monument, to be built of safes and columns taken from the ruins of Chicago. Reproduced from *Lakeside Memorial of the Burning of Chicago* (1872). Courtesy of the J. Paul Getty Museum.

58. William Thornton, Study for dormitories. Thomas Jefferson Papers. Courtesy of Special Collections Department, Manuscripts Division, University of Virginia Library.

59. Thomas Jefferson, Birds-eye-view of the University of Virginia, shaded by Cornelia Jefferson Randolph (1820?). Thomas Jefferson Papers. Courtesy of Special Collections Department, Manuscripts Division, University of Virginia Library.

60. John Neilson, study for 1822 Maverick engraving of the University of Virginia campus. Courtesy of Virginia State Library.

61. Claude-Nicolas Ledoux, Director's house, saltworks at Chaux (1775–78). Photo by Anthony Vidler.

62. H. H. Richardson in monk's robes (c. 1885). All rights reserved, Chicago Architectural Foundation. Reprinted with permission.

63. Louis Sullivan, Golden Doorway of Transportation Building, World's Columbian Exposition. Collection of David R. Phillips.

64. Playroom of Frank Lloyd Wright House, Oak Park (1893). Courtesy of National Center for the Study of Frank Lloyd Wright.

65. Bedroom of Frank Lloyd Wright House, Oak Park. Courtesy of National Center for the Study of Frank Lloyd Wright.

66. Frank Lloyd Wright Studio, Oak Park. Courtesy of National Center for the Study of Frank Lloyd Wright.

67. Thomas Cole, *The Course of Empire*, 1: "The Savage State," or, "The Commencement of Empire." Courtesy of The New-York Historical Society, New York City.

68. Thomas Cole, *The Course of Empire*, 2: "The Arcadian" or "Pastoral State." Courtesy of The New-York Historical Society, New York City.

69. Thomas Cole, *The Course of Empire*, 3: "The Consummation of Empire." Courtesy of The New-York Historical Society, New York City.

70. Thomas Cole, *The Course of Empire*, 4: "Destruction." Courtesy of The New-York Historical Society, New York City.

71. Thomas Cole, *The Course of Empire*, 5: "Desolation." Courtesy of The New-York Historical Society, New York City.

72. World's Columbian Exposition: Fire at Cold Storage Warehouse. Collection of David R. Phillips.

73. Chicago Stockyards at the time of the fair. Collection of David R. Phillips.

74. Illinois Central Van Buren Street viaduct at the time of the World's Columbian Exposition. Photo by C. D. Arnold. Courtesy of the Art Institute of Chicago.

75. World's Columbian Exposition: Crowds arriving at the railroad station on Chicago Day. Courtesy of the University of Chicago Library, Department of Special Collections.

76. World's Columbian Exposition: View west from roof of Liberal Arts Building. Photo by C. D. Arnold. Courtesy of the University of Chicago Library, Department of Special Collections.

77. World's Columbian Exposition: Chicago Day. Photo by C. D. Arnold. Courtesy of the Art Institute of Chicago.

78. "World's Columbian Exposition, Chicago 1893." From the Roosevelt Family Album. Courtesy of the J. Paul Getty Museum.

79. World's Columbian Exposition: View from the Illinois Central tracks showing Administration Building under construction. Courtesy of the University of Chicago Library, Department of Special Collections.

80. World's Columbian Exposition: Grand Basin looking west, 29 June 1892. Photo by C. D. Arnold. Courtesy of the Art Institute of Chicago.

81. Daniel H. Burnham and Edward H. Bennett, *Plan of Chicago* (1909), pl. 131: Elevation showing the group of buildings constituting the proposed civic center. Courtesy of the Art Institute of Chicago.

82. Daniel H. Burnham and Edward H. Bennett, *Plan of Chicago* (1909), pl. 122: Railway station scheme west of the river between Canal and Clinton Streets, showing the relation with the civic center. Courtesy of the Art Institute of Chicago.

83. World's Columbian Exposition: Map of the grounds. Courtesy of the University of Chicago Library, Department of Special Collections.

84. World's Columbian Exposition: Midway work crews. Courtesy of the University of Chicago Library, Department of Special Collections.

85. World's Columbian Exposition: Art Building, northwest corner, 14 July 1892. Photo by C. D. Arnold. Courtesy of the Art Institute of Chicago.

86. World's Columbian Exposition: Wooded Island, looking east, 7 July 1892. Photo by C. D. Arnold. Courtesy of the Art Institute of Chicago.

87. World's Columbian Exposition: Transportation Building, 24

June 1892. Photo by C. D. Arnold. Courtesy of the Art Institute of Chicago.

88. World's Columbian Exposition: View of construction from Illinois Central tracks. Courtesy of the University of Chicago Library, Department of Special Collections.

89. World's Columbian Exposition: Manufactures Building, 11 August 1892. Photo by C. D. Arnold. Courtesy of the Art Institute of Chicago.

90. Central Station, Illinois Central Railroad (1894). Courtesy of the Art Institute of Chicago.

91. World's Columbian Exposition: Agriculture Building at early stage of construction, 6 October 1891. Photo by C. D. Arnold. Courtesy of the Art Institute of Chicago.

92. World's Columbian Exposition: Early state of construction, view northwest from the tower of Fire Engine House. Photo by C. D. Arnold. Courtesy of the Art Institute of Chicago.

93. World's Columbian Exposition: View of the University of Chicago campus from the Ferris Wheel. Courtesy of the University of Chicago Library, Department of Special Collections.

94. University of Chicago campus from Stagg Field. Courtesy of the University of Chicago Library, Department of Special Collections.

95. World's Columbian Exposition: Midway Plaisance, looking west. Courtesy of the University of Chicago Library, Department of Special Collections.

96. World's Columbian Exposition: On the Midway. Photos by C. D. Arnold. Courtesy of the Art Institute of Chicago.

97. World's Columbian Exposition: Midway scene. Photo by C. D. Arnold. Courtesy of the Art Institute of Chicago.

98. World's Columbian Exposition: Yucatan Ruins. Photo by C. D. Arnold. Courtesy of the Art Institute of Chicago.

99. World's Columbian Exposition: View from intramural power house. Photo by C. D. Arnold. Courtesy of the Art Institute of Chicago.

100. World's Columbian Exposition: View east from Ferris Wheel. Photo by C. D. Arnold. Courtesy of the Art Institute of Chicago.

101. World's Columbian Exposition: 60th Street, looking east. Courtesy of the University of Chicago Library, Department of Special Collections.

102. World's Columbian Exposition: interior of Woman's Building. Photo by C. D. Arnold. Courtesy of the University of Chicago Library, Department of Special Collections.

103. World's Columbian Exposition: Ferris Wheel from the University of Chicago campus. Courtesy of the University of Chicago Library, Department of Special Collections.

104. World's Columbian Exposition: Ferris Wheel, base and cabs. Photo by C. D. Arnold. Courtesy of the University of Chicago Library, Department of Special Collections.

105. World's Columbian Exposition: Ferris Wheel. Courtesy of

the University of Chicago Library, Department of Special Collections.

106. Triptych (frontispiece) from H. H. Van Meter, *The Vanishing Fair* (1894). From top: "Vacant site"; "White City"; "After the flames." Courtesy of the Art Institute of Chicago.

107. The White City on fire and in ruins: photographs from H. H. Van Meter, *The Vanishing Fair* (1894). Courtesy of the Art Institute of Chicago.

Index

A

Academy of Fine Arts in New York, 158
Addams, Jane, 203
Adler, Dankmar, 110–11, 136, 167
Administration Building (Hunt), 204, 206–7
AIA. *See* American Institute of Architects
Aldis, Owen, 138
Algren, Nelson, 10
American Academy in Rome, 159
American Architect and Building News (periodical), 223
American Institute of Architects (AIA), 154, 155, 158–59, 164, 167, 223
American Scene, The (James), 185
Andreas, A. T., 27, 86
Andrews, Shang, 240
Antifire laws, 75–76
Antitechnology sentiments, 7
Architecture in Chicago, 10–11, 17–18, 51, 59–60, 61, 74–75, 180–81; and Andreas' history, 86; ballroom construction technique, 73–74; Chicago School, 83, 86, 142–43, 154–56, 158, 160, 213; classical or neoclassical elements in, 196–97, 214; and economic crisis of 1873, 83; fireproof cladding, 103, 138; first building erected after Fire, 22; "form follows function," 113; frenzy to rebuild after the Fire, 63–64, 66; innovation after Fire, 138–39; and literature, 185, 196–97; ornamentation and facades, 78, 114–15, 195–96, 213; "pasteboard" architecture, 77; and poor homeowners, 75–76, 78; pre-fire buildings, *14, 15, 16–17,* 67, 68, 71, 88, *100–104;* pre-fire fragility of, 72–73; ruins, evocative haunting of, 97–98; steel-frame buildings, 110, 138. *See also* Boyce and Superior buildings; Boyington, William W.; Jenny, William Le Baron; Matz, Otto; Richardson, Henry Hobson; Root, John; Skyscrapers; Sullivan, Louis A.; Van Osdel, J. M.; Veiled Lady (legend); Wright, Frank Lloyd
Art, Chicago, 118–19
Art Institute of Chicago, 221
Atwood, Charles, 171
Auditorium Building, 111. *See under* Root, John; Sullivan, Louis A.

B

Baltimore Fire (1904), 2
Bancroft, Hubert Howe, 211
Barnard, George N., 93, 175
Barriers Burned Away (Roe), 30–37,

Barriers Burned Away (Roe), *(cont'd)*
50; characters and city identity,
33–35; as model for Ideal American, 34; theology of, 53
Bauer, August, 74
Beauvoir, Simone de, 10–11
Beaux Arts style, 159, 160, 199
Beecher, Henry Ward, 23
Bell, William, 96–97
Bellow, Saul, 6, 131–32
Besant, Walter, 196–97
Black City, 218, 219. *See also* White
City
Book of the Fair, The (Bancroft), 211
Boston Fire (1872), 2
Bourget, Paul, 118, 144–45, 157,
202, 218
Boyce and Superior buildings, 88
Boyington, William W., 74, 160;
Board of Trade Building, *87;*
Grand Pacific Hotel, 87, 99;
Inter-State Exposition Building,
23, 91–92, *92,* 111
Brooks, Peter, 127–28
Brooks, Shepherd, 127–28
Bross, William: *History of Chicago,*
26, 27–30, 45, 48–49, 50, 72
Brown, Judge Henry, 26
Building Budget (periodical), 223
Building codes in Chicago: opposition to, 75
Burling, Edward, 74; Chamber of
Commerce Building, 89, *99*
Burnham, Clara Louise: *Sweet Clover: A Romance of the White City,*
208–10, 211–12
Burnham, Daniel, 10, 83, 102, 123–
25, 136, 160, 169–70, 195, 205; as
a businessman, 161, 162, 164–
65, 170; and Charles Atwood,
171; Chicago Plan of 1909, 167,
205, 206; classical elements in,
196–97; east-west reorientation
of Chicago, 206; and French
master planning, 171; Masonic
Temple, *64,* 203; as model
for character Howard Roark,
169; portrait of Burnham and
Root, 162–63. *See also* Root,
John; World Columbian Exposition
Burnt Record Act of Illinois (1872),
71
Butler, Charles, 13–14

C

Canetti, Elias, 3
Challenger space shuttle disaster, 7
Chamber of Commerce Building,
89, *99. See also* Burling, Edward
Chamberlin, Everett: See *Chicago
and the Great Conflagration*
Chicago After Dark (Andrews), 240
Chicago and the Great Conflagration
(Colbert and Chamberlin), 21,
25–26, 35
Chicago and the World's Fair (Ralph),
210
Chicago by Day and Night: The Pleasure Seeker's Guide (1892), 240
Chicago Magazine, 74
Chicago: A Stranger's Guide (1866),
211
Chicago's Dark Places (Stead), 242
Cimabue, 162
"Cinders," 65
Cleveland, J. W. S., 49–50
Cliffdwellers, The (Fuller), 130, 176–
79
Cobb, Henry Ives, 221
Colbert, Elias. See *Chicago and the
Great Conflagration*
Cole, Thomas: *Course of Empire, The,*
174–75, *175–79*
Columbia, South Carolina, *93–94*
Commercial Club, 204
Common Lot, The (Herrick), 179, 181,
187–90
Cooper, James Fenimore, 26–27
Course of Empire, The (Cole), 174–75,
175–179
Cropsey, J. F., 156
Currey, J. Seymour, 227

D

Daisy Miller (James), 208
Daley, Richard, Mayor, 149
*Daniel Trentworthy: A Tale of the Great
Fire of Chicago* (McGovern), 60–
61, 78–82, 148
Deaths in the Fire, 18
DeKoven Street, 18
Depression of 1873–1879, 82–83
Destiny. *See* Mythologizing, and
destiny
Dial, The (periodical), 222–23

Disasters and cataclysms, 7–8, 177; as start of new fortune, 28–29; transformed by fiction, 31
Douglas, Stephen A., 220
Dreiser, Theodore, 236, 239
Drought of 1871, 18, 67

E

Edelmann, John, 106
Edwards, Jonathan, 24–25
Elevators, passenger, 137
Emerson, Ralph Waldo, 154
Equitable Building (New York City), 137
Errington, Alderman, 77–78
Evanston, Ill. 78

F

Fales, Mary L., 45
Field, Leiter & Co. Building, 98
Fire, myths of: Prometheus, 3
For Her Daily Bread (Sommers), 240
Fort Dearborn Massacre, 12
Fountainhead, The (Rand), 169
Frank Leslie's Illustrated Newspaper, 70
Frear, Alexander, 46, 50
Frontier town, myth of, 1, 2, 12; Chicago as pioneer town, 18, 43
Fuller, Henry B., 219, 222, 225; on architectural style, 197–98. Cliffdwellers, The, 130, 176–79; Under the Skylights, 181–83; With the Procession, 225–26
Fullerton Avenue, 18
Furness, William Henry, 153–55

G

Galena, Ill.: founding of, 13
Gambler: A Story of Chicago Life (Wilkie), 240
General Relief Committee, 22
Gilman, Arthur: Equitable Building (New York City), 137
Glessner, J. J., 107. See also Richardson, Henry Hobson

Goodspeed, E. J.: History of the Great Fires in Chicago and the West, 51–53, 57, 59
Goodspeed, Thomas Wakefield, 220
Grand Pacific Hotel. See Boyington, William W.
Great Pyramid, 203–204
Grooms, Red, and Gross, Mimi, City of Chicago, 11
Gross, Mimi. See Grooms, Red
Guerin, Jules, 206

H

Hardscrabble: or, Fall of Chicago (Richardson), 58
Harper, William Rainey, 220–21
Harrison, Carter H., Mayor, 198–99
Harrison Police Station, 243
Haughtworth Building (New York City), 137
Hawthorne, Nathaniel, 4
Hayden, Sophia G., 232
Hayes, A. A., 61
Hebard, Mrs. Alfred, 45–46, 50
Heights and Depths (Scanland), 239–40
Herrick, Robert: Common Lot, The, 179, 181, 187–90; Myself, 223–25, 249–50; Web of Life, The, 179
Hesing, Anton Caspar, 76, 85, 112
"High Tension" Electricity, 199
History: and popular imagination, 59; as remembered by the elite, 42. See also Identity, Chicagoan: release from the past; Mythologization
History of Chicago (Andreas), 27, 86
History of Chicago (Bross), 26, 27–30, 45, 48–49, 50, 72
History of Chicago (Brown), 26
History of the Great Fires in Chicago and the West (Goodspeed), 51–53, 57; Chicago as a fortunate Pompeii, 59
Hitchcock, Henry-Russel, 138
Howell, William Dean, 176–77, 191, 208
Hunt, Richard Morris, 158–59; Administration Building, 204, 206–7; portrait of, 162, 163
Hutchinson, John, 47, 50

I

Identity, Chicagoan, 27, 28, 39–40,
192–93, 219; adjusting to trauma
of the Fire, 44, 67, 142, 195, 198–
99; and its architecture, 74, 140,
199, 205; boosterism and denial,
50–51, 66, 72, 128–29, 212; and
characters in Roe's novel, 33–34;
and Columbian Exposition, 205;
contradictions in Chicago, 16–
17, 18, 20; heroic worker, 60; lack
of unified identity, 244; and literature, 31–32, 39, 43, 176; populism and high culture, 220–21;
"Prairie hedonism," 212; and
pre-fire elite, 42, 47; release from
the past, 38, 157. *See also* White
City
If Christ Came to Chicago (Stead), 144,
203, 242
Illinois Central Railroad, Van Buren
Bridge, *199*
Illinois State Association of Architects (ISAA), 167
Industrial Chicago, 89
Industry and commerce: affect of architecture on, 74–75, 89; Chicago
reputation for, 4, 13–14, 23; recovery after Fire, 22, 77, 136
Inland Architect, The (periodical), 223
Insurance Exchange Building, 97
Inter-State Industrial Exposition
(1873) (Boyington), 23, 91–92, *92,*
111
ISAA. *See* Illinois State Association
of Architects

J

Jackson Park (Chicago), 198, 204,
227
James, George Wharton, 242
James, Henry: *The American Scene,*
185; *Daisy Miller,* 208
Jefferson, Thomas: and University
of Virginia, 149–52, *151*
Jenny, William Le Baron, 146–49,
160, 213; Fire monument, *147;*
Home Insurance Building, 74,
110; Portland Block, 89–90, *91,*
170; Second Leiter Store, 110

Johnson, George H., 103, 133, 136
Jordy, William, 138–39

K

Kerford, W. D., real estate office, *22*
Kimball, Edward, 137
King, Aurelia, 47
Kinzie, Arthur, 45
Kinzie, Juliette Magill: and husband
John, 41–42, 164; *Wau-Bun,* 26,
40–41, 52, 58
Kirkland, Caroline, 211
Kirkland, Joseph, 28, 38–39, 70–71,
85, 211

L

Labor disputes, postfire, 240–42
*Lakeside Memorial of the Burning of
Chicago, The* (1872), *20,* 93
Lamb, Mrs. Martha, 53–56; and
E. P. Roe, 55, 56
Land of the Dollar, The (Steevens),
145–46
LaTrobe, Benjamin, 149–51, 160
Ledoux, Claude-Nicolas, 151–53,
153
Legends. *See* Mythologizing
Liebert, A., 93
Lisbon Earthquake (1755), 2
Literature, Chicagoan, 33, 191; re-
sponses to fire, 39, 43–45, 49,
56–57, 60, 81, 185. See also
Cliffdwellers, The (Fuller); *Common
Lot, The* (Herrick); *Under the Sky-
lights* (Fuller); *Vanishing Fair, The*
(Van Meter)
Loesch, Frank J., 38–39
London Fire and Plague (1666), 2
Loop District (Chicago), 65, 199,
203–4, 239

M

Manifest Destiny, 4
Marquette Building, 170–71
Marshall Field Wholesale Ware-
house. *See under* Root, John
Masonic Temple (Burnham), *64,* 203

Matz, Otto, 74, 160; Nixon Building, 90–91, 170
McClean, Robert Craik, 223
McGovern, John: *Daniel Trentworthy: A Tale of the Great Fire of Chicago*, 60–61, 78–82, 148
McKim, Charles F., 195–96 *See also* American Academy in Rome
Meaning. *See* Contradictions in Chicago
Midway Plaisance, 208, 219, 226, 227–36, 230–31, 233, 234, 235; neoclassicism in architecture, 198
Millennial mythology, 2, 4; in Goodspeed's history, 51
Modernity, 13, 58–59; between vision and reality, 14–16, 60–61; and Roe's novel, 36
Money Captain, The (Payne), 225
Moore, Charles, 170, 205
Morgan Park Seminary, 220
Mr. Salt (Payne), 179
Myself (Herrick), 223–25, 249–50
Mythologizing: and actual events, 7, 10; apocalyptic views forged, 13, 19–20, 21–22, 26, 51–52; Chicago's myth of self, 39–40; and destiny, 37; and extremism, 6; fire as purification, 25, 32; in literature, 32–33, 36, 39, 43, 54; popular desire for legends, 6–7, 59; process of, 3, 5–6, 7, 23–24, 26, 60

N

Nielson, John, 152
Nixon Building (Matz), 90–91, 170
Norris, Frank, 239. *Pit, The*, 118
Norton, Charles Eliot, 197
Novels about the Fire. See *Barriers Burned Away* (Roe); *Daniel Trentworthy: A Tale of the Great Fire of Chicago* (McGovern); *Spicy* (Lamb); *Wau-Bun* (Kinzie)

O

Ogden, William, 14, 69
Oldenburg, Claes, 10

O'Leary, Mrs., 1, 2
Olmstead, Frederick Law, 12, 217; landscape development of, 203, 217–18
Origins, myth of: 12–13; and emerging modernity, 13
Ornamentation: Egyptian motifs, 128–29, 171; French motifs, 137

P

Palmer, Potter, 140
Pastoral themes, urban, 20–21
Payne, William Morton, 113, 222; *The Money Captain*, 225; *Mr. Salt*, 179
Peck, Ferdinand W., 111
Photographic, documentary, 2, 3, 95–98. *See also* Barnard, George N.; Bell, William; Liebert, A.
Pioneer spirit, 26–27; combined with Eastern respectability, 33, 79. *See also* Frontier town, myth of
Pit, The (Norris), 118
Poe, Edgar Allan, 4–5
Population of Chicago: growth after Fire, 28
Post (periodical): account of Fire, 19
Post, George B: Manufacturers Building, 203, 213; Western Union Building (New York), 137. *See also* Gilman, Arthur
Poverty: denial of, 50–51; in *Daniel Trentworthy*, 80–81; visible again after Fire, 47–48. *See also* Architecture of Chicago
"Prairie hedonism." *See under* Identity, Chicagoan
Progress: Chicago's Whiggish identity, 48; explosive urban sprawl from, 16, 28; myth of, 4–5, 78, 124; and Thomas Cole, 174, 175
Property abstracts and indexes, 71
Pushkin, Alexander: *The Bronze Horsemen*, 245–46, 248

R

Railroads, 13
Ralph, Julian, 210

Rand, Ayn, 169
Realism, 9, 16
Religious Herald, The, article on the
    Fair, 229
Richardson, Henry Hobson, 107;
    159, 160, 196; Glessner House,
    107–10, *109;* Marshall Field Ware-
    house, *108;* portrait of dressed as
    monk, *163*
Richardson, Major John, 58
Rockefeller, John D., 220
Roe, Edward Payson. See *Barriers
    Burned Away*
Root, John, 83–85, 87–88, 89, 99–
    100, 101–2, 106, 121–31, 136, 160;
    architects and commerce, 123,
    126–27, 130–31; Auditorium
    Building, 107, 110–11; First Regi-
    ment Armory, *110;* Montauk
    Block, 91, *125;* Marshall Field
    Wholesale Warehouse, 107, 115;
    methods of fireproofing, 107;
    Monadnock, *126,* 127–30, 131;
    ornamentation by 128–30; por-
    trait of Burnham and Root, 162–
    63; Reliance Building, *123;* and
    Richardsonian Romanesque,
    123–24; Rookery, 127, *129,* 131,
    132
Rosen, Christine, 85
Ruins. *See under* Architecture in
    Chicago

S

Santayana, George, 209
Scanland, Agnes Leonard, 239–40
Schuyler, Montgomery, 138, 216–17
Sewall, Alfred, 81–82
Sheahan, J. W., 17–18
Sheridan, General, 21, 43
Shortall, John G., 70–72
Sinclair, Upton, 191–92
Skyscrapers, *10;* the Chicago phe-
    nomenon, 138–39; and passen-
    ger elevator, 137–38
Snow, George Washington, 73
Social trauma. *See under* Identity,
    Chicagoan
Sommers, Lilian, E., 240
Spicy (Lamb), 53–56, 58
St. Petersburg, 245–46
Starrett, Paul, 162

Stead, William T: *Chicago's Dark
    Places,* 242; *If Christ Came to Chi-
    cago,* 144, 203, 242
Steevens, G. W., 112–13; *Land of the
    Dollar, The,* 145–46
Stevens, Wallace, 198
Stockyards (Chicago), *198*
Story of Chicago, The (Kirkland), 211
Sullivan, Louis A., 92, 105, 106, 114,
    136, 156, 164, 214–15; artwork in
    buildings, 117–18, 174; Audito-
    rium Building, 107, 111–21; on
    Burnham as businessman, 161–
    62; Carson Pirie Scott Building,
    120, *121;* Chicago Stock Ex-
    change, *114;* democracy and ar-
    chitecture, 117–18; inaccessibility
    of style, 165; last works, 135; and
    motto, Urbs in Horto, 119;
    Transportation Building Golden
    Doorway, *166;* Walker Ware-
    house, *108*
*Suppressed Sensations; Or, Leaves from
    the Note Book of a Chicago Reporter*
    (1883), 240
Survival, archetype of, 2–3
*Sweet Clover: A Romance of the White
    City* (Burnham), 208
Swing, Rev. David, 20, 22, 23, 28,
    57

T

Taft, Lorado, "Death," *10*
Temple of Art, 181, 182
Tesla, Nicola, 199
Thomas, H. W., 85–86
Thoreau, Henry David, 156
Thornton, William, 150
Through the Flames and Beyond, 20
Tribune Building, *66, 67*
Twenty Years at Hull House (Ad-
    dams), 203

U

Under the Skylights (Fuller), 181–83
University of Chicago, 219–20, *221,
    222, 222,* 226; the common and
    high-cultured, 219, 227; early
    bankruptcy of, 220; Rockefeller's

endowment of, 220. See also
   Myself (Herrick)
University of Virginia, *150, 151*

V

Van Brunt, Henry, 124, 159
Van Meter, H. H. See *Vanishing Fair,
   The* (Van Meter)
Van Osdel, J. M.: 160; Court House
   Building, *69,* 68–70; pictures of
   its burning, 70; Reaper Block, *90;*
   Tremont and Palmer Hotels, 88
Vanishing Fair, The (Van Meter), 179–
   80, 246–48, *247, 248*
Veiled Lady (legend), 212
Victorian conflicts, 32
Visionaries, 13, 16
Vulgarism in architecture. *See* World
   Columbian Exposition

W

Ware, William, 159
Wau-Bun (Kinzie), 26, 40–41, 52, 58
Web of Life, The (Herrick), 179
Western Union Building, (New
   York), 137
White City, 202–3, 206, 208, 210,

216, 218, 221, 244; and marshmallow spirituality, 229
White, Horace, 46, 57
White, Stanford, 162
Whitman, Walt, 8–9, 154, 155, 156
Wight, Peter B., 136, 163
Wilkie, Frank B, 82, 106; *Gambler: A
   Story of Chicago Life,* 240
With the Procession (Fuller), 225–26
World Columbian Exposition (1892–
   93), 9–10, 14, 48, 102, 192–94,
   195, *200–201, 204, 213, 214–15,
   218,* 229; Agriculture Building,
   217; Art Building, *212;* "border of
   vulgarities" of, 197, 202–3; Burnham as director, 206; as Chicago's defining moment, 210; Eiffel
   Tower imitation, revolving, 238;
   Ferris wheel at, 236–38, *237, 238;*
   fire at Cold Storage Warehouse,
   189; landscaping of, 217–18; map
   of grounds, *207;* and Midway
   Plaisance, *211,* 227–28, 234–35;
   and women's sculpture, 232
Wright, Frank Lloyd, 114, 115, 132,
   157, 164, 181, 193; architecture as
   cultural criticism, 164; and Daniel Burnham, 170, 171–72, 174;
   Larkin Company Administration
   Building (Buffalo), 133, *134–135;*
   Oak Park period, *172–173,* 173–
   74, 181

University of Illinois Press
1325 South Oak Street
Champaign, IL 61820-6903
www.press.uillinois.edu